EARTH'S TWO-MINUTE WARNING

Today's Bible-Predicted Signs of the End Times

By John Wheeler Jr.

The Leader Company
North Canton, Ohio 44720

Earth's Two-Minute Warning:
Today's Bible-Predicted Signs of the End Times

ISBN 1-886898-04-9

© 1996 by John Wheeler Jr.

Cover design by Jeff Cline
Typesetting by Cathy DeLong

Printed, marketed and distributed exclusively by:
The Leader Company
931 North Main St., Suite 101
North Canton, Ohio 44720
(330) 494-6988

Printed in Canada

Dedication

This book is dedicated to the glory of my Great God and Savior, Jesus Christ, and to the establishment of His everlasting Kingdom.

"The Pharisees also with the Sadducees came, and tempting desired him that he would shew them a sign from heaven.

He answered and said unto them, *When it is evening, ye say, It will be fair weather: for the sky is red.*

And in the morning, it will be foul weather today: for the sky is red and lowring. O ye hypocrites, ye can discern the face of the sky; but can ye not discern the signs of the times?

A wicked and adulterous generation seeketh after a sign; and there shall no sign be given unto it, but the sign of the prophet Jonas. And he left them, and departed.

Matthew 16:1-4

And as he sat upon the Mount of Olives, the disciples came unto him privately, saying, Tell us, when shall these things be? And what shall be the sign of thy coming, and of the end of the world?

Matthew 24:3

Table of Contents

Acknowledgments

I want to thank some of the many people who have made possible the publication of this book. First of all, I am grateful to my wife Cheryl, without whose steadfast support and encouragement so many good things in my life, including this book, never would have happened.

My earliest systematic exposure to the study of Biblical prophecy came from Professor Alan Winkler of William Jennings Bryan College in Dayton, Tennessee, who faithfully transmitted the tenets of end-time Dispensationalism from Dallas Seminary to me shortly after I became a Christian. I learned a great deal of value from Mr. Winkler, and a significant amount of the material in this book is based upon my meticulous notes from his classes. Where I have departed from, omitted, altered or added to his teachings, the responsibility is mine alone.

I am indebted to Pastor Mike Ritzman of Believers' Fellowship Church in Crossville, Tennessee, whose scriptural advice and spiritual support were most beneficial, and to Steve Fitschen, executive director of the National Legal Foundation, who fielded my questions and directed scholarly ideas and observations my way.

Jeffrey Peyton, assistant editor of *Christian American* magazine, provided timely assistance with Internet research; and Ron DeJong, CBN's own "Mr. Fact Sheet," was also quite helpful. My 13-year-old son John Christopher diligently dug pertinent information out of his Mac for me.

I wish to acknowledge also my debt to those many devoted Bible scholars, teachers, and writers whose insights have helped to shape my early thinking as I sought to understand the Scriptures. Hal Lindsey and Derek Prince are two whose names must not be omitted.

And special thanks to all those friends in Christ, known and unknown, whose prayers have covered me for lo, these many years.

Foreword
by Dr. Tim LaHaye

Everyone is interested in the future, from the politicians of both parties to scientists and academics, to us ordinary mortals. We all want to know something about what is going to happen in the next few years. Prophets and soothsayers, mystics and even some preachers, are making claims that can pique the interest of almost anyone — but are they true? That is the question.

This second millennium since Jesus ascended to heaven with the sacred promise, "I will come again, and receive you unto myself," is rapidly coming to a close. Thoughtful people are already asking, "Will His coming be in my lifetime?" Actually, we have been hearing that for years. Now we are more likely to hear, "Will He come before the year 2000?"

There are many reasons for this — the ending of one millennium and the beginning of another is one. Millennial periods naturally spark new interest in the future, which is why I have been expecting renewed interest in end-time prophetic events during the latter half of the nineties. So far I have not been disappointed.

But not only are people getting concerned that we may be coming to "the end of the age," but some, even scientists of renown, see no hope for the continuation of civilization as we know it. They are not basing their thoughts on prophecy, but on the increase of disease, or plagues, for which medical science has no known cure. Others are fearful because it is obvious that some rogue country or group of terrorists, bent on wresting control of world government, could blackmail weak political leaders into submission with the threat of nuclear holocaust. With technological miniaturization to the point that a nuclear bomb could be smuggled into any city in the world in a briefcase, any thoughtful person must ask, What does the future hold for this precarious planet?

That is where the study of Bible prophecy comes in. Over twenty-five percent of the Bible is prophetic, consequently the study of end-time events must be legitimate as long as we start with the Bible. And that is exactly what John Wheeler does. He shows the dramatic events of the future from Scripture, and compares these with current events that can't help but make the reader realize that Christ could come at any time.

Actually, I found this book to be a new, fresh look at end-time events that uses the latest current events to show how soon it could all come to pass. John is an excellent writer who surprised me with his thorough understanding of Bible prophecy. He doesn't set any dates or resort to wild speculation, but he keeps your interest throughout the book and leaves you with the realization that the "Blessed Hope" is still trustworthy and could happen at any time.

This book will help raise the anticipation of the at-any-moment coming of Christ to rapture His Church to be with Himself. Historically, whenever the church at large, or even a local church, has maintained this anticipation of the imminent "Blessed Hope," it has had three effects: 1) Greater evangelistic concern and unction; 2) A desire for holy living in an unholy age; and 3) Increased missionary outreach throughout the world.

That was true in the first three centuries, when the promise of Christ's return drove the early church to preach the Gospel around the then known world. The Second Coming message was lost during the "Dark Ages" when the Catholic church imprisoned the Scriptures and kept them in museums and away from the people for about twelve hundred years. The hope of Christ's return was not re-ignited until after the Protestant Reformation, when the Bible was set loose from its prison so it could again challenge the people.

Not surprisingly, Jewish evangelism was sparked in the seventeenth century, followed by the call to worldwide missions in the eighteenth through the twentieth centuries right up until now, when several missionary agencies are calling for preaching the Gospel around the world in every tongue and to all nations by the year 2000. May I remind you, our Lord promised that the "Gospel of the Kingdom will be preached in all the world and then the end will come" (Matthew 24:14).

It is my prayer that this book by John Wheeler will help raise the anticipation of the fact that Jesus is coming! And may it be quickly. Cetainly our generation has more reason to believe that than any generation before us.

Dr. Tim LaHaye
Washington, D.C.
April 3, 1996

Introduction
The Word of Truth

But of that day and hour knoweth no man, no, not the angels of heaven, but my Father only.

Matthew 24:36

The days in which we live could well be the most exciting times in human history, because the present generation could be the one to witness the triumphal return of the Lord Jesus Christ to this Earth. The Bible says that no man knows "the day or the hour" of Christ's return, but I believe that Jesus intends for His disciples to discern the "signs of the times."

The purpose of this book is to give readers an overview of what those signs are and what they mean from a strictly Biblical perspective, and to show how these things are coming to pass today, literally before our eyes. From natural calamities to international geopolitical developments, the events of our time vindicate the words of the Bible.

The famous humanist philosopher Bertrand Russell once said, "I would not give a fifty-fifty chance for the continued survival of one human being on this planet by the end of this century."[1] His gloomy outlook mirrors that of many other social analysts of modern times.

The *Bulletin of Atomic Scientists* has even established a "Doomsday Clock" to indicate how perilously close mankind is to self-annihilation through nuclear war. In 1996 the large hand of that clock stands ominously at 14 minutes before midnight, although at least one scientist advocated moving it forward to just two minutes before the hour.[2]

To put the world situation into a sports context, the great game of human civilization is almost over. The combatants have struggled across the Earth's continents for almost sixty centuries, but now the final quarter is drawing to its climactic close. The "two-minute" warning has sounded. After only a few more fleeting seconds of intense action, time will run out.

Readers may be surprised to learn that Jesus Christ warned men of these Last Days almost 2,000 years ago, speaking about a coming convulsive period of time that would usher in the end of the world as we know it.

As we draw nearer to that terrible time of trouble known as the Great Tribulation, when a world dictator called Antichrist will rise to power before the Second Coming of the Lord Jesus Christ, I believe that it is appropriate to explain the Biblical revelation of God's plans and purposes in a manner comprehensible to the average man or woman on the street.

Most people in the world today are not Christians. In fact, our present "postmodern" state of civilization has also been termed the "Post-Christian era." God has ceased to be "relevant" for these technological times.

Yet many people sense that our world seems to be spinning out of control, and they wonder if there are any reliable answers to be found anywhere, if there is any way to make some sense out of what is going on in these uncertain times. It is for these people, whether they be professing Christians or not, that this book is written.

I submit to you that the Bible does contain answers that are historically accurate, verifiably true, and experientially relevant for our day. My perspective is unapologetically Christian, and I present what I understand to be God's revealed plan for the Last Days, with the prayer that ultimately these pages may minister not just alarm and fear but also faith, hope and eternal life.

The doctrines contained herein I have inductively gleaned from the Scriptures over the course of fifteen years of Bible study, both formal and personal. I have also studied the teachings of numerous Bible scholars, and church history and tradition have been considered. I have gained some insight into current events from my five-year term as editor of *Christian American*. But my primary source for these doctrines is the Bible itself.

So while this is not an elaborate systematic theology, it is a work derived explicitly from the Bible, and therefore many Scriptures will be quoted and referenced to support the conclusions drawn.

Understanding the Word of Truth

God has revealed His plans and purposes in the Bible, but many people find it hard to understand because the Bible isn't laid out in simple outline form like the owner's manual for an appliance. Yet the Bible is the only reliable standard of authority to which we can turn for answers, and we can legitimately think of it as our "owner's manual" for life.

I have only three basic rules for studying the Bible.

First and foremost, *The Bible is the Truth.* It doesn't just contain some nuggets of truth mixed with a lot of error. I approach the Bible as the inspired Word of God and I accept at face value what it has to say. The Bible claims over 3,800 times to be the Word of God,[3] and if this isn't true, there is no point in reading lies. The New Testament is most explicit about this:

> **"<u>All Scripture is given by inspiration of God</u>, and is profitable for doctrine, for reproof, for correction, for instruction in righteousness: That the man of God may be perfect, throughly furnished unto all good works."**
> **2 Timothy 3:16-17**

I have not accepted or repeated any doctrine merely because it is part of some particular theological system or approved hermeneutic. If what the Bible said didn't fit with the theological system I was studying, the system had to yield to the Word.

The second basic rule of interpretation that I learned early on, and have often heard quoted, bears repeating again here: *If the plain sense of the Scripture makes common sense, seek no other sense.*[4]

Let the words of the Bible simply mean what they clearly say. This has been called by some the "Golden Rule of Biblical Interpretation." It is this "natural" or "literal" approach that my study typically takes.[5]

This does not mean that there may not also be a further spiritual meaning to a given verse or passage. In fact, I am convinced that most Scriptures, being the Living Word of an infinite God, have more levels of meaning than finite human minds can comprehend.

In fact, the Apostle Paul said that the Old Testament account in Exodus of the Children of Israel in the wilderness really had a deeper spiritual meaning and purpose for the later Church.

Paul wrote to the Christians at Corinth (1 Corinthians 10:6, 11):

> <u>Now these things were our examples</u>, to the intent that we should not lust after evil things, as they also lusted....

> **Now all these things happened unto them for en-
> samples: and they are written for our admonition,** upon
> whom the ends of the world are come.

But these added spiritual dimensions of the Word will comple-
ment, not contradict or supplant, the plain meaning of the words.
The events described in Exodus are still true, they really happened.[6]

Where a passage is obviously intended to have a figurative or
symbolic meaning, that meaning should be derived from other
scriptural sources rather than from someone's personal conjecture.

This leads to my third fundamental principle of interpretation:
Let the Scripture interpret the Scripture. God's Word will explain
itself, if you will dig deep enough to find the hidden treasures of
truth buried beneath the surface.[7] The prophet Isaiah reveals
where doctrine comes from:

> **Whom shall he teach knowledge? and whom shall he
> make to understand doctrine? them that are weaned
> from the milk, and drawn from the breasts.**
> **For precept must be upon precept; precept upon pre-
> cept; line upon line, line upon line; here a little, and
> there a little.**
> **Isaiah 28:9, 10**

Having established how we will approach the Biblical record,
we may soon proceed to see what the Bible has to say about the
Last Days. But first, why should we bother to study prophecy, and
does it really matter?

The Importance of Biblical Prophecy

The study of prophecy is important to us because it is important to God—otherwise, He wouldn't have caused one-quarter of
the Bible to be prophecy Scriptures. Of the 66 books in the Bible, 17
deal mainly with prophetic themes. The Bible contains an estimated 165,000 words of prophecy. It would appear that God may
want to tell us something.

In fact, God wants to tell us everything, if we are willing to
take the time to listen. According to the prophet Amos, the entire
plan of human history from Creation to Eternity can be found
in prophecy.

> **Surely the Lord God will do nothing, but he revealeth his secrets unto his servants the prophets.**
>
> **Amos 3:7**

If God has gone to the trouble of putting into writing everything He intends to do throughout the course of human history, it only makes sense that we ought to try to understand what He has said will happen.

Some people don't think that we can really know what is going to happen, that it is all just a matter of guesswork. While it is true that we are not omniscient like God, He has chosen to give us His Word to provide us with the truth and His Spirit to illuminate our understanding of it.

In fact, Jesus said that a particular ministry of the Holy Spirit would be to show His disciples "things to come."[8]

Prophecies Literally Fulfilled

Prophecy validates the truth of the entire Bible, and every prophecy that has thus far been fulfilled has been fulfilled literally and exactly.

The obvious example is the Advent of the Lord Jesus Christ into human history almost 2,000 years ago.[9] His virgin birth as "God with us" was prophesied 600 years in advance by the prophet Isaiah:

> **Therefore the Lord himself shall give you a sign: Behold, a virgin shall conceive, and bear a son, and shall call his name Immanuel.**
>
> **Isaiah 7:14**

At a separate place and time, God revealed to the prophet Micah the exact spot where the baby Jesus would be born. When ungodly King Herod heard from the wise men of the East that the long-awaited Messiah at last had arrived, he immediately consulted the priests and scribes to find out what the Scriptures had to say.[10] They correctly informed him that the prophet had predicted the child could be found in Bethlehem:

> **But thou, Bethlehem Ephratah, though thou be little among the thousands of Judah, yet out of thee shall he**

**come forth unto me that is to be ruler in Israel; whose
goings forth have been from of old, from everlasting.**

Micah 5:2

A thousand years before Christ's birth, God sent the prophet
Nathan to tell King David that the coming Messiah would proceed
from David's line.[11] David later wrote prophetic Psalms about His
crucifixion, and those prophecies were fulfilled exactly, down
to words Jesus spoke from the Cross while the Roman soldiers
gambled for His clothes.[12]

Isaiah 53 foretold the redemptive work of Christ as a suffering
servant, when the religious experts of His day saw and feared Him
merely as a political leader. Like many religious leaders of our day,
they could not understand the prophets' message.

Throughout the New Testament, the early apostles were quick
to point out the manner in which dozens of Old Testament
prophecies had been fulfilled in Christ's life and the emerging
Church. The examples are too numerous to recount here, but even
a cursory reading of the Gospels, and particularly the Book of
Matthew, will amply illustrate this point.

Many of the Old Testament prophecies foretold judgment on
God's people because of their sins, as first Israel was conquered
and led away into captivity by the Assyrians in 722 B.C. Later Judah
was defeated by King Nebuchadnezzar and in 586 B.C. the remaining people were carried away as slaves. The restoration of a remnant of Judah to Jerusalem after 70 years in Babylon was revealed
to the prophet Jeremiah.[13]

God also decreed judgments that have stood fast for millennia
on the enemies of His people, despite the determined efforts of
modern man to circumvent God's will. The ancient seacoast city of
Tyre, a preeminent Mediterranean mercantile center, despite its
vast wealth was destroyed for its idolatry and pride and has never
been rebuilt, just as God said.[14]

God's Word has stood firm for almost 2000 years as the abandoned ruins of Babylon, the most glorious city of the ancient
world, have lain waste according to the prophecies of Isaiah and
Jeremiah. Then Saddam Hussein decided to rebuild the Southern
Palace of Nebuchadnezzar, rediscovered early in the 20th Century
amid the Babylonian ruins of southern Iraq, into a personal palace.
Saddam had 1,000 laborers working seven days a week for four
years to get the job done, but the Gulf War of 1991 stopped those

plans. Hussein apparently intends to make reconstructed Babylon a world class tourist attraction, and some Bible scholars believe that the Antichrist will make the city the seat of his world government, which will be completely and finally destroyed when Christ returns.[15]

If all these prophecies of God, and hundreds more, have been fulfilled literally, by what authority do we presume to say that others will be fulfilled in some other way, or that they no longer apply?

Are we to substitute our finite human understanding in place of God's revealed plans and purposes for the ages?

Such an awesome responsibility I am not prepared to accept.

Prophecy Proves God's Power

Prophecy has been given to men to prove the omniscience of God and His sovereign control over human history. With His absolute power and wisdom, God alone will accomplish His purposes in time and eternity.

> **Produce your cause, saith the Lord; bring forth your strong reasons, saith the King of Jacob.**
> **Let them bring forth, and shew us what shall happen: let them shew the former things, what they be, that we may consider them, and know the latter end of them; or declare for us things to come.**
> **Shew the things that are to come hereafter, that we may know that ye are gods: yea, do good, or do evil, that we may be dismayed, and behold it together.**
> **Behold, ye are of nothing, and your work is nought: an abomination is he that chooseth you.**
> **Isaiah 41:21-25**

The prophecies in the Bible reveal that history is both linear and purposeful, moving inexorably in the direction predetermined by God from the beginning of time. Our awareness of God's active involvement in and redemptive plan for human history gives meaning and purpose to life.

No existential philosophy of nihilism and futility can answer the challenges posed by the fulfilled prophecies of the Bible.

Prophecy Must Be True

The Biblical standard for a prophet was 100-percent accuracy, and there was zero tolerance for error. If someone presumed to speak in the name of the Lord and what he said did not come to pass, or if it did come true but he tried to turn the people away from serving God, he was judged a false prophet and stoned to death.[16]

True Biblical prophecy must be true and cannot fail because it is inspired by the Holy Spirit, Who is God and therefore cannot lie. The Apostle Peter, writing just prior to his death, explained the high level of reverence we are to have for prophecy:

> **For we have not followed cunningly devised fables, when we made known unto you the power and coming of our Lord Jesus Christ, but were eyewitnesses of his majesty.**
>
> **For he received from God the Father honor and glory, when there came such a voice to him from the excellent glory, This is my beloved Son, in whom I am well pleased.**
>
> **And this voice which came from heaven we heard, when we were with him in the holy mount.**
>
> **We have also a more sure word of prophecy; whereunto ye do well that ye take heed, as unto a light that shineth in a dark place, until the day dawn, and a day star arise in your hearts:**
>
> **<u>Knowing this first, that no prophecy of the scripture is of any private interpretation.</u>**
>
> **For the prophecy came not in old time by the will of man: but <u>holy men of God spake as they were moved by the Holy Ghost.</u>**
>
> **2 Peter 1:16-21**

Here Peter affirms that Biblical prophecy comes from the Holy Spirit and that it is even more certain than his own eyewitness account of the Transfiguration of Jesus and God's audible voice speaking from Heaven.[17]

Peter's message to us is clear: you can believe God's Word even more surely than you can believe your own eyes and ears. It was a message Peter wanted to be sure the Church received before he went to be with Jesus.

Systems of Millennial Interpretation

This will not be a learned theological treatise steeped in academic jargon, for there are plenty of those around already. I have listed some in the Bibliography for those who may want to pursue this type of study in greater depth. They have their place but this isn't it.

This is an introductory primer for the common person who wants to know what the Bible says about the Last Days. I'll give you these facts in as simple and straight-forward a manner as I can communicate them.

And I won't get sidetracked into complicated, hair-splitting discussions about minute theological differences between Christians concerning end-time prophecy. I'll simply tell you what the major positions are, and then explain the facts as they are revealed in the Bible.

There are three basic theological interpretations of end-time prophecy, and they deal specifically with the 1,000-year reign of Jesus Christ, known as the Millennium and described in Revelation 20. Theologians disagree about when and even whether this event actually will occur.

1. Amillennialism

Amillennialism, which means literally "no millennium," is actually a misnomer, because the adherents of this doctrine usually believe that the Kingdom is present now in spiritual form, but they deny a literal future Kingdom of 1,000 years on Earth.

Amillennialism is historically a doctrine of the Roman Catholic Church and of the later Reformed churches that grew out of the Catholic tradition. Augustine, Bishop of Hippo, who wrote *The City of God* in A.D. 426, established both the Amillennial theory and the idea that the Catholic Church was supposed to rule on Earth. Augustine thought that the spiritual Millennium started in 350 B.C. and he expected Christ to return in A.D. 650, which of course did not occur.

One thousand years after Augustine, the Reformers fought the theological battle of soteriology, or the means of salvation, insisting that "the just shall live by faith" (Romans 1:17). But they assimilated the Amillennial Catholic doctrine on eschatology, or the study of last things. Many of the followers of Luther and Calvin remain Amillennialists to this day, as is most Calvinist Covenant theology.

To A-mills, most of the prophetic passages in the Bible are an allegory and those Old Testament prophecies which are considered still relevant are transferred from Israel to the Church.

Most A-mills believe the Kingdom of God is now on Earth with the Church, but some think it is Christ's rule in Heaven now with the saints. Either way, the Kingdom of God is now.

But it is a spiritual and not a literal Kingdom, and the Millennium is not literally a thousand years but figuratively a "very long time."

Jesus will come back someday but we don't give it much thought.[18]

2. Postmillennialism

Postmillennialism is the idea that the Church will make the world better, and when it is good enough, then Jesus will come back to rule and reign in person. Meanwhile, if Jesus came back into a sin-filled world, it would be almost like introducing sin into Heaven.

The Church is working hard preaching the Gospel to usher in the Kingdom, which is spiritual today and will gradually become literal at some future time. According to Millard J. Erickson, dean of Bethel Theological Seminary:

> Postmillennialism shares many features with either premillennialism or amillennialism or both. Perhaps its most distinctive feature is its optimism. Premillennialists believe that spiritual conditions will worsen and unbelief increase, and amillennialists tend to think the same way. Post-millennialists believe that through the preaching of the gospel, the world will be Christianized, and with that will come peace and other phenomena of the kingdom of God.[19]

Scriptural support for this view is claimed from Psalms 2, 47, 72 89, and 110, which affirm that "all nations" shall serve the Lord Jesus Christ and that His rule is universal. Postmillennialism is often linked to what is called the "Social Gospel," or the idea that by reforming the institutions of society, the people within that society can also be changed for the better.

Theologian Dr. Loraine Boettner has offered this description:

The millennium to which most Postmillennialists look forward is thus a golden age of prosperity during this present dispensation, that is during the church age, and is to be brought about by forces now active in the world. It is an indefinitely long period of time, perhaps much longer than a literal one thousand years.[20]

Postmillennialism, which places great emphasis on human effort and human progress, was prevalent in some Protestant churches before World War I.[21] Now the theory is in decline, as the idea that things in the world are getting better and better appears increasingly untenable.[22] Most former Post-mills have now switched to Amillennialism.[23]

Today the Post-mill position is held tenaciously by some in the Christian Reconstructionist movement, whose focus is primarily on the restoration of Biblical principles of law and government to politics and public policy. Some theologians consider Post-millennialism to be a key philosophical pillar of Reconstructionist thought, along with theonomy and presuppositional apologetics.[24]

Similarities Between the Two

Postmillennialsim is very similar to Amillennialism in several respects. The emphasis is on how Christians can impact this earthly life now and make a difference politically, socially, and culturally. A lot of sincere Christians who take seriously Christ's command to be "salt and light" in the Earth sometimes buy into this doctrine, and even accuse others, who look for the imminent return of Jesus Christ, of having an "escapist mentality."

Both systems agree that there will be a great apostasy on the Earth, a period of tribulation, and the rise of an Antichrist prior to the end.

Most A-mills and Post-mills do affirm that Jesus' eventual return, however far distant that may be, will be personal and bodily, at the end of an earthly kingdom of indeterminate type and duration. At that time, they believe, there will be one general resurrection of the dead and one general judgment for all people, Christians and non-Christians alike.

To A-mills, the Great Tribulation either occurred a long time ago, at the destruction of Jerusalem, or will come far in the indefinite future, just prior to the Second Coming of Christ. The Great White Throne Judgment and the Eternal State will follow that.

Allegory's Slippery Slope

Some liberal theologians, both Catholic and Protestant, go even further and completely spiritualize both the prophecies and the Gospels, to mean that Jesus is never really coming back because He never really rose from the dead. But the "concept of Christ" can still give us comfort.

While all true Christians recoil in horror from such blatant heresy as this latter departure from the Word, it should be noted that this is just one more step down the slippery slope of allegorical interpretation started by Augustine. The word allegory comes from the Greek "allegro," which means "to speak another." So the allegorical interpretation speaks something other than that which is actually written in the Bible.

The problem with this allegorical method of interpretation, upon which both systems are based, is that Scripture yields to the mind of the interpreter as the basic authority. Since the conclusions drawn by the allegorical method cannot be tested or verified, the words of the Bible become meaningless objectively. The only thing that matters is what they mean subjectively to each individual reader.[25]

This directly contradicts the Apostle Peter, who wrote that "no prophecy of the scripture is of any private interpretation" (2 Peter 1:20).

3. Premillennialism

Premillennialism says that Jesus will come back in person before the Millennium and literally rule on the Earth for a thousand years in visible bodily form with His saints, during which time Satan will be bound and cast into a bottomless pit. At the end of that time Satan will be loosed "for a little season" to tempt men one last time, then finally will be defeated forever by being cast into a lake of fire with all his demon spirits.

This interpretation of the Scriptures draws a distinction between Israel, as the natural people of God in the Earth, and the Church, as the spiritual body of Christ in the Earth. All the Old Testament prophecies given by God to Israel will be literally fulfilled to the Jewish people.

Pre-mills affirm the Rapture of the Church, when all true, born-again Christians—both living and dead—will be "caught up" into the sky to meet the Lord, at which time their mortal bodies will be instantly changed into immortal, glorified resurrection bodies. There will be two separate resurrections and two separate judgments, one each for the saved and the lost, and all the wicked will be cast into the lake of fire for eternal torment.

The Eternal State which follows will be an extension of the literal Millennial Kingdom of Christ on Earth. At the end of time the Earth will be destroyed by fire and there will be a new Heaven and a new Earth.

This view, which will be described in some detail in this book, is derived from a literal reading of the Book of Revelation and other prophetic Scriptures. It is most common in Fundamentalist, Pentecostal, and Charismatic churches, as well as many Evangelical bodies. It is entirely consistent with the teaching of the Apostle Paul, who wrote:

> **Study to shew thyself approved unto God, a workman that needeth not to be ashamed, rightly dividing the word of truth.**
> **2 Timothy 2:15**

Premillennialists disagree among themselves about exactly when Jesus will return, but they all know that the Second Coming is linked somehow to a predicted seven-year period of worldwide plagues and sorrows, the last half of which is known as the Great Tribulation. Pre-tribs say He comes at the beginning, while Post-tribs think He comes at the end. Mid-tribs mostly aren't really sure, so they put Him in the middle and hope for the best. We will examine these positions in greater detail later.

A Biblical Framework

This will not be a line by line commentary on the Book of Revelation, although that book is an important part of this study. But Revelation can only be understood in conjunction with various other Old Testament prophecies, especially the Book of Daniel, as well as a number of New Testament Scriptures.

Remember, as we piece this puzzle together, that doctrine comes "precept upon precept, line upon line, here a little and there a little." It is rare to find a complete doctrine wrapped up in a neat package in only one passage of Scripture. Usually the big picture emerges as numerous Scriptures dealing with similar topics are compared and combined.[26]

But there is a Biblical framework upon which to build the structure of end-time prophecy. That framework is found in the words of Jesus Christ in Matthew 24, a passage commonly known as the Olivet Discourse.

This chapter will be like the trunk of our prophetic tree, and from that trunk will grow the other branches of Scripture that give fullness to our understanding of Jesus' words.

Because of its crucial importance to this study, the text of Matthew 24 is reproduced in full. Parallel passages are Luke 21 and Mark 13.

---

[1]   Quoted by Prof. Alan Winkler, Author's Class Notes, "Prophecy and End Times" (Dayton, Tenn.: William Jennings Bryan College, 1982-83).

[2]   Mike Moore, "Behind the Clock Move," *Bulletin of the Atomic Scientists,* Vol. 52, No. 2, March/April 1996, pp. 17-23.

[3]   Norman L. Geisler and William E. Nix, *A General Introduction to the Bible* (Chicago: Moody, 1968), p. 69. This number includes all the times in the Old Testament when the prophet declared "Thus saith the Lord" or "The word of the Lord came unto me," or something similar, as well as numerous New Testament verses that declare the inspiration of the Scriptures. See also 1 Peter 1:23 and Hebrews 4:12, as well as 2 Peter 1:19-21. In John 6:63 Jesus said, "the words that I speak unto you, they are spirit and they are life."

[4]   I first learned this rule in Prof. Alan Winkler's prophecy class at Bryan College, and most recently read it in Dr. Tim LaHaye's excellent book *No Fear of the Storm* (Sisters, Ore.: Multnomah, 1992), p. 240.

[5]   It is this commitment to "rigid literalism" that Dr. Clarence Bass of Bethel Theological Seminary, a self-described former Dispensationalist who received both his B.A. and M.A. from Wheaton, finds so objectionable. Clarence B. Bass, *Backgrounds to Dispensationalism: Its Historical Genesis and Ecclesiastical Implications* (Grand Rapids: Eerdmans, 1960. Rpt. ed., Grand Rapids: Baker, 1977), pp. 21-27.

[6]   Because this is a very important point, I have included an extended note. Dr. Bill Hamon offers the following explanation of the levels of meaning in the Bible:

"Most prophetic Scriptures have two applications: natural and spiritual; individual and corporate. A prophetic Scripture can apply to natural Israel, the Messiah, and the Church, and not do injustice to the principle of biblical hermeneutics. It can have a natural fulfillment with Israel, personal fulfillment in Jesus, and then a spiritual corporate fulfillment in the Church.

"For instance, examine the Scripture in Hosea 11:1: 'When Israel was a child, then I loved him, and called my son out of Egypt.' The context of the Scripture definitely shows that the prophet is speaking of the time when God led the Nation of Israel out of Egypt. He showed His love by delivering them from their Egyptian bondage and slavery. However, Matthew, in his book (2:15), pulls one phrase from this Scripture to prove that it has a personal application to Jesus the Messiah. The Pharisee and Sadducee theologians could have argued with Matthew that he was taking the Scripture out of context. How could he use it to prove that this Jesus was the Messiah when it was clear that it was speaking of the Nation of Israel? Regardless of the seeming contradiction, the Holy Spirit did inspire Hosea to prophesy this concerning Israel, and also inspired Matthew to apply it to Jesus.

"In the same manner, Hosea 11:1 can be applied personally to a sinner whom Jesus loved and called out of his Egyptian land of satanic bondage. It can also apply corporately to the Church which consists of many of God's sons. At the beginning of the Reformation, God called the Church out of its Egyptian land of religious slavery and dead works which existed during the Dark Ages. His call brought the Church out of Egypt as well as started it on its goal to ultimate restoration." Bill Hamon, *The Eternal Church* (Phoenix: Christian International, [1981]), pp. 131-132.

Dudley Hall, a Spirit-filled Baptist Bible teacher, has an excellent cassette, entitled "When Two World Collide," on this theme. Hall's example: When the Sadducees quizzed Jesus about the resurrection of the dead, He answered them with a seemingly unrelated reference to Moses at the Burning Bush, leaving them speechless. See Mark 12:18-27, Exodus 3:1-6.

[7] If something in the Bible is an allegory, the Bible will tell us so. See Galatians 4:24 and Genesis 16:5 and 21:2 for a true story with an additional allegorical meaning.

[8] Ephesians 1:17-19; 1 Corinthians 2:9-11; John 16:13.

[9] Matthew 1:18-25.

[10] Matthew 2:1-6.

[11] 2 Samuel 7:12-13. This is known as the Davidic Covenant. See also Psalm 89:3-4 and Jeremiah 33:22, 25-26.

[12] Compare Psalm 22 with Matthew 27. See also Psalm 88.

[13] Captivity prophesied, Jeremiah 25:9-13; return prophesied, Jeremiah 29:10.

[14] Judgments on Tyre, Ezekial 26, esp. verses 14 and 21. "Tyre suffered violent destruction in the thirteenth century when the Moslems took it from the Crusaders. The town is in ruins now, consisting of miserable huts and people, about five thousand 'impoverished Metawileth, or Persian schismatics, and Arab Christians.'" Merrill F. Unger, *Unger's Bible Dictionary* (Chicago: Moody, 1966), p. 1121.

[15] Judgments on Babylon, Isaiah 13:19-22; see also Jeremiah 50:3, 13, 39-40 and 51:26-29, 37, 52-58. Unger says: "On October 13, 539 B.C., Babylon fell to Cyrus of Persia and from that time on the decay of the city began. Xerxes plundered it. Alexander the Great thought to restore its great temple, in ruins in his day, but was deterred by the prohibitive cost. During the period of Alexander's successors the area decayed rapidly and soon became a desert....

"In the N.T. Babylon prefigures apostate Christendom, that is ecclesiastical Babylon, the great harlot (Rev. 17:15-18). It also prefigures political Babylon (Rev. 17:15-18), which destroys ecclesiastical Babylon. The power of political Babylon is destroyed by the glorious Second Advent of Christ (Rev. 16:14; 19:17)." Ibid., pp. 115-116.

Babylon, whose ruins are located 55 miles south of Baghdad near the modern town of al-Hillah, Iraq,, ceased to exist early in the Christian era and remained a desert wasteland until the middle of this century. "Restoration of the Emakh temple, and of part of the Ishtar Gate, the Processional Way, and the palace complex was begun in 1958 by the Iraq Department of Antiquities, which has also built a half-sized model of the complete Ishtar Gate at the entrance to the site." *Encyclopaedia Britannica*, 15th ed., s.v. "Babylon," vol. 2, pp. 554-556.

[16] Deuteronomy 18:20-22 and 13:1-5. See also Jeremiah 28:15-17.

[17] Matthew 17:1-6.

[18] "[T]he amillennialist believes in the imminence of Christ's second coming. While this term has many different shades of meaning, it does mean, in general, that the Lord could return virtually at any time.... It should be noted, however, that while this tenet is shared by amillennialists and premillennialists, it does not produce the same mood or tone in the typical amillennialist that it often does in the premillennialist. Thus, the amillennialist seldom bemoans the deterioration of world conditions or condemns the prevalent culture. He has noticeably less preoccupation with the details and sequence of the last things and less curiosity about 'signs of the times.' Indeed, the whole subject of eschatology seems to receive less attention from amillennial theologians than from premillennial theologians, particularly those who are dispensational. Genuine amillennialism has an ethos all its own." Millard J. Erickson, *Contemporary Options in Eschatology* (Grand Rapids: Baker, 1977. Paperback ed., 1987), p. 75.

[19] Ibid., pp. 69-70.

[20] Loraine Boettner, *The Millennium* (Philadelphia: Presbyterian and Reformed, 1957), p. 14.

[21] "Many major denominations eventually incorporated postmillennialism into their creeds. The Augsburg and Westminster Confessions are basically postmillennial. Lutheran, Presbyterian, and Reformed groups have tended to follow this position. The great Princeton school of theology of the nineteenth and early twentieth centuries, represented by the Hodges and Benjamin B. Warfield, staunchly presented this system." Erickson, *Contemporary Options in Eschatology*, p. 61.

[22] "Postmillennialism has suffered a sharp decline in popularity in the past fifty to sixty years. In large part this has resulted more from historical than exegetical considerations. Certain developments seemed to supply empirical evidence that the millennium was not arriving.... Today postmillennialists are, if not an extinct species, at least an endangered species." Ibid., p. 62.

[23] "The recent rise in the popularity of amillennialism can therefore be related to the events precipitating the crisis in postmillennialism.... Conservatives in the historic Reformed groups — denominations like the Reformed Church of America and the Christian Reformed Church, as well as many Presbyterian ones — are primarily amillennial." Ibid., p. 76.

[24] Rodney Clapp, "Democracy as Heresy," *Christianity Today*, XXXI, no. 3 (Feb. 20, 1987), pp. 18-19. See also Steven W. Fitschen, "On Paul and Reconstructionism: Two Views of the Law," (M.Div. research paper, Regent University, 1988). See also Greg L. Bahnsen, *By This Standard: The Authority of God's Law Today* (Tyler, Texas: Institute for Christian Economics, 1985), p. 8, for Bahnsen's denial of Postmillennialism as essential to Reconstructionism.

[25] Dr. Tim LaHaye has made the following astute observations: "I doubt a person could arrive at an a-Millennial or post-Millennial position simply by reading the Bible literally. Instead, a system of interpretation or theology must first be applied to explain away the many promises of the future kingdom age and the one-thousand-year time period mentioned in Revelation 20. Such a system is necessary in order to conclude that no kingdom will arise or that we will take over the world and so improve it that Christ will return to an ideal world already prepared for Him. Both a-Millennialism and post-Millennialism require that systems of belief be imposed on the text of Scripture in order to reach certain conclusions about end-time events....

"This brings us to the heart of what we want to say here. There is such a thing as allowing your theological presuppositions to so determine your hermeneutics (your approach to the Bible) that the theological presuppositions become an authority superior to the Bible itself. The first-century church had no helps or systems for understanding Scripture. Believers just read whatever portion of the Bible they had access to and accepted it. No wonder they were pre-Millennialists, for that is the plain meaning of the Scripture." LaHaye, *No Fear of the Storm*, pp. 235, 239.

[26] "Isaiah's method of teaching, whereby one builds precept upon precept, line upon line, repetition again and again, has proven itself most effective over the years. God's way is so simple that even a child can understand it, it is narrow in that it is the only way to salvation, and it is wearisome to the rebellious in that one must continue daily throughout life to build into his life the divine principles God has given." W.A. Chriswell, ed., *The Chriswell Study Bible* (Nashville: Thomas Nelson, 1979), p. 805.

The Gospel of Matthew, Chapter 24

Matt. 24:1 And Jesus went out, and departed from the temple: and his disciples came to him for to show him the buildings of the temple.

Matt. 24:2 And Jesus said unto them, See ye not all these things? verily I say unto you, There shall not be left here one stone upon another, that shall not be thrown down.

Matt. 24:3 And as he sat upon the mount of Olives, the disciples came unto him privately, saying, Tell us, when shall these things be? and what shall be the sign of thy coming, and of the end of the world?

Matt. 24:4 And Jesus answered and said unto them, Take heed that no man deceive you.

Matt. 24:5 For many shall come in my name, saying, I am Christ; and shall deceive many.

Matt. 24:6 And ye shall hear of wars and rumours of wars: see that ye be not troubled: for all these things must come to pass, but the end is not yet.

Matt. 24:7 For nation shall rise against nation, and kingdom against kingdom: and there shall be famines, and pestilences, and earthquakes, in divers places.

Matt. 24:8 All these are the beginning of sorrows.

Matt. 24:9 Then shall they deliver you up to be afflicted, and shall kill you: and ye shall be hated of all nations for my name's sake.

Matt. 24:10 And then shall many be offended, and shall betray one another, and shall hate one another.

Matt. 24:11 And many false prophets shall rise, and shall deceive many.

Matt. 24:12 And because iniquity shall abound, the love of many shall wax cold.

Matt. 24:13 But he that shall endure unto the end, the same shall be saved.

Matt. 24:14 And this gospel of the kingdom shall be preached in all the world for a witness unto all nations; and then shall the end come.

Matt. 24:15 When ye therefore shall see the abomination of desolation, spoken of by Daniel the prophet, stand in the holy place, (whoso readeth, let him understand:)

Matt. 24:16 Then let them which be in Judaea flee into the mountains:

Matt. 24:17 Let him which is on the housetop not come down to take any thing out of his house:

Matt. 24:18 Neither let him which is in the field return back to take his clothes.

Matt. 24:19 And woe unto them that are with child, and to them that give suck in those days!

Matt. 24:20 But pray ye that your flight be not in the winter, neither on the sabbath day:

Matt. 24:21 For then shall be great tribulation, such as was not since the beginning of the world to this time, no, nor ever shall be.

Matt. 24:22 And except those days should be shortened, there should no flesh be saved: but for the elect's sake those days shall be shortened.

Matt. 24:23 Then if any man shall say unto you, Lo, here is Christ, or there; believe it not.

Matt. 24:24 For there shall arise false Christs, and false prophets, and shall show great signs and wonders; insomuch that, if it were possible, they shall deceive the very elect.

Matt. 24:25 Behold, I have told you before.

Matt. 24:26 Wherefore if they shall say unto you, Behold, he is in the desert; go not forth: behold, he is in the secret chambers; believe it not.

Matt. 24:27 For as the lightning cometh out of the east, and shineth even unto the west; so shall also the coming of the Son of man be.

Matt. 24:28 For wheresoever the carcase is, there will the eagles be gathered together.

Matt. 24:29 Immediately after the tribulation of those days shall the sun be darkened, and the moon shall not give her light, and the stars shall fall from heaven, and the powers of the heavens shall be shaken:

Matt. 24:30 And then shall appear the sign of the Son of man in heaven: and then shall all the tribes of the earth mourn, and they shall see the Son of man coming in the clouds of heaven with power and great glory.

Matt. 24:31 And he shall send his angels with a great sound of a trumpet, and they shall gather together his elect from the four winds, from one end of heaven to the other.

Matt. 24:32 Now learn a parable of the fig tree; When his branch is yet tender, and putteth forth leaves, ye know that summer is nigh:

Matt. 24:33 So likewise ye, when ye shall see all these things, know that it is near, even at the doors.

Matt. 24:34 Verily I say unto you, This generation shall not pass, till all these things be fulfilled.

Matt. 24:35 Heaven and earth shall pass away, but my words shall not pass away.

Matt. 24:36 But of that day and hour knoweth no man, no, not the angels of heaven, but my Father only.

Matt. 24:37 But as the days of Noe were, so shall also the coming of the Son of man be.

Matt. 24:38 For as in the days that were before the flood they were eating and drinking, marrying and giving in marriage, until the day that Noe entered into the ark,

Matt. 24:39 And knew not until the flood came, and took them all away; so shall also the coming of the Son of man be.

Matt. 24:40 Then shall two be in the field; the one shall be taken, and the other left.

Matt. 24:41 Two women shall be grinding at the mill; the one shall be taken, and the other left.

Matt. 24:42 Watch therefore: for ye know not what hour your Lord doth come.

Matt. 24:43 But know this, that if the goodman of the house had known in what watch the thief would come, he would have watched, and would not have suffered his house to be broken up.

Matt. 24:44 Therefore be ye also ready: for in such an hour as ye think not the Son of man cometh.

Matt. 24:45 Who then is a faithful and wise servant, whom his lord hath made ruler over his household, to give them meat in due season?

Matt. 24:46 Blessed is that servant, whom his lord when he cometh shall find so doing.

Matt. 24:47 Verily I say unto you, That he shall make him ruler over all his goods.

Matt. 24:48 But and if that evil servant shall say in his heart, My lord delayeth his coming;

Matt. 24:49 And shall begin to smite his fellowservants, and to eat and drink with the drunken;

Matt. 24:50 The lord of that servant shall come in a day when he looketh not for him, and in an hour that he is not aware of,

Matt. 24:51 And shall cut him asunder, and appoint him his portion with the hypocrites: there shall be weeping and gnashing of teeth.

Chapter 1
The End of the Age

**And as he sat upon the Mount of Olives, the disciples
came unto him privately, saying, Tell us, when shall these
things be? And what shall be the sign of thy coming, and
of the end of the world?**

Matthew 24:3

Wars, plagues, famines, natural disasters, religious apostasy
and intense persecution of the people of God—these are the miserable conditions that will exist on the Earth just prior to the return
of Jesus Christ, according to the Bible.

This isn't a pleasant scenario, but it is the truth. I didn't make
this up, it is written in red ink, in the words of Jesus Himself. He
said in verse 8 that these things would be the "beginnings of
sorrows," or literally the "birth pangs" the world would experience
in the Last Days.

Matthew 24 begins with Jesus talking to His disciples. He had
just told a multitude of people in Matthew 23 of the woes and judgments that were to come upon Jerusalem and He had berated the
Jewish religious leaders for their self-righteous hypocrisy. In fact,
he called them hypocrites seven times in that passage. He also said
they were blind fools, children of hell, and snakes who could not
escape damnation—pretty strong words.[1]

In verse 2 of Matthew 24, Jesus had prophesied that the very
Temple itself—the center of Jewish religious life—would be
destroyed so completely that not one stone would be left on top
of another.[2]

Jesus' disciples were amazed at His radical predictions, and
they wanted to know two things: *when* would all this destruction
occur, and *what* would be the sign of the end of the world, when
Jesus would return?

He spent the next 48 verses answering those two specific questions, and what He said then is still pertinent to us today.

Wars and Rumors of Wars

Jesus began by giving some general information about what things would be like in the Last Days before the end of the world—or literally, in the Greek, at the "end of the age." That phrase has the connotation of the end of a distinct period of time, rather than the ultimate end of everything that exists. So what Jesus is talking about here is the end of the current "age," or the period of human history in which we now live.

He said first, in verse 6, that there would be turmoil on the world political front because of "wars and rumors of wars," with many nations and kingdoms fighting one another. This scenario has been common in human history, but never so widespread as in modern generations.

The 20th Century has spawned an unprecedented escalation in the destructive power of modern warfare and the carnage it produces. World War I introduced modern machine guns and tanks and heavy artillery to the battlefield, as well as poison gas. World War II produced mass destruction from the air and unleashed the awesome power of the atomic bomb to kill hundreds of thousands. The Cold War advanced missile technology and nuclear weapons capable of annihilating all human life on the planet. Hitler, Stalin, Mao Tse Tung, and scores of lesser dictators have combined to make this century the bloodiest in human history.

The total death toll from the five major wars of the 20th Century—World War I, World War II, the Korean War, Vietnam, and the Gulf War—stands at a gruesome 59.5 million.[3]

Today the headlines are filled with reports of conflict in Chechnya and Bosnia and Africa, and despite our oft-expressed desires for world peace, new conflicts continue to spring up around the globe. The Middle East is a powder keg waiting to explode, as Iran and Iraq race to acquire more potent weapons and Israel struggles just to survive.

There have also been three significant international geopolitical developments in this century related to wars, not specifically mentioned in Matthew 24 but found in other prophetic passages. This combination of events makes our time unique in all of human history and causes serious Bible scholars to believe that we are definitely living in the Last Days.[4]

The Rise of Rome

Much of what we can understand about the Last Days comes from the prophet Daniel, a man to whom God repeatedly granted the interpretation of prophetic dreams and visions. Chapters 2 and 7 of the Book of Daniel reveal that at the end of time a ten-nation confederation will arise out of what was once the old Roman Empire.

In Daniel 2, King Nebuchadnezzar had a dream that the prophet Daniel interpreted. In that dream the king saw a vision of a brilliant statue with a head of gold, chest and arms of silver, belly and thighs of brass, legs of iron, and feet of iron mixed with clay. Daniel said that the various metals in the statue represented the successive kingdoms that would come upon the Earth, with Nebuchadnezzar's Babylonian Empire as the head of gold.

> **And after thee shall arise another kingdom inferior to thee, and another third kingdom of brass, which shall bear rule over all the earth.**
>
> **And <u>the fourth kingdom shall be strong as iron</u>: forasmuch as iron breaketh in pieces and subdueth all things: and as iron that breaketh all these, shall it break in pieces and bruise.**
>
> **And <u>whereas thou sawest the feet and toes, part of potters' clay, and part of iron, the kingdom shall be divided; but there shall be in it of the strength of iron, forasmuch as thou sawest the iron mixed with miry clay</u>.**
>
> **Daniel 2:39-41**

Bible scholars have generally agreed that the three successive kingdoms after Babylon were the Medo-Persians, the Greeks under Alexander the Great, and finally the mighty Roman Empire, which officially ended in 476 A.D. A modified form of this Roman juggernaut will arise as a world power in the Last Days. The statue's feet and toes, composed of iron mixed with clay, represent both the strength of empire and the weakness of division, suggesting possibly a powerful but democratic confederation of states under a strong leader.

The statue in Daniel 2 was bright and glorious, a vision representing man's perspective on the nature of these great earthly kingdoms. However, in Daniel 7, the same kingdoms are represented as wild beasts: a lion, a bear, and a leopard, and then a fourth beast described only as "dreadful and terrible, and strong exceedingly."

This vision represents God's perspective. What man sees as great and glorious, God sees as beastly and wicked.

An angel gave Daniel the interpretation of his dream in Daniel 7:

> **Thus he said, <u>the fourth beast shall be the fourth kingdom upon earth, which shall be diverse from all kingdoms, and shall devour the whole earth</u>, and shall tread it down, and break it in pieces.**
>
> **And the ten horns out of this kingdom are ten kings that shall arise: and <u>another shall rise after them</u>; and he shall be diverse from the first, and he shall subdue three kings.**
>
> **<u>And he shall speak great words against the most High</u>, and shall wear out the saints of the most High, and think to change times and laws: and they shall be given into his hand until a <u>time and times and the dividing of times</u>.**
>
> **Daniel 7:23-25**

The fourth kingdom will emerge that will be "diverse from all kingdoms." A strongman dictator, described in Daniel 7:8 as a "little horn," will emerge to consolidate this confederation into a world-wide empire. This man will become the Antichrist, the world's most powerful dictator.[5]

United States of the World

These prophecies are being fulfilled today in Europe, which for 1,500 years has been the cultural descendant of Rome. The European Economic Community (EEC), or Common Market, which is headquartered in Brussels, Belgium, was founded by Jean Monnet on January 1, 1958, with the signing of the Treaty of Rome. Greece became the tenth member nation of the EEC in 1981.

Today there are twelve nations in the Community. Other member nations include France, Germany, Great Britain, Ireland, Denmark, Belgium, the Netherlands, Luxembourg, Spain, Italy, and Portugal. On January 1, 1993, these twelve nations officially became one economic market, uniting 345 million people into a powerful free-trade zone that some believe will soon become the economic champion of the world.

According to an April 1988 article in Forbes magazine, "By the year 2010, the entity that is Europe will be number one in the world economy. The U.S. will be second, China third, and Japan fourth."[6]

The EEC's successor, called the European Union (EU), was brought into being in November 1993 with the ratification of the Maastricht Treaty. The EU is the precursor to a total political union that will effectively become a United States of Europe, with its own currency and government. An entity now called the Western European Union is expected to become the common defense arm of the EU in 1996, gradually replacing NATO.

Germany is the dominant economic and political power in this new unified Europe, which many believe is a model for global government. Hal Lindsey writes, "Germany appears to be moving very quickly now toward becoming, once again, the dominant power in Europe—and Europe is moving rapidly toward becoming the dominant power in the world."[7]

Leon Trotsky, the Russian Communist leader, wrote in his 1918 tract "Bolshevism and World Peace" that: "The task of the proletariat is to create a United States of Europe, as a foundation for the United States of the World."[8] This appears to be happening before our very eyes today.

It is not hard to imagine that a charismatic leader could arise from Europe—traditionally considered the heart of Western civilization—and from there ascend to world dominance. That is what the Bible predicts.

The Rise of Russia

Russia has become a world power only in the 20th Century. In 1905 Russia was defeated by tiny Japan, and in 1917 the Russian army had only one rifle for every three soldiers. But today, despite the Christmas Day 1991 breakup of the Soviet-bloc countries, Russia is a major world military power with a tremendous arsenal of modern Backfire bombers, Typhoon-class submarines, intercontinental ballistic missiles, and nuclear warheads—as well as huge stockpiles of artillery, tanks and armored personnel carriers, and other conventional weapons. And don't forget their chemical and biological weapons, massive quantities of which are still around as well.

Russia has a huge land mass and a current (1993) population of 149 million people, which is expected to increase to 170 million by the year 2075. (Perhaps a hundred million more are in the satellite states of the Russian Federation.) Although these people are still suffering under the crippled economic system left over from their failed 70-year experiment with communist theory, Russia is a major force in the world today and will play a crucial role in end-time events. The Russian sphere of influence still dominates Europe, Africa, Central Asia and the Middle East.

The Russian Federation is unstable today, however, because of continued civil war with Chechnya, where the Russian army has not been successful in suppressing a popular revolt demanding autonomy and independence. This has sent a mixed message to the other 88 regions and republics within the Federation: Moscow wants to retain political control of the territories by military might, but it may not be able to do so.

As the "Chechen disease" spreads across the land, it is causing a widespread collapse of the Federation infrastructure, according to Paul Goble, the foremost Soviet expert in the Bush Administration.

"Some regions don't send in their taxes, other regions don't send in draftees. Nobody obeys any of the laws. Some regions are printing their own money," Goble explained. "This is a country that's just a line on a map, rather than an integral state."

Another question arising from the Checnyan revolt concerns the effective control of the estimated 30,000 nuclear weapons left over from the now-defunct Soviet Union, according to Goble. "The most frightening lesson of Chechnya is that there are a large number of senior generals who are prepared to disobey orders," Goble said. "How confident can we be that Boris Yeltsin actually controls those weapons?"

Gog, Magog, and Rosh

Russia exactly fits the description of a nation called "Rosh" in Ezekial 38 and 39, which along with "Magog" will invade Israel from the far north early in the Tribulation period but will be utterly destroyed on the mountains of Israel. Since nothing like this invasion described in the Bible has ever occurred in the past, we know that it still must be in the future.[9]

The invading Russian armies will be aided by a confederation of allies from Africa and Eastern Europe, which may possibly include Ethiopia, Libya, Egypt, Czechoslovakia, and Poland, as well as Iran (Persia).[10]

Several of the breakaway republics from the former Soviet Union are composed of Islamic peoples, and five of these Central Asian republics have joined into an economic agreement with Iran, Turkey, and Pakistan. In 1992 the republics of Turkmenistan,

Kyrgyzstan, Tajikistan, Uzbekistan, and Azerbaijan joined the Economic Cooperation Organization (ECO), along with Afghanistan. The economic pact makes allies of 300 million people, mostly Muslims, in Central Asia and the Middle East.[11]

Kazakhstan, with its massive oil reserves and a huge cache of nuclear weapons, is an ECO "observer" still trying to get into the European Community, but it is ideologically allied with the Arab Muslims. Iran, flush with cash as the fourth-largest oil producing country in the world, is believed by some already to have acquired nuclear warheads, most likely from Kazakhstan.[12]

The Institute for Science and International Security (ISIS) has confirmed that, while Western intelligence agencies have not yet proven that Iran has nuclear weapons, they have assembled a "substantial body of evidence" suggesting that Iran "is secretly pursuing a broad, organized effort to develop nuclear weapons." As part of this effort, "Iranian agents have traveled throughout the former Soviet Union in search of nuclear materials, 'know how,' and scientists."[13]

According to Hal Lindsey, Iran's master plan, or "Grand Design," is to align the Muslim nations with Russia so that they can all attack Israel together. And it already may be a done deal. Lindsey writes:

> My intelligence sources, who have not been wrong so far about this area, tell me that Russia has already signed an accord with Iran that *will commit them to fight on the side of Islam in the next Islam-Israeli war.*[14]

If indeed it exists, a secret mutual defense treaty between Russia and Iran, targeted against Israel, would certainly fit the end-time scenario of Ezekial 38 and 39. And there may be a man now waiting in the wings in Russia who would love to see that invasion launched.

Master of the World

Vladimir Zhirinovsky is the controversial Russian ultranationalist whose outrageously anti-Semitic pronouncements and anti-American threats have been making headlines worldwide for several years. He is the darling of all the hardline militarists and nationalists in Russia who see their cherished dreams of world empire being forfeited to Yeltsin's free-market reforms.[15]

The name Vladimir means "Master of the World," and Zhirinovsky says that is what he wants to be, leading Russia back to greatness on the world stage. Many have compared his appeal to that of Adolf Hitler in Germany more than 60 years ago, and Zhirinovsky does not discourage the comparison. His 1993 autobiography, apocalyptically entitled *Last Dash to the South,* has been compared in tone and content to Hitler's *Mein Kampf.*

Zhirinovsky spent his early years after college in Georgia, where he was assigned to the Transcaucus Military District Staff Political Directorate. There he gained a knowledge of the southern regions and began to develop the geopolitical philosophy he has articulated in *Last Dash to the South,* which is summed up in the statement:

> All Russia's problems are in the South. So until we resolve our southern problem, we will never extricate ourselves from the protracted crisis, which will periodically worsen.[16]

In 1991, Zhirinovsky ran for president of Russia and came in third, with six million votes. His campaign slogan was: "I will bring Russia up off her knees!" In late 1993, Russia held its first free multiparty elections since 1917, and Zhirinovsky was elected to parliament on the same theme. His Liberal Democratic Party received 25 percent of the 60 million votes cast. He has vowed to defeat Boris Yeltsin in the 1996 presidential elections.

Could "Mad Vlad" Zhirinovsky possibly be elected president of Russia? Discontent is running high among the Russian people, as they are experiencing hard economic times and an unprecedented crime wave, and Yeltsin is now perceived by many to be an ineffectual leader given to Vodka. Such unstable conditions sometimes enable demagogues to rise to power.

If several candidates split the Communist and moderate votes, Zhirinovsky's hardliners could conceivably catapult him into power. If that happens, Russia's massive nuclear arsenal—much of which is still aimed at the United States—will fall into the hands of the man who has said that his vision is for Russian soldiers to wash their feet in the Indian Ocean.

"The last dash to the south, Russia's outlet to the shores of the Indian and Mediterranean Ocean, is really the task of saving Russia," he insists.[17]

Communist Resurgence

But Zhirinovsky is not the pollsters' top pick to knock off Yeltsin in the June 1996 election. That distinction belongs to Gennady Zyuganov, the 52-year-old First Secretary of the Central Committee of the Communist Party of the Russian Federation (CPRF).[18]

The Communists, making a strong political comeback, took first place in the December 1995 parliamentary elections by capturing 35 percent of the Duma seats (157 out of 450). The CPRF platform condemns the 1991 accord that dissolved the Soviet Union and calls for a return to Marxism-Leninism, including the re-nationalization of all property "appropriated against the public interest."

Zyuganov, whose specialties within the former Soviet Communist Party (CPSU) were propaganda and ideology, has positioned himself as a moderate, appealing to popular nationalist sentiments while avoiding direct references to "nationalization" and "communism." However, he advocates the "voluntary restoration" of a "united state," and he is sharply critical of Yeltsin's free-market reforms and land privatization programs.

"We will keep in state hands all that is important for the stable development and security for the country in the areas of industry, energy, transportation and communication," he said in a March 1996 speech.[19]

Zyuganov is supported by a coalition of leftist leaders, including former vice-president Alexander Rutskoi, whose 1993 mutiny against Boris Yeltsin was suppressed with tanks, and former Soviet military leader Valentin Varennikov, who supported the abortive coup attempt against Mikhail Gorbachev in 1991.

General Varrenikov has told former Soviet military leaders to disregard Zyuganov's apparent "sliding toward social-democratic values," which he said was a move of political expediency. "There was no other way if we want to attract other forces to overthrow the current leadership," Varrenikov said. "Keep in mind the party has an unpublished 'maximum program'" which will be revived after the elections, he added.

"Maximum program" was a term used by Bolshevik revolutionaries in reference to their ultimate goal of Communist world domination.[20]

The wild card in the race is former Soviet leader Mikhail Gorbachev, who also has announced his intention to seek the Russian presidency as an independent. "I propose a union of people who want to get rid of the current regime and who do not want to allow the Bolsheviks to return," Gorbachev said. "I represent the party of the majority."[21]

But his popularity at home does not match his international reputation, and he is not expected to win. Hardline Communists and nationalists alike blame Gorbachev for the demise of the Soviet Union and for their subsequent economic woes, social unrest, and rising crime rate.

The winner of the 1996 election—who is quite likely to be someone committed to the hardline Russian nationalist theme and to Communist world domination—will serve for four years, until A.D. 2000.

The Kings of the East

Revelation 16 says that after the defeat of Rosh, the "Kings of the East"—or literally in the Greek, the "Kings of the Rising Sun"—will cross the Euphrates River at the midpoint of the Tribulation period and move into the Middle East with armies numbering 200 million men. There they will fight against the forces of the Antichrist for a period of three and a half years in a grueling military campaign that will culminate at the Battle of Armageddon. The Bible says blood will run "up to the horses' bridles."[22]

When the Apostle John wrote this unlikely prophecy in the Book of Revelation in 95 A.D., there were between 175 and 250 million people alive in the world. For a modern comparison, consider that all the armies of all the nations involved in World War II only totaled about 50 million men. But this massive assault clearly will happen before Jesus comes back in glory.

China and Japan have both developed into world powers in this century. Japan is an economic powerhouse with more than 125 million people packed into a very tiny land area, yielding a population density of 856 people per square mile. Japan's economy has exploded since World War II, until today it ranks second in the world behind the United States.

While Japan has achieved this position of prosperity by focusing its trade efforts on Western markets, especially in America, signs are that the Japanese now are beginning to look to the newly emerging, heavily populated markets of Asia as their future source of untold wealth. China particularly beckons, and the possibility of an economic and political alliance between these two modern "Kings of the East" is very real.

China, with more than 1.2 billion people, is the second great economic success story of the post-W.W.II era. While China occupies a land area only slightly larger than that of the United States, the country has five times as many people. Today the Chinese "sleeping giant" has awakened, and China's economy ranks third in the world behind the U.S. and Japan.

While most of the Chinese people still live in abject poverty by Western standards, their huge numbers nevertheless make them an enticing market. Moreover, their abundance of cheap labor has allowed China to take over the spot formerly occupied by Japan as the world's leading producer of inexpensive consumer goods for the West. The population of China is growing at the rate of 13 percent per year and is expected to reach 1.5 billion by the year 2000.

China was politically aligned with Russia until the 1960s, but the Sino-Soviet split over the correct application of Communist doctrine has established the two as separate powers. Today China has a huge stockpile of conventional and nuclear weapons, as well as the largest standing army in the world. The Chinese now have the capability to field an independent army of 200 million men— the first time in history this has been possible.

But China's huge population also creates a tremendous demand for the Earth's ever-diminishing resources. China will soon need all the grain the world has for export, and all the fish the world's trawlers can catch. As these basic subsistence-level needs continue to escalate, China's nuclear arsenal could pose an awesome military threat to the West.

Today China is the overgrown bully of Asia, intimidating the tiny island of Taiwan with live war games on her virtually defenseless borders and belligerently warning the United States to keep its watching navy vessels out of the way.[23]

Tomorrow China could become the overgrown bully of the world. "I think China has got a chip on its shoulder," commented American foreign policy analyst Jonathan Clarke. "It was badly treated by the West during the 19th century.... I think [it has] a sense that...it's time to get even."[24]

Given this set of circumstances, does anyone seriously doubt what will happen on that future day when the Communist Chinese leaders see the major powers of the world in a position of apparent vulnerability—such as would result from the predicted carnage from massive battles in Israel between the Russian and Arab coalitions, on the one hand, and the armies of the European Antichrist on the other?

Will they hesitate at all to rush across the dried-up Euphrates River with their seemingly endless, unstoppable human waves, making a desperate bid for world domination by seizing the moment of apparent weakness and grabbing for the precious Middle Eastern oil reserves?

Not likely.

These three major political entities—Revived Rome in the form of the rising European Union, an unstable modern militarist Russia, and the overpopulated "Kings of the East"—have risen in conjunction for the first time ever to positions of power and prominence. Thus the scene is set for the Last Days events predicted by the ancient prophets of the Bible.

Pestilence and Disease

From the time of Moses, the Bible has spoken of plagues and diseases such as those with which God smote Egypt in order to force Pharaoh to release the Children of Israel from slavery. The history of our modern times has been dramatically impacted by disease as well.

The Black Death, another name for the Bubonic Plague, killed one-third of the population of Europe, over 50 million people, in just two years between 1348 and 1350. Cholera claimed a million Russian lives in 1848.

In the 20th Century, an estimated 20 million people worldwide died of the Spanish Flu between the years of 1918 and 1919, including half a million Americans. Some scientists anticipate another influenza pandemic any day now, like the Hong Kong flu of 1968 or the Asian flu of 1957, each of which killed 70,000 Americans.

In the second half of this century, most Americans became confident of our society's ability to eradicate the killer diseases of the past with modern "miracle drugs." Antibiotics promised to wipe out tuberculosis, diphtheria, pneumonia, and venereal disease the same way the Salk vaccine has eliminated polio and massive vaccinations have ended the blight of smallpox from mankind. But despite the real advancements of medical science, pharmacology and life-saving technology, there has been a recent reversal of fortunes in our war against disease.

The AIDS Epidemic

Today, virtually the entire continent of Africa is ravaged by AIDS, a deadly disease for which there is no preventive vaccine and no cure, and scientists have not yet calculated exactly how widely this disease may already have penetrated the world population. Studies by the Pan America Health Organization (PAHO), released June 30, 1993, indicate that it's going to get a lot worse before the decade of the '90s ends.[25]

The World Health Organization (WHO), the parent of PAHO, said that there had been 719,894 cumulative reported cases of full-blown AIDS worldwide since the epidemic began in 1981. But taking into account all the unreported cases known to exist, the real cumulative total climbed to about 2.5 million—all of whom had died or were on the verge of dying. By 1994 that estimated number had increased to 4 million.[26]

Since AIDS can have an incubation period of up to 15 years, only about 20 percent of the total HIV infections have yet developed into active AIDS, but it's only a matter of time. This led WHO to another mind-boggling extrapolation: in 1993 an estimated 12.8 to 13 million individuals worldwide were already infected with the HIV virus that most scientists believe leads to AIDS, perhaps in conjunction with other viruses.

Of these 13 million HIV carriers in 1993, more than 8 million were concentrated in the populations of sub-Saharan (Central) Africa, where unsanitary medical conditions and promiscuous sexual conduct combined to fan the epidemic. A news report in early 1996 said that 80 percent of West Africa's Ivory Coast prostitutes are HIV-positive, and 67 percent of the world's actual AIDS cases were believed to be in Africa.[27]

Another 1.5 million HIV cases were located in densely populated Southeast Asia in 1993. There the disease also continues to spread rapidly along the truck routes where HIV-infected prostitutes ply their trade.

"The worldwide situation is deteriorating," said Dr. Jonathan Mann of the Harvard School of Public Health. "We are facing a decade in the 1990s that will be far more difficult than anything we ever saw in the 1980s."

Mann predicted that by the year 2000, Southeast Asia will have passed Africa as the epicenter of the epidemic, with 41 percent of the HIV cases concentrated in Asia, 37 percent in Central Africa, 8 percent in Latin America, and 6 percent in the Caribbean.

WHO officials have predicted that by the year 2000, there will be between 40 and 110 million HIV cases in the world, about one-fifth of whom will manifest the symptoms of full-blown AIDS at any given time. It will be a truly global epidemic, and because the AIDS virus is constantly mutating, there is little chance of developing an effective vaccine against it.[28]

"By the year 2000, heterosexual transmission will predominate in most industrial countries," predicted Dr. James Chin, an epidemiologist who oversees AIDS surveillance at WHO. Chin said that 70 percent of future HIV transmissions will likely occur via heterosexual contact, 10 percent via homosexual contact, 10 percent via intravenous drug use, and the remaining 10 percent from miscellaneous causes such as tainted blood transfusions, accidental infection of healthcare workers, etc.

We cannot yet predict just what the final effects of the AIDS plague on the human race will be, but clearly the situation is far from benign.

Super-Germs on the Loose

Meanwhile, world health authorities also continue to worry over the possibility that something like the virulent Ebola virus, with its 80-percent mortality rate, could break out of Africa and reach major world population centers, creating an instant epidemic that could not be checked.

The popular 1995 movie *Outbreak,* starring Dustin Hoffman, depicts a scenario that could be all too real because of what is called the "global link." Today's highly mobile society makes it possible for disease germs to travel undetected with a jet passenger from continent to continent in a matter of hours, and there is no known way to stop it from happening.

"Public health is a global issue, because what happens in Zaire, what happens in India, affects us almost directly, not indirectly anymore," Dr. David Satcher of the U.S. Centers for Disease Control and Prevention, told a medical reporter recently.[29] To increase awareness among the public and in the medical community, CDC director Satcher has launched a new periodical called *Emerging Infectious Diseases* and put it on the Internet.

Satcher says that infectious diseases "remain the leading cause of death worldwide," noting that "each year more than one million children die of malaria in sub-Saharan Africa alone." In the 1990s, epidemic cholera reappeared in the Americas, after being absent for nearly a century. "From 1991 through June of 1994, more than one million cases and nearly 10,000 deaths were reported," Satcher warned.[30]

Even diseases like tuberculosis, meningitis, pneumonia, and various sexually transmitted diseases that once were considered defeated and dead have re-emerged as antibiotic-resistant strains, or super-bugs that once again threaten human life. A new super-strain of streptococcus has apparently mutated into a virulent "muscle-eating" form that has claimed several lives in the United States. The total cost of infectious diseases exceeds $100 million annually in the United States alone.

Even our advanced medical knowledge and technology may not be able to keep pace with the proliferation of these rapidly mutating diseases, plus the new plagues that may soon arise. Dr. Joshua Lederer, Nobel Prize-winning microbiologist and editor of the *Journal of the American Medical Association*, recently warned his colleagues of the "tinderbox" of a new global epidemic. "We have never been more vulnerable," Lederer said.[31]

Widespread Natural Disasters

Jesus also said in Matthew 24:7 that the Last Days would be a time of great natural calamities, with "famines, and pestilences, and earthquakes in divers places." In a parallel passage in Luke 21:11, Jesus said that "great earthquakes shall be in divers places, and famines, and pestilences, and fearful sights and great signs shall there be from heaven."

Again, we need look no further than the daily news reports to see the hand of God in the wildly fluctuating weather patterns of recent years. Early in February 1995, the "Newswatch" segment of *The 700 Club* indicated that "1995 could prove to be a record-breaking year for weather and natural disasters."[32] By year's end, that grim prognosis had been confirmed. A special report from Reuters News Service in late December proclaimed the sad truth: "Natural Disasters Hit New Record In 1995."[33]

Storms and Floods

Hurricanes, storms, earthquakes, and floods killed thousands and cost billions of dollars in damage to property and crops here in America, and also worldwide. According to Reuters, "The world was shaken by a record number of natural disasters in 1995, with damage from floods, earthquakes, storms, and volcanic eruptions trebling to $180 billion compared with last year [1994]...."

Some of the events cited by Reuters included the January 17 earthquake which killed 6,000 people in Kobe, Japan; the worst floods of this century in Germany and northwestern Europe, including the Netherlands, France, Belgium, Germany and Luxembourg; "an extraordinary frequency of tropical storms" around the world; as well as "various earthquakes, hailstorms, floods and volcanic eruptions throughout the world."

The 600 natural disasters recorded in 1995 took a toll of approximately 18,000 lives, compared to 10,150 killed in 580 incidents in 1994. Munich Re, the world's largest reinsurer, said that "1995 will enter the books as a record year in the history of natural disasters."

Disasters in America in 1995 began with torrential rains and flooding in California, which killed a dozen people and caused an estimated $300 million in damage. The Carolinas and the Ohio Valley also experienced severe flooding and mud slides during the year; and in the Caribbean a record tropical storm season, said to be the worst in half a century, spawned 11 hurricanes. The summer produced a searing heat wave across 19 states that left more than 800 people dead.[34]

The years prior to 1995 also illustrate violent weather trends.

Most people will remember Hurricane Hugo, the giant Category 4 storm (some say it was Category 5 by the time it made landfall) which ripped through South Carolina in the fall of 1989. Eyewitnesses who lived through that event described it as "the wrath of God"—or, alternatively, those who narrowly escaped death called it "the mercy of God." Either way, those on the scene saw the judgment of God in the tremendous physical and financial devastation wrought by that storm.

Hurricane Andrew, the costliest natural disaster in U.S. history, tore across Homestead, Florida, in 1992, and again the property damage was enormous, with insured losses estimated at $15.5 billion. Hurricane Iniki cost another $8.5 billion.

Fortunately, the loss of human life in both storms was minimal. But as the years have passed, the death toll from comparatively minor natural occurrences increased.

A cover story of *Life* magazine called 1993 "The Year of the Killer Weather" and asked "Why Has Nature Gone Mad?" because of the extensive damage, estimated at $4.7 billion, caused by torrential thunder storms, massive mud slides and Mississippi River flooding. Hundreds died and thousands were left homeless across the Midwest and South during the 1993 floods. In 1995 more storms and flooding extended into Texas, along with hailstones the size of baseballs.

The summers of 1993 and 1994 also saw searing heat waves that set records all across America and claimed hundreds of lives. In between were more floods and mud slides in California and raging forest fires across the tinder-dry Northwest timberlands.

In early 1996, two-thirds of the nation was locked in the grip of an unprecedented cold wave that set record lows nationwide. Near the Canadian border, the town of Embarrass, Minnesota, reported a record minus-59 degrees on February 4. Meanwhile, temperatures in the teens extended even to the citrus groves of Florida, devastating the fruit crops.

This cold snap came only weeks after the huge "Blizzard of '96" dumped uncharacteristically huge volumes of snow across the South, the Atlantic Coast, and the New England states. New York and New Jersey broke existing snowfall records that had stood for 50 years.

Some weather analysts attribute the unusual volumes of rain and snow in recent years to the continuing "El Nino" phenomenon, an unusual warming of the Pacific Ocean off the coast of South America. This in turn has been linked to increased volcanic activity in the volatile Pacific Rim region. "El Nino" is Spanish for "the Christ child."

This increasing evidence of instability in weather patterns might be overlooked as merely cyclical phenomena if these were only isolated incidents, but they are just part of a much larger picture.

Famines and the Population Bomb

The United Nations has declared that the world can now tolerate "Zero Population Growth" (ZPG) because there is not enough food to support a larger population. That is why the United Nations

Fund for Population Activities (UNFPA) promotes abortion as a necessary means of birth control in Third World countries around the globe. The UN also supports the "sterile sex" of homosexuality as a positive good in the Earth because that activity does not produce more mouths to feed.[35]

While many believe that these UNFPA claims are specious—there is plenty of food in the world, but often it does not reach the people who need it most because of inept administration, theft and greed, or simply callous manipulation by political leaders—it is a fact that millions of people are starving to death in Third World countries every year.[36]

It has been estimated that one-third of the Earth's population is well-fed, one-third is underfed, and one-third is starving. Who can forget the pictures of emaciated Ethiopians who looked like walking skeletons, or the bloated bellies of the children of Somalia, or the haggard refugees from Rwanda, that have haunted our television screens in the past few years?

It has been estimated that in excess of 50 million people have died of starvation since 1900, with the ruthless forced starvation of "uncooperative" Ukrainian peasant farmers by Soviet dictator Joseph Stalin in the early 1930s accounting for more than 15 million of these.

Other major famines of modern times have included the Irish Potato Blight (1845-51), in which a fungus claimed 1.5 million lives; the Bengal Famine in India, which killed between 1.5 and 3 million in 1943; and the War Famine in China's Henan Province, where between 3 and 5 million perished.

According to the United Nations Food and Agriculture Organization, there are three classifications of hungry people in the world today. Those suffering from acute hunger are on the verge of death from lack of food—there are about 35 million of these in southern Africa now. Those suffering from chronic hunger have inadequate food for health, growth and energy—there are more than 750 million of these in sub-Saharan Africa and South Asia. Those suffering from chronic hunger, or a prolonged shortage of adequate food which shortens their life span, are found everywhere.[37]

And certainly the number of people on the planet is growing.

It took from Creation until 1840 for the world's population to reach one billion. It took only 90 more years, until 1930, for it to double to two billion. By 1960 the population had reached three billion, and by 1975, four billion. By 1993 there were 5.5 billion people in the world, and there were about 6 billion people occupying the Earth in early 1996.[38]

Demographers' project that more than 7.5 billion souls will be living on Earth by the year 2000, after which the population should stabilize at between 8 and 9 billion by 2075 if present birth and death patterns prevail.

The United Nations population experts think these figures are too conservative. They estimate that the Earth will contain 11.3 billion people in 2100 A.D.—if population growth is drastically curtailed from present levels—and up to 14 billion if it is not.

Obviously, the billions of people presently on the Earth, as well as those who will join them in the future, will require food. But the most common cause of famine is either drought or flood conditions that destroy the crops necessary to produce that food. Both of these conditions are predicted for the Great Tribulation period.

The prophet Joel spoke of a time of drought when even the cattle will die because the rivers have dried up, and the Book of Revelation says there will be no rain on the Earth for a period of three and a half years. Great storms will produce both floods and hundred-pound hailstones.[39]

Many scientists today are blaming the "greenhouse effect," caused by the emission of excessive carbon dioxide from automobiles and industry, for some of the unusual weather conditions we now experience. Others say these things are merely the normal fluctuations of variable weather patterns. Still others see a more ominous specter on the horizon.

According to the October 1983 issue of *The Gospel Truth*,

> The U.S. Central Intelligence Agency predicted as far back as 1970 that due to the world's exploding population and predicted adverse weather pattern, that a world dictator will rise to power through revolutions, promising to feed the starving millions.[40]

The Gospel Truth publication goes on to quote another article from the March 1976 edition of the *Smithsonian* magazine, which says:

> The world as we know it will likely be ruined before the year 2000. And the reason will be its inhabitants' failure to comprehend two facts—World food production cannot keep pace with the galloping growth of world population...The

momentum toward tragedy is at this moment so great that there is probably no way of halting it.... No amount of scientific wizardry or improved weather will change the situation.[41]

The unfortunate truth is that the Earth is capable of producing enough food for every person on the planet, but because of the severe judgments that will come upon the world in the Last Days, famine will be everywhere. Food will be so scarce that a loaf of bread will cost a day's wages, and many will starve.[42]

Earthquakes

Earthquakes have become commonplace, with major tremors striking in Japan, South America, Mexico City, and California in recent years. While there have always been earthquakes, their frequency and intensity have increased significantly in the past 200 years, and especially in this century.

Between 1800 and 1906, there were only six major earthquakes recorded. Between 1907 and 1946, there were two or three quakes for each decade. But from 1947 to 1969 there were seven for each decade, and from 1970 to 1980 there were 22 major earthquakes.[43]

According to previously released data from the U.S. Geological Survey, in 1976 there were 79 "significant earthquakes," defined as quakes measuring 6.5 or more on the Richter scale or causing casualties or considerable damage. A decade later, in 1987, there were 76 "significant quakes" and 10 "serious quakes" measuring Magnitude 7.2 or greater.[44]

According to a new book by long-time prophecy analyst Hal Lindsey, "killer quakes worldwide" have increased "more than 30-fold" in the last century. Lindsey describes a "killer quake" as one of Magnitude 6 or greater. In the decade between 1950 and 1960, there were 9; between 1960 and 1970, there were 13; between 1970 and 1979, there were 51; between 1980 and 1989, there were 86; and from 1990 to 1994, there were more than 100.[45]

Sometimes it is difficult to grasp just what these numbers mean, as the definitions of "killer," "serious," "major," etc. seem to overlap, and at times we may be comparing apples with oranges. Nevertheless, some things are clear. According to the latest 1996 data from the National Earthquake Information Center of the USGS, the year 1976 was significant for two reasons: it produced 25 "major" earthquakes of 7.0 or greater on the Richter scale, and also the greatest number of earthquake casualties in recorded history, as the monster Tangshan quake killed an estimated 800,000 people in China.

The NEIC says that it "now locates about 12,000 to 14,000 earthquakes each year, or approximately 35 per day." But the agency stresses that many of these are minor quakes that would have gone undetected before the advent of today's sophisticated seismic monitoring and communications systems. Citing earthquake statistics since 1900 through August of 1995, the NEIC now says that "we expect about 18 major earthquakes (7.0-7.9) and one great earthquake (8.0 or above) in any given year."[46]

The earthquake that shook the seaport of Kobe, Japan, on January 17, 1995, measured only Magnitude 7.2. Still it damaged or destroyed 100,000 buildings, at an estimated cost of $100-130 billion, and killed 6,000 of the 1.4 million residents of that city.

In the aftermath of the Kobe quake, some experts believe that Japan should brace for more destruction in the Tokai region, a heavily populated industrial belt on Japan's Pacific Coast. "We expect a Magnitude 8 earthquake," said seismologist Kunihiko Shimazaki of Tokyo University.

Such a quake, which would be 30 times more powerful than the one that hit Kobe, would likely level Tokyo, killing as many as 60,000 people and injuring 100,000 more, plus causing up to a trillion dollars in property damage. Tidal waves produced by the quake could kill thousands more.[47]

Other earthquakes in 1995 occurred in Australia, Indonesia, and Colombia, all around the Pacific Rim region known as the "ring of fire" because of its seismic and volcanic activity. Residents of California have often felt the destructive effects of this turmoil along the San Andreas fault.

The great San Francisco earthquake of 1906 was estimated at 8.3 on the Richter scale, while the one that hit the Bay Area during the 1989 World Series was "only" 7.1. The latest California tremor, the Northridge quake that hit Los Angeles on January 17, 1994, registered just 6.8, but it killed 61 people. It is expected to cost $30 billion when the damage is repaired.[48]

The Southern California Earthquake Center warns that there is an 86-percent chance that Southern California will be hit by a quake of at least Magnitude 7 within the next 30 years. The USGS predicts a 90-percent chance of a major quake in the San Francisco Bay area by the year 2020.[49]

A San Francisco quake could cause as much as $65 billion in damage, and a major L.A. tremor could top $70 billion. But even worse would be a blow to America's midwestern heartland—a major quake along the New Madrid fault in Missouri could cause devastating damage.

"If that earthquake occurs, the total loss would cost $100 billion— five times greater than the previous greatest disaster," said Jack Weber, head of the National Disaster Coalition in Washington, D.C.[50]

While these possibilities are unpleasant, they are nevertheless likely. The pattern of progressive acceleration of earthquakes and other natural disasters can be expected to continue throughout the Last Days.

Both Old and New Testament prophecies predict terrible earthquakes at various points during the coming Great Tribulation period.[51] Zechariah 14:6 predicts that the Mount of Olives itself will be split completely in two by an earthquake at the moment of Jesus' return. The topography of the land of Israel will be changed and the city of Jerusalem will be flattened. The Dead Sea will be joined to the Red Sea and will finally sustain life. These predictions are more easily understood when we consider the fact that the land of Israel is now known to sit atop a geological region riddled with deep fault lines.

All this adds up to an ever-accelerating pattern of misery and destruction around the globe, and these are just some of the signs Jesus said would accompany the end of the age.

---

[1]   This is a separate teaching, but it should be mentioned that Jesus' opinion of hypocritical religious leaders hasn't changed any, since the Bible says that He is "the same yesterday, and today, and forever" (Hebrews 13: 8). God is looking for true disciples who will "worship Him in Spirit and in truth" (John 4: 24), not in outward appearance only.

[2]   This part of the prophecy was literally fulfilled in 70 A.D. when Jerusalem fell to Roman armies under Titus as the Jewish Zealots' rebellion was crushed. The city was burned and the intense heat of the fire caused the golden dome of the Temple to melt. Roman soldiers literally took the Temple apart stone by stone to get the gold that had run into the cracks. This is just one more example of the literal fulfillment of Biblical prophecy.

[3]   Death toll is from *Academic American Encyclopedia*, Electronic Version (Danbury, Conn.: Grolier, 1995), s.v. "Death."

[4] A comprehensive discussion of the world powers that will arise in the end times can be found in J. Dwight Pentecost, *Things to Come: A Study in Biblical Eschatology*, with an Introduction by John F. Walvoord (Findlay, Ohio: Dunham, 1958; reprint ed., Grand Rapids: Zondervan, 1981), pp. 314-339.

[5] Daniel 11:36-45.

[6] *Forbes* magazine, April 25, 1988.

[7] Hal Lindsey, *Planet Earth— 2000 A.D.* (Palos Verdes, Cal.: Western Front, 1994), p. 226.

[8] Quoted Ibid., p. 227.

[9] "Rosh" refers to an ancient people called the Sarmatians who lived around the Caucasus Mountains between the Black and Caspian Seas. Today this region includes portions of southern Russia, Ukraine, Armenia, Georgia, and Azerbaijan. "Magog" applies to the Scythians, nomadic tribesmen of the Russian steppes who later settled north of the Caucasus Mountains. This region today includes parts of Russia, Ukraine and Central Asia.

[10] Psalm 83:1-4, Ezekial 38:39.

[11] Lindsey, *Planet Earth—2000 A.D.*, p. 181.

[12] Ibid., pp. 179-181.

[13] David Albright, "An Iranian Bomb?" *Bulletin of the Atomic Scientists,* Vol. 51, No. 4, July/August 1995, pp. 20-26.

[14] Lindsey, P*lanet Earth—2000 A.D.*, p. 201.

[15] Information in this section on Zhirinovsky is primarily from Scot Overbey, *Vladimir Zhirinovsky: The Man Who Would Be Gog* (Oklahoma City: Hearthstone, 1994).

[16] Ibid., p. 19.

[17] Ibid., p. 132.

[18] Dmitri Gusev, "Russian Presidential Elections—96," Internet Posting, http://www.cs.indiana.edu/hyplan/dmiguse/Russian/elections.html, April 5, 1996.

[19] Alessandra Stanley, "Russian Communist Aims for Broad Appeal," *New York Times News Service,* March 18, 1996, Internet Posting, April 5, 1996.

[20] Ibid.

[21] *Reuters News Service, St. Petersburg Press,* "Gorbachev Kicks Off Presidential Campaign," Internet Posting, April 5, 1996.

[22] Revelation 16, Daniel 11.

[23] "China Tells U.S. to Stay Out of Taiwan Strait," *Norfolk Virginian-Pilot,* March 18, 1996, p. A-1.

[24] "1996: Changes, Choices and Challenges," *The 700 Club Newswatch Fact Sheet,* January 1, 1996.

[25] Information in this section is from Connie Zhu, "Global AIDS Epidemic Looms: WHO Predicts 40 Million HIV Cases By 2000," *Christian American,* February 1994, pp. 6-7.

[26] "In Ivory Coast, 8 of 10 Prostitutes Carry HIV," *Norfolk Virginian-Pilot,* March 18, 1996, p. A-3.

[27] Ibid.

[28] Some Christians believe that the AIDS epidemic did not originate by accident but that it was deliberately developed by the World Health Organization and intentionally introduced to Africa in smallpox vaccinations. I cannot confirm this hypothesis, I simply mention it her for the benefit of those who may wish to pursue the matter. See William Campbell Douglass, M.D., "Murder on the WHO Express: WHO Murdered Africa," *Frontpage,* Vol. 2, No. 1, 1988 (John Barela, Ed., Today, the Bible, and You, P.O. Box 1722, Broken Arrow, OK 74013, (918) 455-5321).

[29] Marie Joyce, "Q & A," *Norfolk Virginian-Pilot,* April 9, 1995, p. J1.

[30] David Satcher, "Emerging Infections: Getting Ahead of the Curve," *Emerging Infectious Diseases,* Vol 1, No. 1, January-March 1995.

[31] Tom McNamee, "Infectious Disease Threat Rises: Doctors See New Risk of Global Epidemic," *Chicago Sun-Times,* January 17, 1996, p. 3.

[32] "Natural Disasters: Is God Shaking the Nations?" *The 700 Club Newswatch Fact Sheet,* February 6, 1995.

[33] "Natural Disasters Hit New Record in 1995," *Reuters News Service,* December 27, 1995. Much of the information in the following paragraphs is from this source.

[34] "1995 Year in Review: A World Searching for Answers," *The 700 Club Newswatch Fact Sheet,* December 31, 1995.

[35] "The homosexual or the sterile sexual activity is preferred because there is no child that is produced. And this is not a problem for the population controller," explains Cecilia Royals, president of the National Institute for Women. Quoted in "U.N.'s Gender Agenda: How It Undermines the Family," *The 700 Club Newswatch Fact Sheet,* August 3, 1995.

[36] Many leaders of Third World countries resent the intrusion of the United Nations, with the support of the United States, into the family planning policies of their citizens. They would rather have medicine to treat diseases than shelves stocked with birth control devices. Moreover, the basic presuppositions of Zero Population Growth are flawed. "The notion of a worldwide 'population crisis' is a myth. People are not a burden. They are a natural resource." Cal Thomas, "The New American Colonialism," *Christian American,* July/August 1993, p. 30.

[37] Lindsey, *Planet Earth—2000 A.D.,* p. 123.

[38] Current (1993) population and 2075 projections are from *Academic American Encyclopedia,* Electronic Version, s.v. "Population."

[39] Joel 1:17-20; Revelation 8:7, 11:19, 16:21; Ezekial 38:22.

[40] "End Time Weather," *The Gospel Truth,* October 1983, p. 2.

[41] "Head South With All Deliberate Speed," *Smithsonian,* March 1976, quoted Ibid.

[42] Revelation 6:5-6.

[43] Winkler, Class Notes. See also Hal Lindsey, *The 1980's: Countdown to Armageddon* (New York: Bantam, 1981), pp. 29-31.

[44] Associated Press, "Earthquakes Increasing Worldwide," January 1988, referenced in "Judgments — Apocalyptic and Otherwise," *The Gospel Truth,* July 1988, p. 4.

[45] Hal Lindsey, *Planet Earth— 2000 A.D.* (Palos Verdes, Cal.: Western Front, 1994), pp. 83-84. See also Hal Lindsey, *The Final Battle* (Palos Verdes, Cal.: Western Front, 1995), p. xvi. Hal Lindsey's books contain a wealth of valuable information beyond the scope of this author's abbreviated text. I encourage readers who want to know more about the Last Days to study Lindsey's well-researched writings.

[46] "Are Earthquakes Really on the Increase?" National Earthquake Information Center, U.S. Geological Survey, Golden, Co., Internet Posting, February 5, 1996.

[47] "Kobe's Aftermath: Is Any City Safe in the End Times?" *The 700 Club Newswatch Fact Sheet,* December 6, 1995.

[48] Lindsey, *Planet Earth—2000 A.D.,* pp. 84-85.

[49] "Natural Disasters: Is God Shaking the Nations?" *The 700 Club Newswatch Fact Sheet,* February 6, 1995.

[50] "Disaster Protection: Can We Cover Our Losses?" *The 700 Club Newswatch Fact Sheet,* August 16, 1995.

[51] See Isaiah 24:17-23, Joel 316, Revelation 6:12, 8: 5, 11:13, 16:18.

Chapter 2
False Religion
in the Last Days

*For there shall arise false Christs, and false prophets,
and shall shew great signs and wonders; insomuch that, if
it were possible, they shall deceive the very elect.
Behold, I have told you before.*

Matthew 24:24-25

There will be an increase in false religion in the Last Days, and the religious trends all around us indicate that this is rapidly coming to pass.

"In the last days perilous times shall come," warned the Apostle Paul in 1 Timothy 3:1. He also said that men would become both "unholy" and "lovers of pleasure rather than lovers of God."

That about sums up the situation today. Most men simply don't love God. Few even bother to think about God, or to mention His name in any way other than as part of a curse.

The Apostle Paul said specifically that there would be a "falling away," or an apostasy, or literally a defection from truth, before the appearance of the Antichrist.[1] He also told Timothy that "some shall depart from the faith," or literally desert Christ, to follow demons.[2]

Both of those things are happening today in various parts of the world. This condition coincides with a rhetorical question Jesus asked:

*Nevertheless, when the Son of man cometh, shall he
find faith on the earth?*

Luke 18:8

While this last Scripture may be applied most directly to the end of the Great Tribulation period, it is illustrative of the fact that true faith will be diminished in the end times. The Bible predicts several significant developments in the religious world, which could indicate that we are living in the Last Days.

Apostasy From the Faith

Vast numbers of people will depart from the Christian faith in the end times, as many will forsake God completely. This has already happened in the other formerly "Christianized" countries of the world even more than in America, though the trend to theological liberalism is also evident here.

Both Western Europe—including Great Britain and the Scandinavian countries—and Japan have become increasingly humanistic and materialistic. Along with advanced technological development has come prosperity, with the predictable result that money and science have become the new secular gods of this modern age. In Japan, while some hold on to traditional Shinto spiritism, most are merely materialistic.

Missionaries to the Western European countries indicate that most of the people there have little interest in spiritual matters. Religion there is mostly formal traditionalism rather than dynamic living faith.

Atheism was once the official government doctrine in the Eastern European countries previously aligned with the Soviet Union. But there was always a strong though persecuted underground Church in most of these countries, as well as some traces of traditional Eastern Orthodox faith. Revivals have been reported in Russia as well as Albania since the breakup of the Communist bloc in 1989, but still the vast majority of the people in those countries remain unconverted.

The government of China tries, often unsuccessfully, to discourage its huge population from practicing any form of religion, especially traditional religions like Buddhism and Confucianism, preferring that the people concentrate on productive labor. Although an official state-approved form of Christianity is tolerated, the underground house churches in China are persecuted still. These Christian groups, though growing, comprise only a tiny fraction of the Chinese people.

There have been outbreaks of revival all over the world in this century, especially in Africa, Korea, Indonesia, and the Philippines, witnessed by mass conversions and miracles like those recorded in the book of Acts.[3] Still the majority of people in these countries are not Christians.

Hinduism and Buddhism still dominate most of non-Chinese East Asia; Islam is firmly entrenched in Western Asia, Northern Africa and the Middle East; and a mixture of tribal spiritism and Roman Catholicism holds sway in Central and South America.

So despite determined missionary and evangelistic efforts, the vast majority of people in the world remain non-Christian. Statistics from the Christian Broadcasting Network's International Division (now called WorldReach) show that on average only one in six persons exposed to the Gospel actually accepts Christ.

At home in the traditionally "Christian" United States, vital personal faith has gradually been replaced with merely outward religiosity, as many Americans have begun to view God as irrelevant.

"In this great apostasy from New Testament Christianity, we could see a sign which would warrant us in believing that Christ's coming may not be far away," observed Dr. Harold Ockenga, president of Gordon Conwell Divinity School, writing forty years ago.

Dr. Ockenga, a veteran of the ongoing battle to save the fundamentals of the Christian faith in America from encroaching theological liberalism in the first half of the 20th Century, continued, "There has always been some measure of apostasy, and at times that apostasy has been great, but not as it has been in these fifty years."[4]

The Numbers Don't Lie

Unfortunately, the most up-to-date statistics available today bear out Dr. Ockenga's observations from four decades ago.

Researcher George Barna has compiled extensive data documenting the true state of Christianity in America, and his findings have caused many to become alarmed. According to Barna, the American culture is reinventing itself every 3 to 5 years, and what it is becoming is quite different from what it has been in the past.[5]

Mass immigration and modern technology are combining to change both the face and the focus of American life.

In 1993, 52 percent of all immigrants to America came from Mexico and 13 percent came from Asia. One in four Americans today is of non-Caucasian origin, and in most urban areas whites are already a minority. White population growth has essentially stagnated, and African-Americans are increasing by only about

15 percent per year. But both Asian-American and Hispanic populations are growing at about 40 percent per year. By the year 2000, if current trends continue, the ethnic mix in America will be very different from what it is today.

Simultaneously on the educational front, despite the heralded advent of our new "Information Age," personal human achievement is declining. A recent government study revealed that barely 51 percent of the U.S. population is functionally literate, and America's literacy level ranked 49th out of 158 countries in the United Nations. More than a million high school graduates each year cannot read and write at a seventh grade level.

The introduction of large numbers of people from non-Christian cultures, plus the "dumbing down" of American society so that the general population no longer retains any true historical memory of the uniquely Christian roots of this nation, are having a predictable effect—the values that were once considered mainstream are changing radically and rapidly.

People no longer agree on what it means to be an inclusive family. Where once a traditional family consisted of people related by blood, marriage or adoption, that definition is now accepted by just 46 percent of the population. The nouveau definition, which 68 percent embrace, has become "people I care deeply about." The permanent has been replaced by the transitory.

Seventy percent of all Americans now believe that divorce is permissible. One-third expect that they will experience divorce—including a full 50 percent of the 68 million young Baby Busters born between 1963 and 1983. These expectations tend to become self-fulfilling prophecies, as one-third of all children born in America today are born to single mothers.

Barna believes that the decade of the 1990s will determine whether American culture will experience spiritual renewal through the influence of the Church, or whether it will degenerate further into a state of moral anarchy—and the unmistakable trend is definitely toward the latter.

While concepts of "spirituality" are important to the younger generations of Americans, Christianity is not. Syncretism has become the "faith choice" of many in this day of designer religion. Among non-Christians, only 9 percent consider evangelical Christians to be "sensitive" to their needs—instead they are perceived as being "too judgmental."

Almost two-thirds of Americans hold a "very favorable" impression of the American Cancer Society, but only 29 percent feel the same way about the Baptists, and that's the top score. Democrats and Roman Catholics tie at 23 percent each, as do Republicans and Ford Motor Company at 20 percent. The next denomination in line is the Methodists at 18 percent, and it goes downhill from there.

The culture appears to be having more of an impact on the Church than vice versa. Seventy-one percent of all Americans say that there is no such thing as absolute truth—and 68 percent of regular church attenders agree, as do 40 percent of evangelical Christians. Only 34 percent now say that the Bible is the best source for absolute truth.

Although 96 percent of Americans claim to believe in God, closer questioning reveals that only 66 percent actually believe in the Creator described in the Bible. Half of the people believe that Jesus Christ was a sinner, as do one-fourth of self-described "born again" Christians.

Sixty percent of the people surveyed said that good works were sufficient to get them into Heaven, while two-thirds could not name even four of the Ten Commandments.

Of the 265 million people in America, only about 75 million are profession Christians. On any given Sunday, 54 percent of the people attending Protestant churches are not truly born again.

If these numbers don't paint a picture of apostasy in the Last Days, I don't know what does.

One-World Church

Revelation 17 describes a state of affairs that will exist during the Great Tribulation, and a woman referred to by the Apostle John as the "Great Whore" and "Mystery, Babylon." Many evangelical Bible scholars have interpreted this passage symbolically to mean that a false world religious system will form a league with the Antichrist and assist his rise to power.

The Apostle John wrote that men in the Last Days would have "a form of godliness, but denying the power thereof." Combining these two Scriptures gives a picture of a superficial religious structure without true spiritual content, and that description could fit many a dead American denomination today. However, one specific organization now exists which many believe to be the precursor of the "Great Whore" of Revelation 17.

The World Council of Churches (WCC) was formed in 1948 at an ecumenical conference in Amsterdam, with members coming from the old mainline Protestant denominations, including the Methodists, Lutherans, United Presbyterians, Anglican/Episcopalians, and Northern Baptists.[6]

The WCC today consists of eight powerful denominations, each of which designates a percentage of its income to support the WCC. Its American arm is called the National Council of Churches (NCC).

This organization has been instrumental in promoting the World Ecumenical Movement, which ostensibly seeks to fulfill the prayer of Jesus for His disciples in John 17:21, "that they all may be one." Their doctrine of "unity in diversity" is expressed in the slogan: "in essentials unity; in nonessentials liberty; in all things charity." This sounds great.

But critics of the organization say that this superficial unity comes at the expense of sacrificing the distinctive doctrines of the Christian faith, such as the Virgin Birth, the Deity of Christ, the Blood Atonement, the Bodily Resurrection, and the Personal Return of Jesus Christ. Without these fundamental doctrines, the Gospel becomes meaningless and Christianity becomes just another formal religious ritual devoid of spiritual power.[7]

Instead of promoting a scriptural Gospel of salvation, most modern WCC-affiliated denominational seminaries today have degenerated into liberalism. Following the lead of Princeton seminary in the late 1920s, many of their doctrines have plunged headlong into heresy.[8]

For example, many liberal theologians, accepting the "higher critical" method of Biblical textual analysis, now hold that the Bible is a work of men rather than the inerrant Word of God. So it is filled with errors, which only astute scholars can detect. And they endorse Rudolf Bultmann's "demythologizing" of Scripture, saying the miracles are merely myths, for which academics attempt to offer plausible naturalistic explanations.[9]

Not surprisingly, this type of theology has reduced the WCC's emphasis on Christian missionary activities seeking to convert the heathen. That type of activity is now viewed as "imperialistic." In fact, a recent book by an ordained Methodist minister from Sri Lanka, who is also the director of the WCC Sub-Unit on Dialogue, urges that the organization abandon the concepts of "uniqueness and finality" in their presentation of the Gospel.

"Their usefulness is past," the author insists. What is needed now is an acknowledgment of pluralism and common ground with Hindus.[10]

The WCC also has endorsed various types of Marxist-oriented Liberation Theology, or "Theology of Revolution," believing like some left-wing Catholic theologians that political revolution is the only way to reform the social and economic inequities of the world. The WCC has also insisted that "Western capitalism and the profit motive are the major causes of war" and has branded NATO's deterrent policies during the 1980s "as unmitigated an evil as actual war."[11]

The WCC also has supplied funds for almost half a century to communist insurgents in various trouble spots of the world, especially in Africa, and these groups have used those funds to foment social revolution. A January 1983 *Reader's Digest* article entitled "Do You Know Where Your Church Offerings Go?" reported that it had:

> ...discovered and documented that over a two-year period $442,000 in Methodist churchgoers' money alone had been sent to a number of political organizations... "groups supporting the Palestine Liberation Organization, the governments of Cuba, Vietnam, and pro-Soviet totalitarian movements of Latin America, Asia, and Africa, and several violence prone groups in the United States."[12]

There are other recorded instances of WCC support for radical causes that do not appear to be promoting the Gospel as intended by Jesus Christ. In April 1978, for example, the WCC gave $85,000 for "humanitarian purposes" to Patriotic Front guerrillas in Rhodesia, who subsequently slaughtered 35 Christian missionaries and their families.[13]

According to official WCC records, in the first 17 years of its Program to Combat Racism, the Council gave $6,906,545 to more than 100 groups in 30 countries. Of that amount, 70 percent went to political groups devoted to overthrowing the white regime in South Africa "by force and subversion." Three organizations together received $2,292,500, or 36 percent of the total: the African National Congress (ANC), the South West Africa People's Organization (SWAPO), and the Pan Africanist Congress of Azania (PAC).[14]

Considering these facts, we would do well to recall Jesus' teaching that "where your treasure is, there will your heart be also" (Matthew 6:21).

The Vatican Connection

Some believe that, while it is not affiliated with the Roman Catholic Church today, the WCC eventually will merge with Rome. They cite the famous statement by Pope John Paul II that the Protestant "wayward children will come back to the fold." Thus the WCC will be controlled by the Papacy at the time of the Tribulation, when the false religious system they represent will be revealed as the "Great Whore."[15]

It should be noted here that some Bible scholars—especially many of those in the Charismatic Renewal movement—do not endorse this identification of the Vatican as part of the "Great Whore," although this interpretation remains common in Fundamentalist, Pentecostal, and Seventh-Day Adventist doctrine, as well as in some Evangelical theology. The identification of the Pope with the Antichrist has been a recurring theme for Protestants since the Reformation.

Certainly there are many sincere and genuine Christians within the Roman Catholic ranks—although some Catholic doctrines clearly are irreconcilable with Biblical truth—and it would be grossly wrong to mislabel all Catholics as willful followers of the Antichrist.

Some political actions of the Catholic Church throughout history, however, have been anti-Semitic, and others have been anti-Christian.[16] Despite the historical antipathy between Protestants and Catholics—especially those sore grievances provoked by the notorious Inquisitions of the Counter-Reformation period—the Vatican today remains one of the most steadfast and vocal opponents of the pro-abortion and pro-homosexual agendas now being promoted by radical social reformers in the United Nations and elsewhere.

The Catholic Church also affirms vital Biblical doctrines such as the sanctity of life and the value of traditional marriage, as well as the deity of Christ; His virgin birth and sinless life; His crucifixion, death and bodily resurrection; and His physical return at some future time.

Nevertheless, there is some legitimate cause for concern that the Vatican may one day run amok, and this possibility has been articulated by the Pope himself and chronicled by a faithful Jesuit, Malachi Martin. In 1990 Martin wrote a book with the provocative title, *The Keys of This Blood: The Struggle for World Dominion Between Pope John Paul II, Mikhail Gorbachev, and the Capitalist West*. This book raises two interesting points.

First, according to Martin, Pope John Paul II has been unable to purge from within his own church structure the seeds of doctrinal liberalism. While this means something different to a traditionalist Catholic theologian than it does to a Protestant Biblicist, the net effect is still apostasy from whatever vestiges of the true Christian faith may remain. By 1981, three years after he took office, John Paul realized that:

> Already whole sections of the Church in France, Austria, Holland, Germany, Spain, England, Canada, the United States, and Latin America had fallen precisely into unfaith. There subsisted only a faithful remnant of practicing Catholics.... An intricate and self-protective network of actively homosexual priests, nuns, bishops, and some cardinals now throttled all attempts to reform morals. Contraception was advocated explicitly or implicitly by a plurality of bishops, and abortion, together with divorce, was connived at....
>
> Most frightening for John Paul, he had come up against the irremovable presence of malign strength in his own Vatican and in certain bishops' chanceries. It was what knowledgeable Churchmen called the "superforce." Rumors, always difficult to verify, tied its installation to the beginning of Pope Paul VI's reign in 1963. Indeed, Paul had alluded somberly to "the smoke of Satan which has entered the Sanctuary"—an oblique reference to an enthronement ceremony by Satanists in the Vatican. Besides, the incidence of Satanic pedophilia—rites and practices—was already documented among certain bishops and priests as widely dispersed as Turin, in Italy, and Southern California, in the United States. The cultic acts of Satanic pedophilia are considered by professionals to be the culmination of the Fallen Archangel's rites.[17]

It would appear, not only from this passage but also from the whole tone of Martin's book, that unless John Paul II soon does something drastic to reassert his authority within the Catholic Church, his potential successor could well be someone not at all devoted to Christ. Should an active Satanist ascend to the Papal throne—which is likely since the Pope is over 70 years old—and should an ecumenical alliance between the Vatican and the liberal Protestant denominations actually occur, the possibility for a scenario similar to that described in Revelation 17 appears very real.

The second point revealed by Martin is John Paul II's belief that some dramatic supernatural event is going to occur very soon, which will have the effect of causing all the religions of the world to accept him as their authentic spiritual leader. This event will be linked to a series of wars and economic and natural disasters, as well as a period of apostasy and unbelief, first predicted in 1917 by an appearance of the Virgin Mary in Fatima, Portugal. Those predictions are said to match a similar vision of the future which John Paul II himself had in August 1981, while he was recovering from an assassination attempt.

Coincidentally, the attack on the Pope had occurred on May 13, the official feast day of the Virgin Mary as Our Lady of Fatima. John Paul II had previously consecrated himself especially to Mary, and he believes that it is she who spared his life that day for a purpose of divine destiny. Now 73 years old, he expects to be alive when Jesus returns before the year 2000.[18]

According to Martin, Russia is the key to these cataclysmic events.

> The chastisements were meant to punish the nations for their ungodliness and abandonment of God's laws. The whole dire process could be averted—need not happen, in fact—if two requests of Mary were granted. One: that whoever would be Pope in 1960 (actually it was John XXIII) should publish the text of the "Third Secret" for the whole world to read and know. Two: that then the Pope, with all his bishops acting collegially, should consecrate Russia to Mary. Russia, according to the text of the "Third Secret," was the regulator of the timetable.[19]

Because the preceding conditions were not met by his predecessor, John Paul II believes that the calamitous events which have been predicted are unavoidable. However, "some mitigation of the coming tribulations—but only a mitigation—could be achieved by merely consecrating the world to Mary, 'with a special mention of Russia.'"

This the Pope did on May 13, 1982, at Fatima.[20]

False Prophets, False Christs, False Religions

Jesus specifically warned His disciples to beware of false Christs and false prophets in the Last Days. His words are worth repeating, because this warning was the very first thing out of Jesus' mouth when He answered His disciples in Matthew 24:4, and He quickly repeated it three times.

> **And Jesus answered and said unto them, _Take heed that no man deceive you_.**
> **_For many shall come in my name, saying, I am Christ: and shall deceive many_....**
> **_And many false prophets shall arise, and shall deceive many_....**
> **_For there shall arise false Christs, and false prophets, and shall shew great signs and wonders; insomuch that, if it were possible, they shall deceive the very elect_.**
> **_Behold, I have told you before._**
> **Matthew 24:4-5, 11, 24-25.**

Jesus seems to be telling us that a lot of pseudo-spiritual religious deception will be going on in the Last Days, and the ignorant and unaware will be deceived by the multitude of false prophets and false Christs who will arise. We are going to look at some of the various false religions, cults, and doctrines that dominate our modern American culture.

Unfortunately, it is beyond the scope of this book to explore this crucial topic in depth, so a brief overview here will have to suffice.

False Prophets

People have an intense curiosity about the future, often fueled by the uncertainties of the present and the tragedies of the past. They tend to be fascinated with the promise of supernatural insight into things to come. So pervasive has this fascination become that 900-number ads for "psychic hotlines" and "psychic friends networks" can be found on many television channels, and these spiritual quests are often endorsed by entertainment celebrities and other prominent people.

Perhaps most telling about the spiritual tenor of our times was the revelation by Ronald Reagan's former chief of staff, Donald Regan, that First Lady Nancy Reagan regularly consulted astrologers for psychic advice on behalf of her husband, and that his schedule as President was subject to her whims based on his astrological charts. Mrs. Reagan later admitted that this was so, and that the President was aware of it, but she said she didn't see anything wrong with "hedging our bets" this way.[21]

Popular Psychics and Seers

Popular interest has recently rekindled in the 400-year-old writings of Nostradamus, a French Roman Catholic born in 1503. Nostradamus was a true Renaissance man who obviously had a glimpse of things to come. His predictions of modern airplanes, submarines, and periscopes were unique to his time. He predicted that Great Britain would fade as a world power after 300 years, before England had arisen as an empire. He named America and Hitler (Hisler) before they existed. He predicted a great war to begin in 1999, describing bombs and flame-throwing tanks.[22] Today we see his name on the front covers of supermarket tabloids virtually every week.

Edgar Cayce was a famous clairvoyant of a generation ago. Cayce made several famous predictions that came true, such as the exact date when World War II would end and the date of the future assassination of President John Kennedy in 1963. Cayce believed in reincarnation and was convinced that he had once lived on the long-lost continent of Atlantis, which he said had been destroyed by a nuclear explosion.[23]

Cayce, also known as the "sleeping prophet," was able to heal people of diseases the doctors of his day couldn't cure. He did this by a process known as "channeling," in which he went into a deep trance and allowed the "voices of his past lives" to speak words of wisdom through him. He produced an estimated 16,000 of these "readings," as he called them. He also taught others to channel their past lives.

Cayce claimed to have received his psychic gifts from an encounter with a bright figure dressed in white who appeared to him one day when he was seven or eight years old while he was reading the Bible in the woods. He died in 1945 but his son carries on his psychic heritage through the Association for Research and Enlightenment, based in Virginia Beach, Virginia. People still come from all over the world to learn about Cayce and his metaphysical secrets for unlocking a person's psychic power.[24]

Jeane Dixon is the most famous psychic of our time, and it is said that her predictions have an accuracy rating of over 50 percent, far greater than most professing clairvoyants. She predicted the death of Franklin Roosevelt, the Communist takeover of China, the partitioning of India, the orbiting of the Russian satellite *Sputnik,* and the fall of Nikita Kruschev.

Defying all the conventional wisdom of the day, she correctly predicted in January of 1948 that Truman would defeat Dewey in the coming November presidential election, astonishing the political pundits. She has also accurately predicted many events of lesser importance, from the winners of horse races to theatrical hits.

She is said to have warned John F. Kennedy not to go to Dallas in 1963 because he would be killed there, but he failed to follow her advice. She had seen in a vision in 1952 that a young, blue-eyed Democratic President in 1960 would be killed. Her prophecy was printed in *Parade* magazine on May 13, 1956. Kennedy was shot on November 22, 1963.

A slogan written by Jeane Dixon, which appeared in the *Army Journal* of 1946, reads: "It's not what your country can do for you; it's what you can do for your country." In 1961, newly-elected President Kennedy used a slightly modified version of that slogan in his inaugural address.[25]

There is no question that people can gain access to information about the future through psychic means. From King Saul in the Bible, who met his doom after consulting the "witch [medium] of Endor," to Shakespeare's MacBeth, who died after Birnam Wood moved according to the witch's prediction, we see that throughout recorded history supernatural insight into the future has been accepted and documented.

But what is the source of this psychic power? While both the United States and the Russians have had their secret intelligence agencies working overtime for years trying to develop a way to turn "parapsychology" and "ESP" to military purposes, this field really has nothing to do with traditional science. It is a spiritual matter, and the power behind these supernatural manifestations comes from either God or the Devil.

The common thread between all the psychics, whether of the past or present, is their denial of the Deity of Jesus Christ and the sufficiency of His Blood Atonement on the cross for the redemption of mankind.

They may claim to be "Christian," they may even go to church, they may affirm that Jesus was a good man or a great moral teacher, or even call Him a prophet or "a god"—but at some point every false prophet will deny the fundamental identity of Jesus Christ of Nazareth as the only true Messiah of God and Savior of the world, Who has come in the flesh and is coming again. This is the mark of a false prophet and a false religion.

Edgar Cayce believed in the Hindu doctrine of reincarnation, which directly contradicts the Biblical teaching that "it is appointed unto man once to die, but after this the judgment" (Hebrews 9:27). Reincarnation has no place for judgment. It holds that individual souls continue basically to recycle themselves on the Karmic wheel until eventually everyone attains a blessed extinction in Nirvana, merging with the Godhead.

If this be true, of course, the Bible is false, Jesus is a liar, and men never really needed a Savior after all.

Visions From the Serpent

Jean Dixon claims to be a Christian who prays and attends daily Mass at a Catholic church. But in her authorized biography, *A Gift of Prophecy,* she tells of a dream she had on July 14, 1952, in which a huge snake crawled into her bed and wrapped itself around her body, gazed into her eyes and filled her with a sense of "peace on earth, good will toward men."[26]

In the Bible, the Apostle Paul encountered a female fortune teller at Philippi (Acts 16:16-18). This woman was described as a "damsel possessed with a spirit of divination," but the Greek says literally "a spirit, a Python." When Paul rebuked the spirit, it left the damsel and she could no longer tell fortunes. Jean Dixon has with her own mouth described the demonic nature of her psychic powers, which apparently were passed to her by a "sweet old gypsy" who gave her a crystal ball when she was eight years old.

Because this book is concerned with end-time events, I will mention three other visions Jean Dixon has had which may have some relevance. These visions have also been described by renowned Bible scholar Dr. Merrill F. Unger in his excellent book, *Demons in the World Today.*

Mrs. Dixon had her second vision while she was praying and meditating in St. Matthew's Cathedral in Washington. She was about to burn candles when "a mass of purple and gold balls...floated upward and...encircled the knees of the statue of the Virgin Mary, rising gently... enveloped her breast and head, like an uplifted halo." The rest of the cathedral vision caused her to declare: "A remarkable peace overcame me and I knew that a council of our church would soon bring together under the roof of the Holy See in Rome the religions and nationalities of all the world." Four years later the Roman Catholic Church began the fulfillment of her vision in the Ecumenical Council of 1962 (cf. Revelation 17:1-8).

In her third vision, the seeress saw the papal throne vacant and the papacy suffering violence, a prophecy clearly outlined in Revelation 17:15-18, when the political power of the endtime destroys the ecclesiastical power headed up by Rome.[27]

Apparently Jean Dixon's two visions described above had to do first with the establishment and later the destruction of the world religious system of the Last Days—although the vision of violence to the papacy could have application to any attack upon that office at any time, such as the 1981 assassination attempt on John Paul II by a Turkish radical believed to have been acting on behalf of Bulgaria and ultimately the Soviet KGB.

Dixon's fourth vision is also of special interest. Quoting Unger:

The fourth vision, which the seeress believes to be the most important of all, was received February 5, 1962, when a rare conjunction of the planets took place and astrologers were forecasting some great event.

At this time strange things began to occur in Mrs. Dixon's home. Lights began to dim and flare. As she gazed toward the East before sunrise she saw an Egyptian Pharaoh and Queen Nefertiti stepping out of the sun's rays. Cradled in the queen's arms was a baby in rags, in stark contrast to the gorgeous robes of the royal couple.

While the seeress gazed entranced, the couple advanced toward her and extended the baby, whose eyes were full of wisdom, as if offering it to the entire world.

Soon the baby grew and became a man before Mrs. Dixon's eyes. A small cross which had formed above him began to grow in size until it extended over the earth. Then people of every race were seen kneeling and adoring this man. Her interpretation was:

"A child, born somewhere in the Middle East shortly after 7 a.m. (EST) on February 5, 1962, will revolutionize the world. Before the close of the century he will bring together all mankind in one all-embracing faith. This will be the foundation of a new Christianity, with every sect and creed united through this man who will walk among the people to spread the wisdom of the Almighty Power."[28]

Unger's immediate comment about Dixon's fourth vision was that the person she had described was not the Savior but the Antichrist. And a few years later, when she published her own autobiography, Dixon still included the vision but reversed her interpretation of it, saying that "There is no doubt in my mind that the 'child' is the actual person of the Antichrist, the one who will deceive the world in Satan's name."[29]

Was the Antichrist really born in 1962, as Dixon now says? Will the Roman Catholic Church unite the world's religions? Perhaps both visions are true, as some of Dixon's other prophecies have been. But we cannot seek our information from the serpent, who has symbolized Satan since the Garden of Eden. Our only reliable source of knowledge is the Word of God and the understanding given to us by the Holy Spirit Who wrote it.

Marks of a False Prophet

As has been mentioned, God's standard for a prophet is 100-percent accuracy. Human beings make mistakes but the Spirit of God does not. So even a high percentage of accuracy on important matters does not establish a person as a genuine prophet of God. And even the standard of complete accuracy is not sufficient if the prophet seeks to turn the hearts of the people aside to worship other false gods.[30]

Any so-called prophet who does not point people to Jesus Christ as the only source of salvation is essentially pointing them to a false god of some sort, and a false hope of security apart from the only true God.

It is interesting to note how often the psychics' accurate predictions involve major calamities like airplane crashes, fires, etc. Almost all of them deal with death and destruction. One possible explanation could be that Satan and his demons are prophesying the plans they want to bring to pass.

Two other things should be mentioned about false prophets.

First, they are often motivated by greed. The Apostle Peter warned about this right after he had finished affirming the authority of the Bible:

> **But there were false prophets among the people, even as <u>there shall be false teachers among you, who privily shall bring in damnable heresies, even denying the Lord that bought them</u>, and bring upon themselves swift destruction.**
>
> **And many shall follow their pernicious ways; by reason of whom the way of truth shall be evil spoken of.**
>
> **And <u>through covetousness shall they with feigned words make merchandise of you</u>: whose judgment now of a long time lingereth not, and their damnation slumbereth not.**
>
> **2 Peter 2:1-3**

Peter said that "through covetousness" these false prophets would "make merchandise" of the people of God with false teachings, and the result would be that the unbelieving world would reject the Gospel. And you will notice that the distinguishing characteristic of their "damnable heresies" was "denying the Lord that bought them."[31]

Second, these false prophets will often try to make people into disciples of themselves rather than disciples of Jesus Christ. The Apostle Paul warned the elders of the Church at Ephesus about the danger of "grievous wolves" who would arise, "speaking perverse things, to draw away disciples after them" (Acts 20:28-30).

An obvious example of someone who fits both of these descriptions was Jim Jones, the preacher who departed from the Bible and began to teach all manner of heresy, building an empire called the People's Temple, with a large following and great personal wealth in the process. The end result was the tragedy in Jonestown, Guyana, where U.S. Congressman Leo Ryan and his investigative group were murdered and more than 900 other people died after drinking poisoned Kool-Aid at Jones' direction.

Another was the cult leader David Koresh, who built a following for himself from the ranks of the disenchanted but later led these devoted Branch Davidians to fiery deaths in the tragic conflagration at Waco in 1993.

By contrast, the true prophet of God will seek to turn men's hearts to Christ, the only One who can save men's souls. Jesus said, "If I be lifted up from the earth, I will draw all men unto me" (John 12:32). While this verse applied literally to Jesus' death on the Cross, it also applies spiritually to our representation of Him to the world. The true prophet will lift up Jesus, not himself, and will seek the glory of God, not his own personal wealth.

False Christs

Related to the false prophet is the false Christ, the person who claims that he himself is the Savior or one of many saviors. This is what Charles Manson told his gullible followers, who foolishly submitted themselves to him and thereby came under his evil spell, before he sent them out to commit the bloody Tate and LaBianca murders.

Yet another is Louis Farrakhan of the Nation of Islam, who seeks to mobilize Black people to follow him with racist rhetoric and anti-Semitic sentiments, claiming to be both Jesus and Elijah. Farrakhan regularly applies to his ancestors and to himself the messianic prophecies of the Bible that are intended to describe the Lord Jesus Christ. "Who is Jesus, who is Elijah? Jesus and Elijah are one and the same," Farrakhan said in a recent speech. "I am that Elijah that was to come and now is."[32]

Jesus said that many false christs and false prophets would arise and would deceive many people with supernatural signs and wonders. Cult expert Dave Hunt, author of *The Cult Explosion,* reports that this has happened in an unprecedented way in our time.

There have always been a few false christs, but never the *many* that Jesus predicted would appear just before His second coming. The prophecy has only been fulfilled within the last decade. There are now literally hundreds, if not thousands, of cult leaders who claim to be the Messiah. Even Jim Jones, in spite of his hatred of the Bible and Christianity and his sworn allegiance to Marxism, pretended to be Jesus Christ.[33]

Perhaps the most famous false christ of our day is Lord Maitreiya, a New Age messiah whose advent was announced by an extremely well-funded public relations campaign. On April 25, 1982, full-page ads in major newspapers around the world heralded the headline: "The Christ is Now Here" and identified him as "the World Teacher, Lord Maitreiya, known by Christians as the Christ." The spokesman for Lord Maitreiya—who has not yet been personally revealed to the world—is a London artist named Benjamin Creme.

According to *The Gospel Truth*, a prophecy newsletter which has thoroughly investigated the manifestation of this new "christ":

> The word "maitreiya," in the ancient Indian language, Sanskrit, means "friend." Evidently, this is not his real name, but an assumed title used to imply that he is the friend of all mankind. According to pre-revelation propaganda by Benjamin Creme and the Tara Group, Maitreiya was born 2,600 years ago in the Himalaya Mountains. Since that time, he supposedly has been evolving into the perfect spiritual being, until he has become a god, the messiah of the world.[34]

On Sunday, March 21, 1982, the *Denver Post* published an interview by Jack Kisling with Benjamin Creme about the Lord Maitreiya. An excerpt from that interview reads as follows:

> ...[Creme] explained that by The Christ he means not Jesus Christ, but the Master of Wisdom of whom Jesus and such other spiritual leaders as Mohammed, Brahma, and Krishna are disciples....
>
> Asked what will happen after the great galvanic day, Creme said progress will be slow but steady. World needs and world resources will be reassessed and redistributed and the groundwork for a single global religion will be started and probably flower fully within 20 years.
>
> "Won't the advent of a single world religion annoy the hierarchies of all the current orthodox religions?" I asked.
>
> "More than that," he said with a smile. "They will be shocked. I daresay they will be among the last to accept the new age."
>
> But, he said confidently, it will come, anyway, because it must. "We will begin to live," he said .... "as potential gods."[35]

What is being described here is world socialism and a world religion where men will be "as gods." To discover the source of this idea that men will become as gods, one need only consider what Satan told Eve in the Garden of Eden as he was enticing her to sin against her Creator. Satan's lie to the woman was simple:

> **Ye shall not surely die: For God doth know that in the day ye eat thereof, then your eyes shall be opened, and <u>ye shall be as gods</u>, knowing good and evil.**
> **Genesis 3:4-5**

Satan's lies have not changed from ancient times until now. The same subtle thread runs through contemporary feminist theology, as well as all New Age/Theosophical doctrines, all of which have their demonic roots in Eastern mysticism. But there is an infallible standard in the Word of God by which these concepts can be judged.

> **Beloved, believe not every spirit, but <u>try the spirits, whether they are of God</u>: because many false prophets are gone out into the world.**
> **Hereby know ye the Spirit of God: Every spirit that confesseth that Jesus Christ is come in the flesh is of God:**
> **And <u>every spirit that confesseth not that Jesus Christ is come in the flesh is not of God: and this is that spirit of antichrist</u>, whereof ye have heard that it should come; and even now already is it in the world.**
> **1 John 4:1-3**

Jesus Christ is not just one of the great teachers of the past, another spiritual leader equal to those so-called "avatars" who have also appeared in other religions. He is not one of many "ascended masters." He is God, the Creator of all things. That is His distinctive and exclusive claim, and if it be not true, then Jesus is not a great teacher but a blatant liar.

The greatest heresy of our day is the encroaching New Age doctrine that finds some truth in all religions and absolute truth in none. This will be the basis for the world super-religion of the future under the Antichrist.

False Religions

Cult religions of all kinds have proliferated in the last hundred years or so, although the world has always been filled with major religions that are antithetical to the teachings of both Judaism and Christianity.

Christianity may most accurately be viewed as the completion of Judaism, since Jesus the Christ was and is actually the long-awaited Jewish Messiah foretold by the prophets of the Old Testament.

So to say, as some have done, that Judaism is a "cult" is Biblically and historically inaccurate. However, to equate traditional Judaism, without an acknowledgment of Jesus as the Messiah, as a true religion acceptable to God today is equally erroneous. The Apostle Peter—himself a Jew—stated clearly—to an audience of Jews—on the Day of Pentecost:

> **Be it known unto you all, and to all the people of Israel, that <u>by the name of Jesus Christ of Nazareth, whom ye crucified, whom God raised from the dead</u>, even by him doth this man stand here before you whole.**
>
> **This is the stone which was set at nought of you builders, which is become the head of the corner.**
>
> **<u>Neither is there salvation in any other: for there is none other name under heaven given among men, whereby we must be saved</u>.**
>
> **Acts 4:10-12**

There is just one standard of salvation for all men in all places at all times, be they Jews or Gentiles—faith in Jesus Christ, the only begotten Son of God. This is the exclusionary aspect of Christian doctrine which makes it so unpopular with the modern multiculturalists who preach inclusion, tolerance and diversity as supreme virtues.

God does recognize the free will of individual men and women, and acknowledges their right to make their own moral choices, and so do Christians. But that does not mean that all religions are equally good, right, or acceptable to God. According to the Bible, that is simply not true.

All religious roads do not lead to Heaven.

Pseudo-Christian Heresies

In America and England, the rise of cults has usually begun as a departure from traditional orthodox Christian doctrine. Unitarianism and later Universalism arose as Congregationalists gradually abandoned the fundamental Christian doctrines of the blood atonement and the new birth for a more inclusive theology that allowed everyone to be saved.

It took less than two generations for the descendants of the Puritans in New England to begin forsaking the faith of their fathers, as the "Half-Way Covenant" was instituted in Massachusetts by the year 1662. This allowed church membership—and consequently voting privileges—for individuals who had been baptized as infants but had never professed a personal conversion experience. Before 1700 these "halfway" members were also allowed to partake of the Lord's Supper in the hope that they might thereby be converted. Spiritual vitality rapidly waned from the church.[36]

Another ecumenical milestone was reached in 1992, when members of the Unitarian Parish, which was once a conservative Congregationalist body, voted to readmit as members two dead witches from the past. Rebecca Nurse and Giles Corey had been excommunicated in 1692 from the First Church of Salem, Massachusetts, the first and longest continuing Protestant fellowship in America. The action came as part of the 300th anniversary of the Salem Witchcraft trials, which had resulted in the executions of 20 people accused of consorting with Satan.

According to *World* magazine, the 20 former witches were being honored with a stone marker to commemorate "the enduring lessons of human rights and tolerance." Approximately 10 percent of the 35,000 current residents of Salem are now witches who practice the pagan Wicca religion.[37] This ceremony followed a previous resolution by Massachusetts Governor Michael Dukakis designating occult bookstore owner Laurie Cabot as the "official witch" of Salem.

False Gospels, Angels of Light

Many cults arise from extrabiblical revelation, as in the case of the mystic treasure-digger Joseph Smith, who couldn't find a church that suited him, so he prayed fervently for God's direction. In 1820, while praying in the woods, Smith claims to have been visited by "God the Father" and "God the Son," who like Smith were displeased with the current crop of Christian churches and therefore appointed him their newest prophet to set things right in the world.

In 1823 Smith received an angelic visitation at his bedside from a spirit named Moroni, who revealed to Smith the esoteric doctrines that became the *Book of Mormon* and spawned the misnamed Church of Jesus Christ of Latter Day Saints. This cult believes that some men will one day become gods like Jesus and rule their own planets.[38]

The Apostle Paul warned Christians pointedly about the dangers of receiving "another Jesus" because "Satan himself is transformed into an angel of light."[39] Nothing in the Bible is put there by chance. Every word inspired by God has a purpose and a reason. Paul also wrote:

> But <u>though we, or an angel from heaven, preach any other gospel unto you than that which we have preached unto you, let him be accursed</u>.
>
> **As we said before, so say I now again, If any man preach any other gospel unto you than that ye have received, let him be accursed.**
>
> **Galatians 1:8-9**

As we consider the supernatural spiritual sources of many of the heretical teachings that have infiltrated the professing Christian church over the years, the seriousness of the apostle's words become clear.

Other well-established American cults include the Jehovah's Witnesses, who deny Christ's atonement and hope to be among the fortunate 144,000 souls who eventually make it to heaven; the Christian Scientists, who claim that sickness and disease is merely the product of negative thoughts; and the Theosophists, who are actually spiritist mediums in the Hindu tradition seeking to contact the dead.

Recent pseudo-Christian cults include the Way, the Worldwide Church of God, the Unification Church, Unity, and the Children of God. These cults and others like them often gain gullible converts from the ranks of disenchanted former church-goers who are looking for a place with some spiritual life. Spiritual seekers sometimes drift into the clutches of cults after leaving one or more of the spiritually dead, so-called Christian churches that claim to represent Jesus to the modern world.

Feminist Theology

Dr. Walter Martin, whose book *The Kingdom of the Cults* is the definitive work on modern pseudo-Christian cults in America, has noted:

> It is one of the strange historical peculiarities of the saga of cultism that at least six cults were either started by or were influenced in a major way by the allegedly weaker sex: Christian Science, Mary Baker Eddy; Unity, Myrtle Fillmore; Spiritism, the Fox sisters; Jehovah's Witnesses, Marie Russell; Theosophy, Helen Blavatsky and Annie Besant; The Peace Mission Movement [Father Divine], Sister Penny and Faithful Mary [Viola Wilson].[40]

Martin, like many traditionalists in the Church, believes that heretical doctrines can proliferate more easily where female teachers exercise spiritual authority. While this may not always be true, some mainline Christian denominations already have felt the impact of feminist theology and have begun to depart from orthodox Christian doctrines and to embrace New Age concepts and ungodly contemporary moral ideas.

Consider this sad but enlightening recent example:

> National staff and leaders of the Presbyterian Church (USA) gathered with feminist leaders from other World Council of Churches denominations to destroy patriarchal religion and worship the goddess "Sophia," according to an article in the January/February issue of the *Presbyterian Layman.*
>
> Repeated themes in the November 4-7 conference, "Re-Imagining 1993," included destroying traditional Christian faith, adopting ancient pagan beliefs, rejecting Jesus' divinity and His atonement on the cross, creating a goddess in their own image, and affirming lesbian lovemaking.
>
> According to the *Layman,* 24 PCUSA national staff members registered for the event. The denomination's Bicentennial Fund was the largest source of financial support for the conference with a $66,000 grant....
>
> Delores Williams, professor at Union Theological Seminary in New York, told the group, "I don't think we need a theory of atonement at all. I think Jesus came for life and to show us something about life...I don't think we need

folks hanging on crosses and blood dripping and all that weird stuff....

Melanie Morrison, co-convenor of CLOUT (Christian Lesbians Out Together), told the group that liturgists in her church read from the holy book of Isaiah and then from "a holy book" written by a lesbian author....

The conference finished with a "milk and honey" ritual instead of the Lord's Supper. The women recited the litany, "Our maker Sophia, we are women in your image, with the hot blood of our wombs we give form to new life...with nectar between our thighs we invite a lover...with our warm body fluids we remind the world of its pleasures and sensations...with the honey of wisdom in our mouths we prophesy a full humanity to all the peoples.[41]

In a similar vein, the Evangelical Lutheran Church of America issued a 21-page first-draft social statement in 1993 entitled "The Church and Human Sexuality: A Lutheran Perspective." That draft report

...endorses homosexuality and suggests that marriage, though desirable, is optional for committed couples.

The report presents the perspective of "those of us who are gay and lesbian Christians" and calls on the church to "challenge stereotypes" of gays and lesbians, and to challenge the idea that all homosexuality is contrary to God's law....

The report, sent to 19,000 pastors and church leaders in late October, has drawn sharp criticism from the conservative wing of the 5.2-million member denomination.[42]

Not to be outdone, the 1,100 delegates of General Convention of the Episcopal Church who met in Arizona in 1991 refused to discipline those bishops who had ordained openly homosexual priests.

Conservatives had proposed that the church discipline those bishops who ordained homosexuals, but after many priests rose to speak openly about their own homosexuality, the group adopted the attitude that the church should not attempt to legislate the matter....

The compromise resolution cut short the attempted censure of Bishop Ronald Haines of Washington, D.C., and

Asst. Bishop Walter Righter of Newark, N.J. Haines had ordained an openly lesbian woman in June and Righter a gay deacon in September.[43]

And then of course there is the case of Episcopal Bishop John Spong of New Jersey, whose book *Recapturing the Bible From Fundamentalism* attracted widespread attention when he wrote that the Apostle Paul was really a "self-loathing and repressed gay male." Pat Buchanan hit the mark with his commentary on the bishop's unfortunate flight of fancy:

> I am trying, he says, to make homosexuals more comfortable in the church. But active homosexuals, like active adulterers, are, in Christian doctrine, leading a life of sin. And it is not an expression of Christian love to make a sinner feel more comfortable about a life that can lead directly to the loss of his immortal soul.[44]

Obviously, not all Episcopalians, not all Lutherans, and not all Presbyterians believe like those responsible for the examples cited above. But there is an obvious trend developing here that does not portend well for the future of the denominations in question, or for other Christian groups that open the door to these destructive doctrines.

Major World Religions

Islam, Buddhism, and Hinduism are the other major world religions, and various sects and cults of all kinds have splintered off of them.

Islam, concentrated principally in Northern Africa, the Middle East, and Central Asia, also extends into portions of India, Malaysia, Indonesia, and the Philippines. With more than one billion adherents, Islam is the fastest growing religion in the world, and the ultimate goal of many zealous Moslem fundamentalists is to make it the only one, by violent conquest if necessary. Today one out of every five people in the world is a Moslem.

Islam began as a Christian heresy founded by a successful young Arab businessman named Ubu'l Kassim, who was born in Mecca in 570 A.D. While meditating and praying in a cave, he received a visit from a being claiming to be the angel Gabriel, who changed Kassim's name to Mohammed and dictated to him in Arabic the teachings now contained in the *Koran*. Those writings are believed by Moslems to be the "undefiled and uncreated word of God," concentrated on the idea that there is only one true God, Allah, and that Mohammed is his final prophet.[45]

While Islam accepts Abraham, Moses, and Jesus as prophets, and claims to affirm parts of the Bible, it denies that Jesus is the Son of God and "reduces him to a mere human prophet, inferior to Mohammed himself." Therefore, despite being a monotheistic religion which emphasizes prayer and traditional morality, Islam "bears a strong demonic stamp."[46]

Buddhism in theory is a practical, man-centered way of life originally taught 2,500 years ago by Prince Siddartha Gautama, the Buddha, who is believed by his followers to have descended from heaven to save mankind. He did not teach about God because he accepted the Hindu idea that "The true self is God and God is the true self."

The Buddha defined his "way" in the Four Noble Truths and the Eightfold Path, which are intended to produce individual enlightenment and avoidance of suffering through meditation and right living.

Buddhism is most prevalent in China and other countries of the Far East, where it is often mixed with Confucianism, Taoism, and other spiritist ritual practices like Shinto nature worship. In actual practice it is idol worship, "notably in Tibet and Mongolia where demonic phenomena such as spirit-worship, divination, magic, and sorcery abound."[47]

Hinduism is an ancient religion—believed to be the oldest in the world—concentrated mainly in India, where its adherents constitute 90 percent of the population. Modern Hinduism, which is "a syncretism of Brahmanism and Buddhism," is a sexually degenerate, pantheistic and also polytheistic religion with literally thousands of gods who are thought to dwell in both animate and inanimate objects.

Like Buddhism, Hinduism accepts the doctrines of reincarnation and *karma* and embraces the caste system, in which a person's station in life is predetermined. After death an individual may be reborn countless times in different forms, working out his personal *karma* on the wheel of life until finally achieving purification and Nirvana—which is not glorification in heaven with God, but rather extinction of individual consciousness and absorption into the Brahma, or World Soul.

The principal Hindu god is Krishna, the King of serpents and Prince of demons. In the Hindu's sacred book, the *Bhagavad-Gita,*

Krishna says, "Take whatever road you will, it will lead to me." He also declares, "Whatever god a man worships, it is I who answers the prayer."[48]

The voice of Krishna is the voice of Satan, speaking from the oldest false religion in the world. Apart from Jesus Christ, all roads do not lead to Heaven, they lead to Hell.

New Age Cults

The mystical concepts which underlie the various Eastern religions like Hinduism and Buddhism are also behind all the New Age cults currently proliferating in formerly Christian cultures like the United States.

As people find that their gnawing questions are not being answered by humanism and their deepest spiritual needs are not being met by materialism, they begin to look for answers and to seek satisfaction in the supernatural realm. But all too often their quest, because it does not begin with the God of the Bible, leads them to the snare of pagan cults. And since there are only two sources of supernatural power in the universe, these people find themselves unwittingly in the clutches of Satan.

Pat Robertson has succinctly defined the spiritual parameters of the '90s in his popular book *The New Millennium*. Robertson writes:

> The 1990s will not be a decade dominated by rationalism or science, but a decade of religious faith. We are entering the age of the supernatural.
>
> What we don't know yet is what form the religious faith will take. Will the world embrace the claims of Jesus Christ and the truths of the Bible, or are we to expect the world to turn to an "Age of Aquarius" dominated by the Hindu religions and led by mystic holy men in touch with demonic spirits known as "ascended masters"?[49]

These various New Age cults include groups emphasizing yoga, reincarnation, transcendental meditation, chanting, channeling, mind control, astrology, horoscopes, fortune telling, spiritism, necromancy, dreams, ESP, telepathy, telekinesis, clairvoyance, magic, hypnosis, ouija boards, Tarot cards, and the like.

Perhaps the most prominent example in America is the New Age Mecca centered in the lovely resort town of Mount Shasta, California, a picturesque community of just 3,600 people. The quaint village streets are lined with all types of New Age stores and places of worship and teaching. New Agers believe that "the ascended masters from the earth, who have gone on to a higher life—as Jesus did—are filtering light through Shasta Mountain to this planet," explained devotee Dawn Fazenda.

"I saw beautiful temples of the world's religions...Judaism, Islam, Christianity, Hinduism, Taoism—all with people, many people, coming and getting a sense of the heart of these different faiths," said Swami Vandana Jyoti, who wants to establish the Shasta Center for Universal Peace (CUP) there, in obedience to a vision from God.[50]

New Agers generally believe that the world is approaching the "Millennial Dawn" of a new era, and that the year 2000 will usher in the Age of Aquarius, a period of enlightenment and universal peace. Interestingly, the Age of Aquarius is believed to follow and to supplant the current Age of Pisces, which like the Christian church is symbolized by a fish.

While some of these New Age activities may appear to be "spiritual" and may in fact produce altered states of consciousness, feelings of well-being, and even supernatural experiences, they are all occult in nature and demonic in origin. Cult expert Dave Hunt has explained that behind all of these experiences lies the lust for personal power.

> Fundamental to the consciousness revolution is the ancient teaching of shamanism, or witchcraft—that there is something infinitely more powerful than atomic power, a mystical Force that pervades the universe and which can be activated by the minds of those initiated into its secrets. Those who learn to control this Force become Gods, to whom all things are possible.[51]

The Bible is clear that these occult practices are forbidden by God:

> **When thou art come into the land which the Lord thy God giveth thee, thou shalt not learn to do after the abominations of those nations.**
>
> **There shall not be found among you any one that maketh his son or his daughter to pass through the fire, or that useth divination, or an observer of times, or an enchanter, or a witch,**

> Or a charmer, or a consulter with familiar spirits, or a wizard, or a necromancer.
> <u>For all that do these things are an abomination unto the Lord</u>: and because of these abominations the Lord thy God doth drive them out from before thee.
> Thou shalt be perfect with the Lord thy God.
> Deuteronomy 18:9-13

The Bible says that both these occult sins, and those who do them, are abominations to God. They bring a curse. The person who engages in these activities, whether knowingly or unknowingly, places himself under the influence of the demonic realm and risks coming under demonic bondage as a result. According to occult expert Kurt Koch,

> [I]t is particularly easy for those who engage in occult practices to fall victim to demonic subjection. Such practices include visiting a fortune-teller who has occult powers, spiritistic enquiring of the dead, charming, the reading of books on sorcery and horoscopes, superstitious practices, as for example the wearing of amulets or so-called letters of protection, and even the use of a rod or pendulum if it is allied to clairvoyance....[52]

It doesn't matter if a person did these things with the sincere desire to find some esoteric version of "truth," or was just dabbling in the occult "for fun." Derek Prince has compared this to "counting the teeth on a tiger, just for fun." The end result is the same, and it is demonic bondage.

That may sound far-fetched, but I can sound this warning on the basis of my own personal experience. It is possible for a person to trespass on the Devil's territory, without the complete protection of God, and come under the Devil's control. I know, I have done it. And I can tell you now, it is bad news. In my particular case, it was hell on Earth.

In my personal encounter with the Satanic supernatural, years ago before I became a Christian, I unwittingly confronted the demonic realm on my own—and it was a terrifying experience that easily could have destroyed me. Because I ignored God's warnings, I entered Satan's spiritual domain, and I was vulnerable.

But thankfully, mercifully, God in His sovereign grace intervened and preserved my life. I am convinced that, without His divine intervention and protection, I would not be writing this book today.

That is why the Bible warns us as Christians always to

> **Be sober, be vigilant; because <u>your adversary the devil walketh about as a roaring lion, seeking whom he may devour</u>:**
> **Whom resist steadfast in the faith, knowing that the same afflictions are accomplished in your brethren who are in the world.**
>
> **1 Peter 5:8-9**

Some preachers want to tell you that this Devil is a toothless old lion and there isn't anything to worry about from him, but they are mistaken. I have felt those teeth and they are quite sharp. The Bible says he is looking for someone to devour. If you give him the chance, he will devour you.

Now this is not intended to minister fear, because the disciples of Jesus Christ do have authority over Satan and do not have to be afraid of him. But that authority applies only to those individuals in a particular spiritual faith position in Christ, and it is not automatic.

Let me repeat that again, so you won't miss it: *it is not automatic.*

One cannot dabble in the occult without consequences. If you presume upon the grace of the Lord, if you ignore the clear precepts and requirements of the Word of God, you do so at your own peril.

You could very easily be devoured by the powers of darkness.

——————

¹ 2 Thessalonians 2:3, Greek *apostasia,* Strongs #646.

² 1 Timothy 4:1; Greek *aphistemi,* Strongs #868.

³ For a first-person account of the miracles in the Indonesian revival, see Mel Tari, as told to Cliff Dudley, *Like a Mighty Wind* (Carol Stream, Ill.: Creation House, 1971).

⁴ Harold J. Ockenga, *The Church in God: Expository Values in Thessalonians* (Westwood, N.J.: Revell, 1956), p. 281.

⁵ Information in this section is from seminar material by George Barna, *Understanding Ministry in a Changing Culture* (Glendale, CA.: Barna Research Group. Ltd., 1994). See also the video by George Barna, "Current Trends in Culture and Religion" (Gospel Light, Ca.: Gospel Light, 1996).

⁶ The Southern Baptists are the largest Protestant denomination which has refused to affiliate with the NCC and WCC.

⁷ "When the modernist approaches Christ, he interprets Him in the form of a natural birth out of wedlock, as mistaken in His teaching, as wrong in His claims about His deity and destiny, and as a mere man who made an impact upon His age which was interpreted in legendary clothing of miracles. They believe that He died as a martyr and that His body remains in the grave but that His influence lives on today." Ockenga, *The Church in God*, p. 277.

⁸ "The way of salvation for the modernist is to follow the example of Jesus and live a self-denying, sacrificial life of service. Thus he also will come to God.... The possibility of the new birth is totally denied by the modernist.... The great work of the church is to reform society through the social gospel." Ibid., pp. 277-278.

⁹ "Modernism was the result of the impact of the scientific method in theology. Men turned to induction, to discovery, to generalization from particulars, and they substituted this for the method of receiving divine revelation and thinking God's thoughts after Him. Consequently, they accommodated their views of religion to science. The supernatural was bowed out and everything was explained on the ground of naturalism." Ibid., p. 276.

¹⁰ Wesley S. Ariarajah, *Hindus and Christians: A Century of Protestant Ecumenical Thought* (Grand Rapids: Eerdmans, 1991), pp. 210-216.

¹¹ "The Council opposed the U.S. Strategic Defense Initiative and supported all of Chairman Gorbachev's arms control proposals. The posture, advice, and wording of WCC statements on nuclear arms throughout the period closely paralleled that of the secular nuclear freeze movement and other peace campaigns that were supported directly or indirectly by the Soviet Union." Ernest W. LeFever, *Nairobi to Vancouver: The World Council of Churches and the World, 1975-87* (Washington, D.C.: Ethics and Public Policy Center, 1987), pp. 71-77.

¹² "Do You Know Where Your Church Offerings Go?" *Reader's Digest*, January 1983.

¹³ LeFever, *Amsterdam to Nairobi: The World Council of Churches and the Third World* (Washington, D.C.: Ethics and Public Policy Center, 1979), pp. 1-2.

¹⁴ LeFever, *Nairobi to Vancouver*, p. 120.

¹⁵ Rome is identified by Revelation 17: 9, "The seven heads are seven mountains." Rome is known as the "City of Seven Hills" because of its unique topography.

The colors of the Papacy are scarlet and purple, as described in Revelation 17: 4. The Vatican sent "unofficial observers" to the ecumenical conference in Amsterdam.

[16] For an account of the abuses of Christians at the hands of the Vatican, see William Byron Forbush, ed., *Fox's Book of Martyrs* (Grand Rapids: Zondervan, 1967).

[17] Malachi Martin, *The Keys of this Blood: The Struggle for World Dominion Between Pope John Paul II, Mikhail Gorbachev, and the Capitalist West* (New York: Simon and Schuster, 1990), p. 632.

[18] Ibid., pp. 626-638.

[19] Ibid., p. 631.

[20] Ibid., p. 636.

[21] Donald T. Regan, *For the Record: From Wall Street to Washington* (New York: Harcourt, Brace, Jovanovitch, 1988), pp. 70-74, 90, 93, 290, 300-301, 344, 359, 367-370. See also Nancy Reagan with William Novak, *My Turn: The Memoirs of Nancy Reagan* (New York: Random House, 1989), pp. 32, 44-55, 134.

[22] Stewart Robb, *Prophecies on World Events by Nostradamus* (New York: Ace Books, 1961). Robb also has written other books on Nostradamus.

[23] Some information in this section about Edgar Cayce and Jeane Dixon is from James Bjornstadt, *Twentieth Century Prophecy: Jeane Dixon, Edgar Cayce* (New York: Pillar Books, 1976). For more on Cayce, see also George A. Mather and Larry A. Nichols, *Dictionary of Cults, Sects, Religions, and the Occult* (Grand Rapids: Zondervan, 1993), pp. 27-30.

[24] Mather and Nichols, *Dictionary of Cults, Sects, Religions, and the Occult*, p. 27.

[25] Bjornstad, *Twentieth Century Prophecy*, p. 30.

[26] Ruth Montgomery, *A Gift of Prophecy* (New York: Morrow, William & Co., 1965), p. 26. See also Merrill F. Unger, *Demons in the World Today* (Wheaton: Tyndale House, 1971), p. 68. Unger comments: "Amazingly, Mrs. Dixon considers this first vision a key to the others. In Scripture the serpent is a symbol of evil (Genesis 3:1; Revelation 12: 9-12; 20: 1-3), and its appearance in this key vision suggests that deceptive spirits are indeed the source of her revelations (1 Timothy 4:1; 1 John 4:1-2)."

[27] Unger, *Demons in The World Today*, pp. 68-69. Dixon's quotes are referenced as being from Gordon Lindsay, *Jean Dixon—Prophetess or Psychic Medium?* (San Antonio, Tex.: Christian Jew Publications, n.d.), p. 23.

[28] Ibid., p. 69. Dixon's quote is from Montgomery, p. 181.

[29] Ibid., pp. 69-70. Dixon's quote is from Jean Dixon, *My Life and Prophecies* (New York: William Morrow, 1969), p. 203.

[30] Deuteronomy 13:1-5.

[31] See also Jude 11.

[32] "Radical Islam: Growing Threat To Black America?" *The 700 Club Newswatch Fact Sheet*, March 6, 1996.

[33] Dave Hunt, *The Cult Explosion* (Irvine, Cal.: Harvest House, 1980), p. 252. This thoroughly researched book on modern cults and their Hindu roots is highly recommended.

[34] Hutchings, "Is Maitreiya the Antichrist?" *The Gospel Truth*, July 1982. p. 3. The nefarious Satanic network behind the organized effort to establish a New Age messiah has been described in detail by Constance E. Cumbey, *The Hidden Dangers of the Rainbow* (Shreveport, La.: Huntington House, 1983).

[35] Quoted Ibid.

[36] Thomas A. Askew and Peter W. Spellman, *The Churches and the American Experience: Ideals and Institutions* (Grand Rapids: Baker, 1984), pp. 35-36.

[37] "Salem Church Accepts Dead Witches as Members," *Christian American*, November/December 1992, p. 31.

[38] Walter R. Martin, *The Kingdom of the Cults* (Minneapolis: Bethany, 1977), pp. 150-152. Dr. Martin's book contains a wealth of material on the major established cults in America.

[39] 2 Corinthians 11:3-4, 13-15.

[40] Martin, *The Kingdom of the Cults*, p. 223. Martin further comments: "The history of Theosophy then, is marked indelibly by the imprint of the female mind, which, ever since Eve, has apparently been vulnerable to forbidden fruit and the tantalizing tones of various varieties of serpents.

"It should be remembered that the Apostle Paul strictly enjoined the Christian Church to forbid women the teaching ministry, especially when men were available to meet this need:

"'Let the woman learn in silence with all subjection. But I suffer not a woman to teach, nor to usurp authority over the man, but to be in silence. For Adam was first formed, then Eve. And Adam was not deceived, but the woman being deceived was in the transgression' (1 Timothy 2:11-14).

"It can be clearly seen from the study of non-Christian cults, ancient and modern, that the female teaching ministry has graphically fulfilled what Paul anticipated in his day by divine revelation, and brought in its wake, as history tells us, confusion, division, and strife. This is true from Johanna Southcutt to

Mary Baker Eddy to Helena Blavatsky and the Fox sisters, all of whom were living proof of our Lord's declaration that 'if the blind lead the blind, both shall fall into the ditch' (Matthew 15:14b)" (p. 225).

[41] Paul English, "PC(USA) Promotes Goddess Worship," *Christian American,* February 1994, p. 19.

[42] Evangelical Press News Service, "Lutherans Endorse Same Sex Unions," *Christian American,* January 1994, p. 26.

[43] National and International Religion Report, "Episcopal Leaders Compromise on Homosexual Issue," *Christian American,* September/October 1991, p. 10.

[44] Pat Buchanan, "Recapturing: Bishop Spong's Latest Heresy," *Christian American,* March/April 1991, p. 13.

[45] See Galatians 1:8-9 and 2 Corinthians 11:3-4, 13-15.

[46] Unger, *Demons in the World Today,* p. 166.

[47] Ibid., p. 164.

[48] Ibid., pp. 159-160. See also Hunt, *The Cult Explosion,* p. 78.

[49] Pat Robertson, *The New Millennium: What You and Your Family Can Expect in the Year 2000* (Dallas: Word, 1990), p.73.

[50] "New Age in America: Building Spiritual Sanctuaries," *The 700 Club Newswatch Fact Sheet,* November 8, 1995.

[51] Hunt, *The Cult Explosion,* p. 12.

[52] Kurt Koch, *Occult Bondage and Deliverance* (Grand Rapids: Kregel, 1976), pp. 138-139. Dr. Koch continues: "However, it is not only the active engagement in occult sins like those we have just mentioned which leads to demonic subjection, but one frequently finds that people whose parents and ancestors have practised sorcery also fall under the ban of the devil. In fact, powerful sorcerers and mediums often seek to transfer their occult powers over to some relative or friend, be it an adult or child, before they die. Later the people onto whom the powers have been transferred suddenly become aware of their strange inheritance.

"And so, in all these ways either knowingly or unknowingly, man lays claim to the services of the devil. His motive may vary from a desire for something that has previously been denied him, be it wealth or some form of worldly fortune, to a desire to uncover the future which God in his purposes has hidden from him. But whatever it may be, Satan is only too willing to oblige, although in the end the result is always disastrous."

Chapter 3
The Days of Noah

But as the days of Noe were, so shall also the coming of the Son of man be.

For as in the days that were before the flood they were eating and drinking, marrying and giving in marriage, until the day that Noe entered into the ark,

And knew not until the flood came, and took them all away; so shall also the coming of the Son of man be.

Matthew 24:37-39

Will spiritual conditions in the world at the end of this age be about like they have always been, or will they be significantly different? The Bible gives some definite and perhaps surprising answers to that question.

Besides the various natural phenomena, international political developments and religious trends which can be viewed as signs of the end of the age, there are also social and cultural conditions which closely match those predicted for the Last Days.

Jesus said that conditions in the world just before the time of His return to Earth would be as they were in "the days of Noah." The Bible describes that ancient time in some detail in Genesis 6, starting in verse 5.

And God saw that <u>the wickedness of man was great in the earth, and that every imagination of the thoughts of his heart was only evil continually.</u>

And it repented the Lord that he had made man on the earth, and it grieved him at his heart.

And the Lord said, I will destroy man whom I have created from the face of the earth; both man, and beast, and the creeping thing, and the fowls of the air; for it repenteth me that I have made them.

But Noah found grace in the eyes of the Lord.

These are the generations of Noah: Noah was a just man and perfect in his generations, and Noah walked with God.

And Noah begat three sons, Shem, Ham, and Japheth.

<u>The earth also was corrupt before God, and the earth was filled with violence.</u>

And God looked upon the earth, and, behold, it was corrupt; for all flesh had corrupted his way upon the earth.

And God said unto Noah, The end of all flesh is come before me; for the earth is filled with violence through them; and, behold, I will destroy them with the earth.

Genesis 6:5-13

Wickedness, evil thoughts, corruption, and violence—these are the conditions which the Bible says existed during the time of Noah, before God in judgment sent a great flood to destroy the Earth. We may assume from Scripture that these same types of evil things will be prevalent on Earth in the Last Days. The New Testament paints a similar picture to the Genesis account. The Apostle Paul wrote about how things will be:

This know also, that <u>in the last days perilous times shall come,</u>

For men shall be lovers of their own selves, covetous, boasters, proud, blasphemers, disobedient to parents, unthankful, unholy,

Without natural affection, trucebreakers, false accusers, incontinent, fierce, despisers of those that are good,

Traitors, heady, high-minded, lovers of pleasure more than lovers of God;

Having a form of godliness but denying the power thereof: from such turn away.

2 Timothy 3:1-5

These words, combined with those of Genesis 6, conjure in the mind an image of total depravity, and that word can accurately be said to apply to many aspects of our postmodern, "Post-Christian" culture at the end of the 20th Century. Biblical prophecy closely matches this degraded civilization.

Degraded Modern Civilization

"Wickedness," "evil thoughts," and "corruption" are words which characterize much of the popular entertainment culture today. Major corporations produce and market movies and music which pander to the basest of human instincts and desires, ranging from the merely lewd to the openly Satanic.

Some people blame Hollywood for turning out a steady stream of filth that poisons the minds of our children. Certainly a generation raised on the current crop of major movies and the nihilistic images and lyrics of MTV will grow up with a warped view of what is normal, right and good.

Wicked Music

There is no excuse, other than consuming greed, for huge corporations such as Time-Warner to distribute pernicious rap music like Ice-T's *Body Count* album, which contains the songs "Cop Killer" and "Bowels of the Devil." These songs have lyrics that glorify stalking and killing police officers and casually murdering other people over trivial offenses. "Cop Killer" got the nation's attention in 1992 when a fellow with that tape in his cassette deck shot and killed an unsuspecting Texas state trooper who had stopped him for a traffic violation.[1]

Or take 2 Live Crew's *As Nasty As They Wanna Be*, which portrays all women as "bitches" and "ho's." Lead singer Luther Campbell's lyrics, with their debased emphasis on violent sex, are believed to have contributed to the brutal beating and gang-rape of a young female jogger in Central Park a few years back by a pack of teenage thugs on a "wilding" spree. They bashed her head in with bricks and an iron pipe and left her for dead, with 80 percent of her body's blood supply spilled on the ground. The precious boys later explained that they were "just having fun."[2]

These are just two of the many sordid examples of the degenerate music to which many of our children are exposed. Whether it is rap, heavy metal, or the newer forms of punk rock and grunge music, the messages in the lyrics all too often reinforce the worst in human nature—murder, suicide, drug abuse, rebellion, violence, degradation of women.[3]

Some songs emphasize deviant sexual themes, like forced oral sex at gunpoint, fantasy and masturbation, prostitution, lesbianism, sado-masochism, anal sex, and human excrement. Others glorify bizarre occult practices, and there is even a new category called Black Metal Music that openly promotes Satanism.[4]

Luther Campbell insisted that his songs were not obscene, and at least one jury in Florida agreed with him. And he has denied any responsibility for what others do after listening to his lyrics. But the connection between human behavior and music is well established.

Before he died of a drug overdose, the late rock superstar Jimi Hendrix said that "Music is a spiritual thing of its own. You can hypnotize people with music, and when you get them at their weakest point, you can preach into the subconscious what we want to say."[5]

When you think about these things, it is easy to understand why Jesus told His disciples to "Take heed what you hear" (Mark 4:24).

So some of our political leaders, like Dan Quayle and even Bill Clinton and Bob Dole, were on target to call into question the motives and the agenda of the "cultural elite" whose unwholesome influence is eroding the moral foundations of decency and traditional family values.

But in a larger sense, the blame does not lie with Hollywood alone, or even with the rappers. The corporate executives say that they are simply businessmen catering to the public's desire. If there were no market demand for these products, they wouldn't be so profitable to produce.

And the street rappers insist that their music doesn't incite people to do bad things, it just reflects the kinds of things people from their ghetto world are already naturally doing. Art imitates life, in its rawest form.

Neither of these excuses is satisfactory, of course, but each contains an element of truth. People crave the depraved and perverse, and that which they crave spurs them on to greater depravity and perversity. Then life begins to imitate "art," and the spiral downward into the cesspool becomes a self-perpetuating cycle of moral corruption.

Moral Corruption

The problem with "traditional family values" is that no one can define precisely what they are. Within the conservative, sometimes Christian, so-called "pro-family" movement, it is simply assumed that everyone believes the same thing in a warm, fuzzy kind of way.

The fact is that values must be based on something absolute and objective in order to have any enduring strength and binding force. The laws of God in the Bible, and specifically the Ten Commandments, have been the bedrock of western civilization for 2,000 years. Judeo-Christian concepts of justice and legitimate authority shaped the English Common Law and later the American Declaration of Independence, with its recognition of inalienable rights bestowed upon men by their Creator.

These Biblical foundations of authority, based upon the righteous character of a holy God, are morally superior to the depravity and human sacrifice practiced by all pagan cultures, both ancient and modern.

But these foundations have been abandoned in our day, as the Supreme Court expelled God from the public schools in 1962 and 1963, when they ruled that prayer and Bible reading in school had become unconstitutional. Today the moral precepts of the Ten Commandments can no longer hang upon the walls of our children's public classrooms.

Yet many people can't seem to understand why the generation that reached adulthood in the '60s and '70s turned out so rootless and rebellious.

Could this "destructive generation," as former counterculture leader David Horowitz has termed the 60s radicals, possibly foreshadow an "unholy" generation of children that will be "disobedient to parents," as the Apostle Paul predicted?

And is it merely a coincidence that those same turbulent years were a period of such social trauma for America? One President assassinated and another driven from office in disgrace. Political leaders assassinated, cities burned in urban rioting. Humiliation in Vietnam, rampant drug abuse at home. Casual divorce and widespread venereal disease. Teen pregnancy and abortion on the rise. Plummeting test scores and soaring crime rates.

Bill Bennett released his *Index of Leading Cultural Indicators* back in 1993. This statistical study showed empirically the measurable decline of American culture in the 30 years since 1960. "Over the last three decades we have experienced substantial social regression," Bennett wrote.

While our population has increased 41 percent, our violent crime rate has increased 560 percent. While our inflation-adjusted spending on education has increased 225 percent, our teen suicide rate has doubled and average S.A.T. scores have dropped by 80 points. While our Gross Domestic Product has nearly tripled, so has the number of children living in single-parent homes. Both the divorce rate and the number of illegitimate births have quadrupled.[6] Bennett tells one story that sums it all up:

> Over the years teachers have been asked to identify the top problems in America's public schools. In 1940 teachers identified talking out of turn; chewing gum; making noise; running in halls; cutting in line; dress code infractions; and littering. When asked the same question in 1990, teachers identified drug abuse; alcohol abuse; pregnancy; suicide; rape; robbery; and assault.[7]

Did these sweeping social problems really arise as a result of the Supreme Court's ruling on school prayer? Many believe that is exactly what happened, and much more besides.

Steven W. Fitschen, executive director of the National Legal Foundation, has accurately observed that the *Roe v. Wade* decision of 1973, which legalized the feminist goal of "abortion on demand and without apology" throughout the United States, was "both a consequence of and a judgment for" that Court's earlier decision to abandon God.

Now, 23 years and approximately 35 million murdered babies later, we continue to sacrifice our children on the altar of the god of pleasure, just like the ancient Israelites who abandoned God and caused their children to "pass through the fire" to the demon Molech.[8]

Every day of the year in America, 1,000 illegitimate babies are born to unwed teenage mothers, on average, and that statistic is disturbing. But more disturbing still is the fact that another 4,000 are aborted. Every day.

All that righteous blood cries out from the ground to God for judgment, and yet we continue storing up wrath to ourselves because neither the people nor their elected leaders have either the moral commitment or the political will to stop it.[9]

Jesus said in Matthew 24:12 that in the Last Days "iniquity shall abound." That iniquity has its roots in the abandonment of God's moral law, and the lack of spiritual discernment that follows. We often think of moral corruption as being synonymous with sexual sins, but while the two are related, they are not the same thing. It is first the erosion of our basic moral values that later produces the proliferation of our sexual corruption.

Sexual Corruption

We live in a day that glorifies Madonna, the "Material Girl," and makes a multimillionaire of an alleged chronic child molester like superstar Michael Jackson. Our society is saturated with sex, from the billboards along the highways to lingerie ads in our newspapers to suggestive television commercials and steamy soap operas. Late-night television features a multitude of invitations for callers to partake of the vicarious pleasures of telephone sex.

And of course every form of raw and explicit sex is available in porn shops, in movies, in videos, on pay TV, and on the Internet. Prostitution is readily available in almost every American city by simply opening up the Yellow Pages for extensive listings of massage parlors, "escort" services, and so-called "gentlemen's clubs." The world's oldest profession is prospering.

Sex is not evil in itself. God created sex, and like everything else He created, it was "very good." But men have cheapened and degraded what God intended as a holy sacrament of the marriage covenant. Our sex-saturated society is rapidly losing virtually all traces of godly restraint, sexual purity and fidelity. Instead we are abandoning commitment and virtue, and degenerating into an openly hedonistic people.

Paul wrote that men in the Last Days would become "incontinent," or without self-control, and "lovers of pleasure more than lovers of God." Those phrases accurately describe the self-centered mindset developing in our modern world. If you don't believe me, just turn on the TV talk shows some afternoon and try to stomach some of the gross sins and perversions openly confessed and accepted there. "I'm okay, you're okay," is the rule.

America's descent into total depravity is not yet complete, but our culture is on that slippery slope, as an egocentric philosophy of moral relativism continually penetrates our children's minds.

Abortion: A New American Institution

Radical feminists proclaim the "equal rights" of women to fornicate, commit adultery, and practice prostitution without legal sanction. They further insist that all women should be allowed to abort their unborn babies, for any reason or for no reason at all, at any stage of their pregnancy, and at government expense. Gradually society at large is acceding to each of these depraved demands.

The Supreme Court's legalization of abortion in 1973 was just the beginning, as subsequent court decisions at every level have limited the rights of state legislatures to restrict abortion in any meaningful way. The Court, by a margin of 5-4, reaffirmed *Roe v. Wade* in 1992 with their surprise *Planned Parenthood v. Casey* decision, which essentially said that abortion at any time from conception to birth is a basic American right.

"This is an outrageous example of judicial tyranny," said Pat Robertson, president of the Christian Coalition. "The majority opinion is totally at odds with both the Constitution and the wishes of the American people. It is unbelievable."

Other pro-life Christian leaders were even more graphic in their condemnation of the Supreme Court majority's ruling.

"They have betrayed God, they have betrayed the pro-life movement, they have betrayed the children," said Randall Terry, then the leader of Operation Rescue. "History will remember them as sinister cowards who did not have the courage to do what is right."[10]

In 1994 Congress passed the Freedom of Access to Clinic Entrances Act (FACE), which restricts the First Amendment rights of pro-life demonstrators to rally near abortion clinics. So far lower courts have allowed FACE to stand, though the Supreme Court has not yet ruled. The American legal system is advancing the feminist's pro-abortion agenda.

But the feminists' best friend is Bill Clinton. On January 22, 1993, just two days after he took the oath of office, the new President began to fulfill his campaign promises to the pro-abortion lobby that helped elect him.

While more than 100,000 pro-life demonstrators marched in the snow outside on the 20th anniversary of *Roe v. Wade*, Clinton met with feminist leaders inside the White House and signed executive orders that removed the last remaining vestiges of federal regulatory restraint on legal abortion in America. This action prompted pro-life leader Rep. Chris Smith (R-NJ) to dub Clinton the "Abortion President."

"Mr. Clinton is the first president in the history of America to be an advocate for abortion and gay rights," said pro-life leader Rev. Patrick Mahoney of the Christian Defense Coalition. "These views, among many others of the new Administration, are in direct conflict with the teachings of the Bible and the Church. It is a disgrace for the president-elect to portray to the American public that his public policies will have as their foundation Christian principles."

Clinton's orders reversed policies of both the Reagan and Bush administrations that prohibited any form of abortion advocacy counseling at federally funded Title X family planning clinics, thus funneling $37 millions of tax dollars annually into the coffers—and ultimately into the coffins—of Planned Parenthood clinics. Clinton also ordered doctors at U.S. military bases worldwide to perform abortions for members of the armed services and their dependents, and he directed the Department of Health and Human Services to expedite approval for the importation of the controversial RU-486 abortion pill from France.

Clinton restored U.S. funding for the United Nations Fund for Population Activities, which supports and encourages abortion as a means of birth control in ostensibly "overpopulated" Third World countries. He also changed the U.S. immigration rules to deny political asylum to refugees fleeing the coercive one-child family planning policies of China, which are enforced by mandatory abortion and involuntary sterilization.

Clinton also reversed the Bush-era ban on federal funding for fetal tissue research. Clinton's action opened the door for the widespread resumption of gruesome "D & X," or partial-birth, abortions under the sanitized sanction of medical science.[11]

In this late-term medical procedure, which is intended to supply "fresh" fetal material for researchers, labor is induced and the baby is partially delivered, with only the baby's head remaining inside the mother's body. Then doctors insert a long needle into the base of the baby's skull and siphon out the brains from the still-living child. The brain matter is used for research on Parkinson's disease and other things.

Despite intense opposition by pro-abortion feminist groups, Congress finally by a narrow margin passed a bill banning partial-birth abortions late in 1995. But as this book is going to press, Clinton has threatened a veto, and there are not enough pro-life votes to override.

Civilized nations around the world recoiled in horror from the crude medical experiments performed by Nazi doctors on concentration camp inmates during World War II, and those who made lamp shades from the dead victims' skin were deemed guilty of "crimes against humanity."

The only difference between then and now is about 50 years.

Gay and Lesbian "Pride"

President George Bush always appeared to be a decent enough kind of guy. He campaigned hard on the "family values" theme and he held the line, commendably, against abortion to the bitter end. But Bush did for the gay agenda what Clinton did for the feminists—he gave it legitimacy through the White House.

On April 23, 1990, Bush signed the "Hate Crimes" Bill, intended to provide special protection to individuals or groups who were the targets of KKK-type, hate-driven violence. "Enacting this law today helps us move toward our dream," Bush said, "a society blind to prejudice, a society open to all." Who can disagree with something that sounds so fair?

The problem is, language in the Hate Crimes Bill can be construed to interpret Christian preaching against sodomy as an act of "hatred" against homosexuals because it makes them feel guilty and damages their self-esteem. No joke. Some government agencies as far back as the midpoint of the Reagan administration have suggested that churches which persist in this type of "harassment" should forfeit their tax-exempt status.

"A lot of people have been hood-winked," warned Sen. Jesse Helms (R-NC). "This bill is the flagship of the homosexual/lesbian legislative agenda." Thanks to George Bush, the homosexual leaders gaily sailed that big pink boat right into the Rose Garden.

For the first time in American history, openly professing leaders of the homosexual movement were invited to the White House for a signing ceremony. Bush's top liaison to the religious community, a committed Christian named Doug Wead, objected and was fired for his trouble.[12]

Later that summer they were back again for the signing of the Americans with Disabilities Act, which classified the deadly AIDS disease as a "disability" against which no employer could "discriminate." Thus AIDS became the world's first politically protected disease.

Since then homosexual activists have "come out of the closet" with a vengeance and have now openly demand special "civil rights" protection so that no one can even dare to say that, according to God's Word, homosexual sodomy is still a sin. That kind of judgmental rhetoric is now condemned as intolerant, politically incorrect "hate speech."[13]

Homosexuals also want society to sanction their illicit sexual unions with gay and lesbian marriage ceremonies, and they want new laws to force employers to pay spousal benefits for their "domestic partners."

When average American voters in Colorado resisted with the passage of the Amendment 2 referendum restricting special rights for homosexuals, the Colorado Supreme Court declared the lawfully expressed will of the people to be unconstitutional. The U.S. Supreme Court affirmed that decision in 1996. Meanwhile, "gay rights" activists launched a well-financed media campaign to falsely portray Colorado as the "Hate State."[14]

Politicians without moral principle pander to the gay lobby, as when New York City mayoral candidate Rudy Giuliani marched in the Gay Pride parade alongside the delegation of pedophiles from NAMBLA (North American Man-Boy Love Association) in 1993. Massive Gay Pride rallies in Washington, D.C., have attracted thousands in recent years, including several openly homosexual members of Congress.

Visitors to our nation's capital on April 25, 1993—just three years after that first historic Rose Garden visit by gays—were confronted with the sight of 300,000 bare-breasted lesbians, French-kissing men, and sado-masochistic "masters" in black leather garb leading around their submissive "slaves" with chains and spiked dog collars—all this on the Mall and the lawn of the Washington Monument, just outside the White House.[15]

Similar annual events in San Francisco, where the Gay Pride celebrations first started as huge homosexual block parties in the city's gay districts, regularly include top city leaders. A video of one such parade shows a high-ranking federal government official, Clinton appointee Roberta Achtenberg of HUD, fervently kissing her lesbian lover, Mary Martin, who also happens to be a San Francisco municipal judge.[16]

The San Francisco parades often include transvestite drag queens and gay men and lesbian women in varying stages of public nudity. Anti-Christian slogans are evident, and some male cross-dressers have even donned nuns' habits for the event—adding black fishnet stockings and garter belts in a blatant mockery of purity and chastity.

Their "gay pride" is a defiant fist flouted in the face of a Holy God.

Bill Clinton has done his part to advance the gay agenda, too. He actively sought the gay vote in 1992, and on May 20 at the Palace Theater in Hollywood he campaigned on the theme: "I have a vision, and you're part of it."[17] Once elected, he tried his best to allow gays openly into the military, and he invited a dozen gay activist leaders to meet with him for three hours in the White House to address their "concerns." Clinton has also filled his Administration with homosexuals, though not all of them are admitting their sexual orientation publicly. Not yet, anyway.

Paul said that in the Last Days men would be "without natural affection," and he warned of the especially defiling effects of homosexuality, which produces in men and women a "reprobate mind," so that they can no longer discern the error of their ways but must continue blindly on to judgment. The continuing debilitating plague of AIDS on the homosexual community is ample evidence of the tragic truth of this passage.[18]

Today in America it is deemed politically incorrect to render a moral judgment on sexual sins of any kind, and especially on homosexual and lesbian activities, which are now taught in the college classrooms of our state universities under the guise of "diversity" and "multiculturalism." "Tolerance" has been enshrined as a virtue superior to the Word of God.

It needs to be stated plainly that God's opinin of sin has not changed just because man's has. God still views homosexuality the same way He did when He destroyed Sodom and Gomorrah, and His response to modern man's defiance is likely to be the same. The major earthquake that rocked San Francisco during the 1989 World Series could have been a divine warning rather than a mere coincidence.[19]

Lawlessness and Violence

Violence pervades our lives. Paul wrote that men in the Last Days would become "fierce" and "despisers of those that are good."

We see that trend in the violence all around us every day. We saw it in April 1995 with the truck bomb that blew up the Alfred P. Murrah Federal Building in Oklahoma City. We saw it with the assassin's bullet that felled Yitzhak Rabin in Israel just before Christmas in 1995. We see it in the news reports of terrorist attacks, or another deadly package from the Unabomber. Every day, around the world, one million people die, and many of those deaths are violent.

We have already discussed the violence of war in this century, but the threat of domestic violence is, for most of us, even more real on a daily basis. The rate of violent crime in America surpasses that of other industrialized countries, and the FBI says that eight out of ten Americans will be the victims of violent crime during the course of their lifetimes.[20]

Every day in America, 135,000 of our children show up at school with some kind of weapon. Gangs terrorize the streets of our inner cities with impunity. More than 250,000 Americans have been murdered in the past ten years, and experts say it's going to get worse.

"There's a demographic double-whammy that's going to hit us," warns Northwestern University criminologist James Fox. "Not only are today's violent teenagers maturing into even more violent young adults, but they're being replaced by an even larger group of teenagers behind them. There is trouble ahead unless we prepare for it now."[21]

But in an unstable society with increasing numbers of broken homes, and children growing up without fathers, turning the tide against violence is an uphill battle. The social infrastructure seems to be disintegrating.

Human Waste

Much of the violence we experience is pointless, brought on by stress. Husbands and wives argue at home, kids fight at school. Life goes on.

But some is more serious, though provoked by trivial matters. Each daily newspaper tells another senseless story. Someone is cut off in traffic, so he pulls out a pistol and kills the other driver. Teenagers fight over a basketball game, and someone ends up dead on the court, stabbed or shot or beaten with a baseball bat. A drug deal turns sour, and people are killed. A ten-year-old boy shoots his little sister because she won't do what he says.

We have all read about these kinds of things. We shake our heads over the human waste, and we say, "How sad."

Extreme Reactions

Then there are the incidents that have understandable causes but produce extreme reactions. Lorena Bobbitt severs her husband's penis because she says he beat and raped her. A fired postal employee returns to work and murders his boss and several co-workers before turning the gun on himself. A spurned lover or angry ex-spouse kills the object of his unrequited love and maybe a half dozen of her relatives in the process. The Menendez brothers shoot their mother and father with a shotgun to inherit a $14 million dollar fortune, then say they were driven to do it by previous child abuse.

We deplore these events but we understand what causes them. There is an obvious motive: bitterness, revenge, jealousy, money. We shake our heads at the human tragedy, and we say, "How awful."

Low-Grade Depravity

Other things we read about make us angry because of the low-grade depravity of human nature they reveal. Often they involve child abuse, as in the case of the parents who fed their small children fried rats and cock roaches and sexually abused them. Or the boyfriend who kept his lover's 12-year-old daughter locked in a box in the dark closet.

Or Susan Smith, who drowned her two small sons in the lake and told police they had been kidnapped, pleading tearfully for their return for days before the horrible truth surfaced.

Or the L.A. gang that surrounded a family car that got lost on a dead end street called the "street of killers"—they shot into the car and killed a four-year-old child before the frantic family could escape.

When we read these accounts, we get very angry. We slam our fists on the table and exclaim, "This is sick! How could they _do_ that!"

Pervasive Evil

But there is another kind of violence, and we read about it with increasing frequency these days, as well. It is much more frightening because it is so evil, so depraved, and so completely alien to everything humanity holds to be decent. Because it is so random and so pointless and so totally unpredictable. And because it strikes across every strata of society, and that means we ourselves are vulnerable.

This category includes well-known incidents like the Manson cult's bloody murders of actress Sharon Tate and her unborn child, and then later the LaBiancas, in California in 1969.

Or the Luby's Cafeteria massacre in Texas in 1991, when a heavily armed gunman crashed his pickup through the plate glass window of a busy restaurant and methodically began to execute people, killing 22 defenseless victims in 10 minutes before turning the gun on himself.

Or the bizarre case of Jeffrey Dahmer, who kidnapped young boys and homosexually abused them, then killed them and dismembered their bodies. He froze the body parts, eating some of them later. His known victims numbered 17 before he was caught, convicted, and then beaten to death in prison by another inmate.

Or the terrible recent tragedy in Dunblane, Scotland, where a deranged man murdered 16 five-year-old children and a teacher in a kindergarten gym class before turning the gun on himself.

There are other cases, less well known but just as disturbing. A woman meticulously decorated her house for Christmas, then on Christmas Eve she stabbed her husband and two children to death as they slept, tucked them neatly into bed, and later called her sister-in-law to tell her what she had done. Police said she was under stress because of unpaid bills.

Or the couple who wanted a baby but didn't have one, so they killed a pregnant woman and cut open her abdomen to steal the unborn child.

Or the teenage boys who picked up a young girl hitchhiking to her grandmother's house, then took her to a remote area where they beat and then stabbed her 180 times, cutting off her fingers for souvenirs before tossing her off a cliff. The ringleader said she was a sacrifice to Satan.

Encroaching Fear

When we read of these things—and we all know that this is just a minute sampling of the growing number of such incidents that could be listed here—when we read of these things, we simply sit in stony silence. We cannot express what we feel. The revulsion. The pain. The fear.

What we feel is beyond words, almost beyond comprehension. Yet there it is, with an Associated Press byline, the gory facts spread before us right there on the breakfast table, next to the orange juice and toast.

"It's insane," is our first semi-numb reaction. And then, almost casually, because we don't really want to know, we think, "I never used to read about stuff like that. Now I hear about it all the time. What's going on here? What's happening to the world?"

What is happening is a society in decline, a society that has forsaken God. A generation that has been indoctrinated with the nihilism of MTV and the existential mentality of *Natural Born Killers*. A generation that has seen Schwarzenegger waste so many human "targets" that it has become desensitized to the reality of blood, and pain, and human death.

What is happening is a society where human life has no intrinsic value, because men are not created in the image of God, because we all came from monkeys. Where children are not a blessing but a burden and a curse, because there are too many people on the planet already.

Where the future has no purpose because there is no plan. Where life has no meaning because there is no God.

Where the spirit of death, having been given official government sanction to kill 4,000 unborn babies a day, has broken forth and demanded more. Has subtly permeated the minds of the living and slyly turned them to its will. Has infiltrated our lives, along with encroaching fear.

What is happening, my friends, is the Last Days.

Drugs, Demons and Satan Worship

Pat Robertson has described what he thinks will happen spiritually during the 1990s. Like many other Christian leaders, he believes that there will be increased spiritual conflict during the days that lie immediately ahead. In his best-seller, *The New Millennium,* Robertson says:

> The manifestation of satanic power is going to come at us—that is, at Bible-believing Christians—in such a way we would not have believed it possible. But I also believe that during this decade there will be a counter-balancing Christian revival of the power of God's Holy Spirit.[22]

The days of Noah were a time of intense wickedness and evil upon the Earth, and the Last Days will be like that as well. One manifestation of this evil will be a marked increase in occult activity and demonic influence just prior to the return of Jesus. The Apostle Paul described how it will be:

> **Now the Spirit speaketh expressly, that <u>in the latter times</u> some shall depart from the faith, <u>giving heed to seducing spirits, and doctrines of devils</u>....**
> **1 Timothy 4:1**

The Scriptures quoted above have a special meaning for me because God used those words to bring me understanding in a time of personal confusion and trouble. The ultimate result was deliverance and freedom.

My Personal Testimony

When I first heard those words from the Bible, back in the summer of 1980, I was a voluntary patient in a mental hospital recovering from what the doctors called a "psychotic break." I called it a supernatural encounter with the Devil. Either way, I was there trying to regain my mental balance after the darkest experience of my life.

But more important than mere recovery, I wanted to know *why* my mind had suddenly snapped. Although I was not a born-again Christian, I was praying to God for answers and reading the Bible.

One day I walked into the hospital day room, where some of the other patients were watching television. A program called *The 700 Club* was on, and a preacher named Pat Robertson was reading the Scriptures quoted above. After he finished reading, Robertson looked at the camera and said something like, "I believe we're going to see a lot of this in coming years. We're going to see more and more *drug-induced demonic possession.*"

Those four words—"drug-induced demonic possession"—got my attention, because that sounded like exactly what had happened to me. Through a combination of prolonged drug abuse including cocaine and PCP, plus participation in a wide variety of occult practices ranging from fortune-telling with cards to meditation and the cultivation of personal clairvoyance, I had come under Satan's control.

I knew that fact as surely as I knew that I was alive. I also knew that, if God hadn't answered when I called on Him in desperation, I surely wouldn't be alive. Beyond that, I really didn't have a clue. As you might imagine, trying to tell this bizarre tale to the doctors didn't get me very far. (It is too surreal to repeat here, either, so we had better just move along.)[23]

I called *The 700 Club* and talked to a counselor, who prayed with me over the phone and then sent me some tracts on "Occult Bondage and Deliverance." Those tracts said that people who commit certain occult sins will come under the control of demons.[24]

I read the tracts but dismissed them, because they said that I had to receive Jesus as my Savior, and I wasn't interested in that. I was interested in developing my personal psychic powers so that I could stand up to the assorted witches and sorcerers I had encountered.

After leaving the hospital, I continued my spiritual quest. I still prayed and read the Bible, but I was heavily into cocaine. I was searching for God, but I still wanted the power. I began studying occult literature.

A casual friend of mine, a serious warlock said to have an altar to Satan in his bedroom, tried to recruit me into his camp. "We've been watching you," he told me one day as we stood beside the bluff behind his Lookout Mountain mansion. "You have a lot of spiritual power. You should join up with us."

I was interested but unconvinced, though he said that he only used his occult powers "for good." I told him I would think about it. He loaned me a book on curses and I left, but I already had a gut feeling that his way would not take me to God.

I continued doing drugs while searching for God, and I would stay up all night snorting cocaine and reading occult books. One night, while we were partying and smoking free-base cocaine, my new girlfriend saw me reading the book on curses. Inexplicably, she looked at me and said, "I don't think you're crazy, and you're going to find your answers. But if I were you, I'd find out about Jesus first, before the witches." If ever there were evidence for the sovereignty of God, that unlikely incident is it.

I wasn't interested in Jesus at first, because I saw powerlessness in the lukewarm religion of many of my relatives. But the occult books I was studying said that Jesus was a great sorcerer like Solomon and Moses before him. I began to read the Bible to find out how Jesus did His magic tricks.

But when I began to read the Gospels, I found myself confronted with the claims of Christ. Rather than affirming the universal truths of all religions, Jesus said that all the so-called messiahs who came before Him were "thieves and robbers," and that He was the only way to God.

"I am the way, the truth, and the life: no man cometh unto the Father, but by me," Jesus insisted. He spoke of a mysterious spiritual process of being "born again," apart from which no person could enter Heaven.[25]

A few months later, on my 32nd birthday, I was saved. It happened in a biker's duplex in North Miami Beach, with a chopper in the living room and a picture of the Devil on the wall. I had been up all night partying with a go-go girl from the Easy Pieces Lounge. The Scotch whiskey and the free-base cocaine were spread out on the table in front of me when, at 10:15 a.m., with the sarcastic go-go girl watching in disbelief, I prayed and asked Jesus to forgive my sins and be my Savior.

Two hours later, after a spiritual battle that was without question the most intense experience of my life—after claiming the Blood of Jesus against the powers of darkness that were controlling my life—I received massive deliverance. The demons left me with a great convulsive shudder that racked my body. The Holy Spirit rushed in like a fountain gushing up in my chest, and I was free for the first time in my memory.

As I began seriously to study the New Testament for the first time, I found that my experience exactly matched what it had to say:

> **Giving thanks unto the Father, which hath made us meet to be partakers of the inheritance of the saints in light:**
> **Who hath <u>delivered us from all the power of darkness,</u> and hath <u>translated us into the kingdom of his dear Son:</u>**
> **In whom we have <u>redemption through his blood,</u> even the forgiveness of sins....**
> **Colossians 1:13-14**

That encounter with Jesus in Miami ended my search for God and began my walk with Him. Leaving behind drugs and occultism, I married the girl who had told me to "find out about Jesus first." We now have seven beautiful children and a new life in Christ.

As I have read the Bible and understood its truths, I have come to realize that my friends and I had been spiritually blinded by the Devil. We were living in lust and sin apart from God, yet we didn't realize it. I had told everybody that I was free to live my own life as I saw fit, but I didn't know that I was really a slave of Satan, controlled by his demons.

It was only after Jesus set me free from Satan's grip that I came to understand what my long-time folk hero Bob Dylan had meant when he appeared on *Saturday Night Live* way back then and sang, "You've gotta serve somebody. Now it might be the Devil, or it might be the Lord, but you know you're gonna have to serve somebody."

Satan Worship

There have always been witchcraft covens and other groups that have made the conscious choice to serve the Devil. From the time of Babylon until the present there have been those who have practiced magic and sorcery. The Chaldeans were occult astrologers, and every ritualistic mystery religion the Earth has ever known has its roots deep in that demonic past.

But today the glorification of Satan has become more open. Anton LaVey founded the Church of Satan in San Francisco and wrote *The Satanic Bible*. LaVey had decided that Christians were hypocrites who denied their true, carnal human natures. So he created a church where magic, lust, greed, and the drive to power are virtues. Here people can just be what they really are, without pretense or hypocrisy. The idea seems to be catching on.

In 1968 Roman Polanski directed the hit film *Rosemary's Baby*, which was about a Satanic plot to produce an Antichrist. Ironically, in 1969 Polanski's pregnant wife, actress Sharon Tate, was brutally murdered by Charles Manson's Satanic cult, along with her unborn child.

Today over 325 different musical groups or performers have some type of Satanic or occult connection, according to Eric Barger's *Rock Music Rating System*.[26]

The rock group KISS looks like a band of warlocks. Their name is supposed to be an acronym for Kings In Satanic Service. Other rock groups like Iron Maiden, Black Sabbath, Motley Crue, Van Halen, Blue Oyster Cult, Merciful Fate, Slayer, Megadeth, and many others have lyrics and videos which openly glorify the Devil. Some have album covers which depict his grotesque demons.

Grindcore and Death Metal bands, along with Black Metal Music, focus on the themes of death, murder, and suicide. The message is clear in the names of some of these groups: Deicide, Sadus, Morbid Angel, Carcass.

Even the seemingly innocuous but ever-popular Eagles allegedly have some connections with Satanist Anton LaVey, whose face appears on the cover of their *Hotel California* album.

A few years back, the *Encyclopaedia Britannica* called belief in a "person called Satan" an "erroneous idea." Today the pendulum has shifted, and the society is saturated with belief in the Devil. A series of "Damien" movies in the late 1970s and early 1980s essentially glorified the emerging Antichrist. Steven King's chilling horror novels top the best-seller lists, denoting a popular preoccupation and fascination with evil.

Teenage students addicted to *Dungeons and Dragons* act out the instructions of their "dungeon master" in gruesome real-life murders. Police find Satanic literature and symbolism connected to ritual killings. Witchcraft openly flourishes. The spiritual stage is being set for the explosion of Satanic supernaturalism that will produce the Antichrist.

Those involved in the overt worship and service of Satan are in grave peril. Once the Devil has a person in his clutches, he does not easily release them. More and more people are paying the price of their pacts with Satan.

> But above all, <u>a conscious subscribing of oneself to the devil, particularly with one's own blood, will result in a terrible form of demonic subjection and oppression</u>. Formal contracts with the devil of this nature take place much more frequently than one would care to think, but fear prevents many people from confessing what they have done. The motive behind this surrendering of one's life and soul to Satan is usually the desire to have some special wish fulfilled.[27]

But despite Satan's very real power, the power of God through Jesus Christ is infinitely greater. There is no Satanic pact and no human curse that cannot be broken by the power of the Blood of Christ at Calvary.[28]

Sorcery and Drugs

It has been said that drug abuse is the number one social pathology of the 20th Century. Addiction to and trafficking in drugs are contributing factors in the proliferation of other crimes ranging from prostitution and petty burglary to armed robbery and murder. Today's bloody gang wars and drive-by shootings, most of which have some connection to drugs, make the old Prohibition-era gangsters look tame by comparison. Police have started to call the Miami area "Dodge City" because of the running drug wars between the Cubans and the Colombian "cocaine cowboys."

Some people don't think the Bible says anything about drugs because they can't find the word in the concordance. But in the Book of Revelation, speaking specifically about the Last Days, there are several references to "sorcery." In the Greek, the word for sorcery is "pharmakia," from which our modern English word "pharmacy" is derived.

Drugs have always been connected with witchcraft and sorcery. Potions, spells, charms, and rituals frequently have some type of drug at their core. Hallucinogens have been used as the sacraments of pagan religions since time began.

Drugs are bad. They open a person's mind to demonic influence. God has built a hedge of protection around men's minds to keep their state of consciousness in the material world in which they live. When men breach that barrier, they find themselves in a different spiritual dimension. There they are vulnerable, out of their natural element, like the cliched "fish out of water."

The Bible is clear about the danger: "Whoso breaketh an hedge, a serpent shall bite him" (Ecclesiastes 10:8). When a person lets down the God-given barriers of his will and opens his mind to the spirit world, he will get poisonous demonic results.

"The domination of the human psyche by demons...is the real danger in drug use," cult expert Dave Hunt has explained. Hunt also observes that "hallucinogens produce the same mystical experiences that Hindus and Buddhists have been enjoying for thousands of years through yoga and transcendental meditation." Hunt quotes the noted scientist Sir John Eccles, whose research on the brain won him a Nobel Prize. Eccles describes the brain as "a machine a 'ghost' can operate."[29]

That is what happens in drug abuse. Men give their minds over to the operational control of demons. The experience can give the illusion of power or enlightenment, but the true result is bondage. Side effects often include misery, depression, mental illness, and even suicide.

My drug of choice was cocaine. I used cocaine continuously for almost 10 years and I loved it. Cocaine became such an idol in my life that I used to tell my friends that I felt that it was almost sacrilegious to cut it.

I also used to say that cocaine is a very powerful but subtle drug, and it should be used moderately in order to appreciate its subtlety.

Looking back now, after not having used cocaine for 15 years since I became a Christian, I see that I was more correct than even I knew at the time. Having now read Genesis 3, I know that the serpent is "more subtil than any beast of the field which the Lord God had made."

Cocaine is Satan's drug of choice, too.

Sons of God, Daughters of Men

As we have already seen from Scripture and as we have abundantly demonstrated from the events of our lives, ours is a time of ever-increasing lawlessness, violence, and wickedness.

Some believe that things will continue on pretty much as they are until suddenly, unexpectedly, Jesus just shows up one day. People will be buying and selling, marrying and giving in marriage, and things will be pretty much business-as-usual.

But I believe there is more to it than that. The Bible says that God destroyed the Earth and all the people in it in Noah's day because of their great wickedness. God repented of ever creating these people, whose every thought was only to do evil constantly.

When Jesus comes back in judgment at the end of the age, it will be at the close of a period of Great Tribulation such as has never been experienced on the Earth before, a completely unique segment of human history. The Bible says that this period is the time of God's wrath on the world, a time of misery and slaughter, and except those days were cut short, not a single living soul would survive.

What is it that will provoke this outpouring of God's wrath, just as it was provoked in the Days of Noah? The answer to this question is clearly revealed in the Scriptures in the first four verses of Genesis 6.

> **And it came to pass, when men began to multiply upon the face of the Earth, and daughters were born unto them,**
>
> **That <u>the sons of God saw the daughters of men, that they were fair; and they took them wives of all which they chose</u>.**
>
> **And the Lord said, My spirit shall not always strive with man, for that he also is flesh: yet his days shall be an hundred and twenty years.**
>
> **And <u>there were giants in the earth in those days</u>; and also after that, when the sons of God came in unto the daughters of men, and they bare children unto them, the same became <u>mighty men which were of old, men of renown</u>.**
>
> **Genesis 6:1-4**

Here the Bible says that a particular activity was going on. The "sons of God" were cohabiting with and marrying the "daughters of men," who were then giving birth to a race of giants—these later became "mighty men, men of renown" in the Earth.

That the daughters of men were ordinary human women seems pretty clear, but who were these "sons of God"? Some suggest that these are the godly descendants of Adam and Eve's third son, Seth, as opposed to the wicked descendants of Cain.[30]

This explanation does not account for the fact that only Noah and his family were found righteous in God's sight, and everyone else was devoted to wickedness. The Bible does not describe a large group of righteous people on the Earth at this time.

Furthermore, the Hebrew words which are translated as "sons of God" are *bene Elohim,* a phrase which consistently in the Old Testament is translated "sons of God" but always has reference to angels.[31]

I believe that this verse refers to the fallen angels who were expelled from Heaven with Lucifer at the time of his initial rebellion against God. One-third of the angels of Heaven followed Lucifer—who is now known as Satan—and these fallen angels are the demon spirits who serve him.[32]

These same demons are described in the New Testament as "the angels that sinned" in 2 Peter 2:4-5. Additionally, Jude 6-8 says this:

> **And <u>the angels which kept not their first estate, but left their own habitation</u>, he hath reserved in everlasting chains under darkness unto the judgment of the great day,**
>
> **Even as Sodom and Gomorrah, and the cities about them in like manner, <u>giving themselves over to fornication, and going after strange flesh</u>, are set forth for an example, suffering the vengeance of eternal fire.**
>
> **Likewise also these <u>filthy dreamers defile the flesh, despise dominion</u>, and speak evil of dignities.**

The Bible speaks here of angels who left their appointed place of habitation and committed some great sin that has resulted in their being bound in chains under darkness until the day of judgment. These creatures, because of the magnitude of their sin, today do not enjoy even the freedom of the common demons of Satan.[33]

Moreover, the passage links by example the perverse sexual activities of Sodom and Gomorrah, mentioning "going after strange flesh" and those who "defile the flesh" and "despise dominion," or God's established order. I believe this passage clearly speaks of the cohabitation of demon spirits with human women in the days of Noah.[34]

Their offspring, the "giants," are in the Hebrew *nephilim,* which literally means "fallen ones." According to Dr. Unger, the Septuagint translation of this word is "not 'giants' but of mixed human and angelic birth, like the Titans of Greek and Roman mythology, who were partly human and partly divine—angelic."[35]

It appears obvious that God is saying he destroyed the Earth in the days of Noah because the human inhabitants of the Earth, in addition to all their other sins, had defiled the created order of being by submitting themselves sexually to intercourse with demon spirits and producing a mongrel race of beings neither fully human nor completely angelic.

The "mighty men of renown" from this mongrel race were known to every ancient pagan people, and they became the heroes of their various folk tales, which we in modern times have called mythologies.

But the Bible says it happened just this way.

Star Wars, E.T., and UFOs

In occultism these demons are called *incubus* and *succubus,* and this is a real phenomenon, though not very widespread today.[36]

In Noah's day, apparently, voluntary human sexual interaction with demons was much more common, though by no means universal. Not all human offspring were *nephilim,* and life was more than one continuous orgy. People apparently still carried on many of their normal daily activities, as Jesus used the examples of eating and drinking, marrying and giving in marriage, working in the field and grinding at the mill.

But I suggest to you that we are much closer to this time than you might think. As the society continues to degenerate around us, and both promiscuous fornication and blatant homosexual perversion become more commonplace, men and women will sink to ever lower levels of depravity.

Romans 1 is clear that, as men forget God and descend into idolatry, they are given over first to sexual sin, then to perversion, and finally to a reprobate mind, where they can no longer discern good from evil. This is the spiritual process of degeneration now at work in our godless world.

I was in the lobby of a Holiday Inn on I-75 somewhere in Kentucky a few years back, and I was looking at the magazines on the newsstand. The headline of a cheap tabloid caught my eye: "I Had An E.T. Baby!" The story was about a woman who claimed to have been abducted by space aliens, taken aboard a spacecraft, and forced to have sex with the creatures. She claimed to have become pregnant by the aliens and to have borne a child.

Now I certainly can't vouch for the veracity of her story, but it illustrates a point. People are starting to think in these terms. Next time you go through the check-out line at the grocery store, glance at the tabloid covers. The odds are, you'll see something about a space alien or a UFO. There may even be a doctored photo of a hideously ugly creature that looks like something from a *Star Wars* episode. You're looking at a demon.

The movie *E.T.* was a masterpiece of Satanic genius, yet many Christians flocked to see it, and sent their children. The message of *E.T.* was simple: there are kind, gentle, intelligent beings out in space, from civilizations far more advanced than our own, and they would like to use their superior wisdom to help us out with all our problems.

They can't reveal themselves to us, though, because we Earthlings are too uptight and suspicious. But the trusting little child, who accepts the nice space alien as his friend, received special supernatural powers.

This movie and others like it are, in my estimation, part of a process of mental conditioning designed to lower the natural defenses of a whole generation of young people, many of whom are already growing up violent and rebellious and alienated from God. To such an amoral generation "without natural affection" and driven by lust, "going after strange flesh" will not seem wrong or dangerous, but rather exciting and adventurous.

I stood on the sidewalk in front of a video rental store just the other day, and there in the window was a large, glossy, color poster advertising the movie *Species*. The creature depicted had the face of a seductive, somewhat sinister-looking woman, but her body was covered with coarse, reptile-like skin, there were long claws on her fingers, and she had a tail.

Inside the store, I walked down long aisles of videos. There was a whole section on alien encounters of one kind or another, and the jacket descriptions revealed a recurring theme of lost civilizations on distant planets and mutant alien races seeking to contact Earth. Right beside these videos was another section devoted to witchcraft, occultism, and Satanism. Immediately past that section were the horror movies featuring, among other gory things, bloody stabbings and gruesome chain saw murders.

Apparently even the stock clerk at the video store was able to see the obvious connection between the demonic themes of these movies.

There has been too much research done on UFOs, and too many documented experiences by too many people, for us to dismiss these phenomena as either hoaxes or the products of someone's overactive imagination. Something is happening, we just need to define what it is.

Cult expert Dave Hunt has quoted Dr. Jacques Vallee, an astro-physicist and computer scientist as well as a respected UFO expert, as saying that "the phenomena reported by [UFO] witnesses involve poltergeist effects, levitation, psychic control, healing and out-of-body experiences.... Furthermore there is a connection between UFOs and occult themes in their social effects."[37]

Hunt goes on to say that

> After 18 years of careful investigation of UFOs, Dr. Vallee comes to some startling conclusions in *Messengers of Deception,* his sixth book on the subject: 1) that UFOs are real but probably not physical; 2) that they are part of some evil scheme for the victimization of earthlings; and 3) that one of the major purposes is to <u>manipulate human con-sciousness and to program us psychologically for some ultimate deception.</u>[38]

Prophecy expert Hal Lindsey agrees with Hunt and Dr. Vallee in their identification of extraterrestrials as demons, and offers his own explanation for why these things are happening at the present time:

> I definitely believe there have been accurate sightings of UFOs. There may even have been actual encounters with intelligent beings on these crafts. But, let me reiterate: These creatures are not space aliens. They are demons. And I believe the UFO phenomenon is all part of a Satanic plot to set up a great deception....
>
> And why? Because something truly dramatic, sensa-tional, and spectacular will be necessary in these endtimes to ensure that a skeptical world buys into the new world religion the Bible predicts will be in place before the second advent. Something remarkable must occur to deceive the entire population of the world and line them up—eagerly—behind a god-man political and spiritual leader.[39]

The common theme of the New Age movement with its false Messiah, Maitreiya, is that the more advanced "ascended masters" are going to come and help us out, and their superior wisdom will solve all our problems. This is all part of the same demonic deception. There will be rampant demonic activity in the Last Days, and it is already underway.

The mastermind behind this ungodly conspiracy is Satan himself, preparing the minds of the people to accept his coming Antichrist and all the supernatural evil that accompanies him. The Bible plainly says that Satan is "the prince of the power of the air."[40]

In my estimation, it will be this wanton abandonment of all moral restraint on the part of the human race that will trigger the outpouring of the wrath of God during the coming Tribulation period, just as it did during the ancient days of Noah.

A Wicked Generation

In Proverbs 30 the Bible speaks of a particularly wicked generation that will come upon the Earth:

> **There is a generation that curseth their father, and doth not bless their mother.**
> **There is a generation that is pure in their own eyes, and yet is not washed from their filthiness.**
> **There is a generation, O how lofty are their eyes! and their eyelids are lifted up.**
> **There is a generation, whose teeth are as swords, and their jaw teeth as knives, to devour the poor from off the earth, and the needy from among men.**
> **Proverbs 30:11-14**

These Scriptures describe a violent, lawless, and degenerate generation which does not even accord basic respect to their parents, let alone allegiance and loyalty. This agrees with the words of Jesus in Luke 21:16, when He warned that in the Last Days family members would betray one another to death. It gives me no pleasure to write this, but I believe that such a generation has been born in the offspring of the Baby Boomers.

As the older generations of Christians die out—the Boomers' parents and grandparents—with them will die a vast repository of the genuine Christian faith. Those who will remain will be today's predominately humanistic, materialistic, and agnostic Boomers, most of whom have forsaken the historic faith of their fathers but in whom residual traces of decency remain. This is our contemporary "cut-flower" civilization.

But the Boomers' children, and even grandchildren, are now growing to adulthood without learning any consistent Biblical basis for morality. These children are being taught situation ethics under the guise of "values clarification" in our public schools, and they are learning that their greatest needs are self-esteem and self-actualization.

Self-denial and self-discipline are no longer in vogue. Generation X is really the "ME" generation, which has extolled immediate self-gratification as the highest good to which people can aspire.

As these children are constantly bombarded with images of sex and violence, more and more they will begin to act out in real life what they have already vicariously experienced repeatedly in fantasy. Drugs, Death Metal music, and occult demonic deception will warp their perceptions of good and evil. Increasingly, objective reality in the physical world will be shaped by the distorted images from the video stores and MTV. It is naive in the extreme too assume that children can constantly consume such garbage without having their minds polluted by it and their subsequent actions conditioned by it.[41]

What we are seeing now is just the beginning of a period of physical violence and spiritual chaos that I believe is going to come upon the Earth quickly and escalate much more rapidly than we can presently imagine.

I do not believe that it will take many decades for this to occur.

=>●<=

[1] Oliver North, "Bucks Over Bodies," *Christian American,* September/October 1992, p. 25.

[2] John Wheeler Jr., "Record Labeling: Censorship or Common Sense?" *Christian American,* Winter 1990, pp. 4-5.

[3] For a wealth of background information on the rock music culture, see Bob Larson, *Rock: Practical Help for Those Who Listen to the Lyrics and Don't Like What They Hear* (Wheaton, Ill.: Tyndale House, 1982).

[4] For information about the openly Satanic musical influences to which contemporary young people are being subjected, see Charles G.B. Evans, *Teens and Devil Worship: What Everyone Should Know* (Lafayette, La.: Huntington House, 1991).

⁵ "Use Laws to Get Labels on Dangerous Lyrics," *USA Today*, January 10, 1990, p. 8A.

⁶ Statistical information from William J. Bennett, *The Index of Leading Cultural Indicators* (Washington, D.C.: Heritage Foundation/Empower America, 1993), pp. i-ii.

⁷ Ibid.

⁸ Leviticus 18:21, 24-30.

⁹ Genesis 4:10-11; Leviticus 18:21, 28.

¹⁰ All quotes and information on *Casey* are from Connie Marshner, "Post-Casey Chaos," *Christian American*, September/October 1992, pp. 1, 4.

¹¹ All information about Clinton's actions is from Paul English, "Pro-Lifers March in Washington: Clinton Signs Pro-Abortion Directives," *Christian American*, March 1993, p. 11.

¹² Information on Bush's bringing gays to the Rose Garden is from "Bush Opens White House to Homosexual Leaders," *Christian American*, Summer 1990, p. 5.

¹³ Connie Zhu, "Gays Seek Federal Civil Rights Law," *Christian American*, January 1993, p. 3. See also Tony Marco, "Are Gays an Oppressed Minority?" *Christian American*, February 1993, p. 5.

¹⁴ John Wheeler Jr., "Colorado Law Blocked: Battle Shifts to Courts as Boycott Fizzles," *Christian American*, February 1993, pp. 1, 4.

¹⁵ March organizers were disappointed because they wanted a million people. Cliff Kincaid, "Gay Pride March Backfires," *Christian American*, July/August 1993, pp. 16-17.

¹⁶ Marshall Wittmann, "Achtenberg Confirmed to HUD," *Christian American*, July/August 1993, p. 12. After her confirmation as Assistant Secretary for Fair Housing and Equal Opportunity at HUD, the highest government position ever held by an open homosexual, Achtenberg was honored as "Woman of the Year" by the Washington, D.C.-based homosexual magazine *The Advocate*. See *Christian American*, February 1994, p. 18.

¹⁷ "Clinton Courts Homosexuals," *Christian American*, July/August 1993, p. 14.

¹⁸ Romans 1:26-32; Leviticus 18:22-30; 1 Corinthians 6:9-11.

¹⁹ Genesis 19:1-29.

[20] "Lifetime Likelihood of Victimization," Technical Report, U.S. Department of Justice, Bureau of Statistics, March 1987. Referenced in Bennett, *Index*, p. 3.

[21] "America the Violent: Bringing Our Nation to Its Knees," *The 700 Club Newswatch Fact Sheets*, August 9, 1995.

[22] Robertson, *The New Millennium*, p. 75.

[23] I have since been told by a Christian psychologist with whom I discussed this experience that the PCP was probably the precipitating factor, since it is not excreted though the kidneys like other drugs but is stored in the body's fat cells, where it builds up and could be released in extremely high levels by a triggering situation of stress. This agrees with Hunt, who says that PCP, more commonly known as Angel Dust, "has an obviously demonic effect." Hunt, *The Cult Explosion*, p. 35.

[24] Some people in our highly rationalistic age do not like to admit the reality of demons, but the Bible plainly speaks about them often. According to Bible scholar Merrill F. Unger, "In view of the Bible's silence regarding the origin of demons, the best supported deduction from scriptural hints is that demons are fallen angels." Unger, *Demons in the World Today*, pp. 15-16. See also *Unger's Bible Dictionary* (Chicago: Moody, 1966), pp. 259-261.

[25] John 14:6; John 3:1-17.

[26] Eric Barger, *From Rock To Rock* (Lafayette, La.: Huntington House, 1990), p. 45.

[27] Koch, *Occult Bondage and Deliverance*, p. 138.

[28] For the true story of one woman's escape from the powers of Satan, see Doreen Irvine, *Freed From Witchcraft* (Nashville: Thomas Nelson, 1973).

[29] Hunt, *The Cult Explosion*, pp. 24, 31-38. Hunt also says, "In the normal state of consciousness, the human spirit or mind is the 'ghost' that operates the brain.... In an altered state of consciousness, however — achieved through drugs, hypnosis, yoga, TM, or other similar means — this normal connection is loosened , allowing an alien mind to operate the brain. This alien mind could be a human being who has hypnotized the subject, or it could be a spirit being, such as a demon. The extent to which the latter occurs in hypnosis may be far greater than commonly imagined. Psychiatrists who use hypnosis do not want to admit the possibility at all, although they have no evidence to deny it."

[30] This is the view of Dr. Chriswell and some other conservative Bible scholars. W.A. Chriswell, ed., *The Chriswell Study Bible* (Nashville: Thomas Nelson, 1979), p. 14.

[31] For example, in Job 1:6 and 2:1, the "sons of God," who are clearly angels, come before God, and Satan is among them. This is the view of Dr. Unger, who

says that "the breaking down of God-ordained orders of beings (cf. 2 Pet. 2: 4-5; Jude 6) is the only exegesis of this passage that will satisfy its scope." *Unger's Bible Handbook*, p. 48.

[32] Isaiah 14:12-17; Ezekial 28:11-19; Revelation 8:10. See also Unger, *Demons in the World Today*, pp. 13-17.

[33] Dr. Unger elaborates: "These are thought by many scholars to be 'the sons of God' (fallen angels or demons) who co-habited with mortal women, producing moral chaos in God's established order of created beings. Their crime was so enormous that these lawless spirits (demons) and perhaps their monstrous offspring, were punished with imprisonment in Tartarus, the Greek nether world, comparable to hades, rather than in the regular prison of demons — the abyss. The flood may have been another indication of the enormity of their crime, in which God destroyed the offspring of this bizarre union." Unger, *Demons in the World Today*, pp. 16-17.

[34] "To translate it literally would make the passage say that members of the heavenly company selected choice women from the earth and set up marriage relationships with them, literally and actually. This can be the only interpretation of Job 1:6.... In light of the facts and the accurate rendering of the words of the text, we conclude that some men of the heavenly group (angels or messengers) actually took wives of the earthly women. They used superior force to overpower them, to make the conquest complete. The 'sons of God' were irresistible (cf. II Pet. 2:4; Jude 6)." Charles F. Pfeiffer and Everett F. Harrison, eds., *The Wycliffe Bible Commentary* (Chicago: Moody, 1962), pp. 11-12.

[35] Unger, *Unger's Bible Handbook*, p. 48.

[36] Win Worley, *Conquering the Hosts of Hell*, (Lansing, Ill.: HBC Publications, 1977), p. 39. Pastor Worley writes: "There are vicious sexual spirits which can molest and torment susceptible individuals. Those attacking females are called *incubus* and those concentrating on males are called *succubus*. They often come into prominence in connection with witchcraft spells, love potions and other curses of lust. They can also operate when people consciously and habitually experiment with sexual sin."

[37] Hunt, *The Cult Explosion*, pp. 19-20.

[38] Ibid.

[39] Lindsey, *Planet Earth—2000 A.D.*, pp. 72, 78.

[40] Ephesians 2:2.

[41] Serial killer Ted Bundy before his execution testified to the addictive and defiling effects of pornography, which came to control his thoughts and led him ultimately to commit heinous crimes. The message is the same for everyone: "Garbage in, garbage out."

Chapter 4
The Days of Restoration

> Repent ye therefore, and be converted, that your sins may be blotted out, when the times of refreshing shall come from the presence of the Lord;
> And he shall send Jesus Christ, which before was preached unto you:
> Whom the heavens must receive until the times of restitution of all things, which God hath spoken by the mouth of all his holy prophets since the world began.
> Acts 3:19-21

The Bible says that there is a time which has been spoken about by every prophet of God from the beginning of the world. That is the "time of restitution of all things." A better modern word would be "restoration." All of God's prophets have spoken about a coming time when "all things" will be restored. Bible teacher Derek Prince explains it this way:

> This is the climactic period of this age, a period when God is putting everything back in its right place and its right condition. And sometime in conjunction with this period, at a day and an hour that no man knows, the return of Jesus Christ will take place.[1]

There is a multiple restoration contemplated in this verse. First God is restoring some things in the Earth, prior to which Jesus Christ must remain in Heaven. But God is also restoring the Earth and everything in it to its original condition prior to the Fall, and this can be accomplished only by the Lord Himself when He returns.

In this chapter we will consider one of the most important aspects of God's current process of restoration in the Earth—the restoration of God's natural people Israel.

The Restoration of Israel

A truly distinctive development of the 20th Century, and one which has aptly been termed a "miracle of history," is the restoration of the Jewish people to their traditional homeland in Palestine. After 1,800 years of being scattered abroad across the face of the Earth with no place to call home, the remnants of the Children of Israel are finally settled back in the Biblical "land of Canaan" that God gave to Abraham in Genesis 12.[2]

Appreciation for the significance of this historic event is crucial to the correct understanding of end-time Bible prophecy, and the fact that it has occurred in this generation could mean that people now living will witness the personal return of Jesus Christ in glory.

Judgment and Dispersion

There are literally hundreds of Old Testament prophecies dealing with the return of Israel to the land in the Last Days after a period of God's severe judgment on their sins of national apostasy, which punishment was first predicted by Moses.[3]

That judgment began with the defeat of the idolatrous Northern Kingdom of Israel by Assyria in 722 B.C. The Assyrians carried away all the inhabitants of Israel as slaves, and for approximately 2,700 years the descendants of those tribes have been scattered abroad over the face of the Earth without a home.

After King Solomon's death, the Southern Kingdom of Judah also fell to Babylon in three stages, beginning in 606 B.C., when the first captives were led away. Nebuchadnezzar finally destroyed the city of Jerusalem in 586 B.C. and took both the Temple treasures and the remaining people to Babylon as spoils of war.

The prophet Daniel was among the early Babylonian captives, and it was while he was in Babylon that he had his prophetic visions of the Last Days, which are instrumental to our understanding of the prophecies of the Book of Revelation.

In 539 B.C. the Medo-Persian King Darius conquered and slew King Belshazzar of Babylon. His successor, King Cyrus, allowed a remnant of the Jews to return to Jerusalem after 70 years of captivity, and in about 445 B.C. King Artaxerxes Longimanus issued an edict permitting them to rebuild the city and the Temple. The descendants of these returnees from Babylon occupied Israel in Jesus' time.[4]

But also included in God's judgment was the later destruction of Jerusalem in 70 A.D. by Roman legions under Titus, and the subsequent dispersion of the remaining Jews across the globe, known as the Diaspora.

This was predicted by Jesus in Luke 21:24:

> *For Jerusalem shall be trodden down of the Gentiles until the times of the Gentiles be fulfilled.*

According to the Bible, the "times of the Gentiles" began in 586 B.C. when King Nebuchadnezzar carried the last captives away to Babylon. There have been a succession of Gentile powers with rulership over that city from then until modern times. The Gentile period will last until the Messiah personally rules in the Holy City.[5]

We will discuss the importance of this prophetic timetable more fully in subsequent sections of this study.

Worldwide Persecution

The Jews' sojourn in the world often has been a time of intense persecution, yet they have miraculously retained their ethnic identity as a unique race, preserving their language and their religious and cultural traditions. Still their suffering has been immense, as the Jews have frequently been despised, scorned and rejected by the people of the lands where they have lived. Sometimes they have been violently abused.

Anti-Semitism is nothing new. It has been going on in the world for over 3,000 years, as the Egyptians tried to drown the Jews' male babies at birth during the time of Moses before the Exodus. Later the Babylonians tried to burn them, and the Persians wanted to hang them.

In the 20th Century Hitler finally tried to exterminate them all in the concentration camps of his grotesque "Final Solution." Nazis during World War II killed an estimated six million Jews— approximately one-third of all the Jews in the world at that time.

Historical population records indicate that in the year 1800, there were 2.5 million Jews in the world, and by 1939 that number had grown to 16.7 million, of whom 56.8 percent lived in Europe. But by 1946, the total number of Jews in the world had been reduced to only 10.7 million by the Nazi Holocaust.[6]

Despite this kind of savage anti-Semitism, God preserved the Jews as a distinct people and eventually brought them back into their homeland, an event unique in human history. In fact, a fairly widespread resurgence of anti-Semitism in contemporary Europe has recently been contributing to the return of even more Jews to Israel each year.

Never before have a totally displaced people been restored to their national inheritance in this manner, and this fact bears witness to the sovereign control of God over the affairs of men, as well as His faithfulness to perform the covenant promises of His Word.[7]

Zionism and the Land

The return of the Jews to the Holy Land marked the end of a half century of efforts by Zionist nationalists to find international support for a native Jewish homeland, starting in 1897 with the first World Zionist Conference in Basle, Switzerland.

The resettlement started in earnest in 1914, when thousands of Jews began to migrate to Palestine, buying land there and establishing communes called "kibbutzim." By 1919, just 65,000 Jews were trying to eke out an agricultural existence from farms in the deserts and swamps.

Great Britain issued the Balfour Declaration in 1917, announcing that country's support for a Jewish homeland in Palestine. U.S. President Woodrow Wilson also endorsed the plan.

On December 9 of that same year, British General Viscount Allenby captured Jerusalem from the occupying Turks. Allenby, a Scotch Presbyterian, was a committed Christian who did not want to see the Holy City laid waste by war as had happened so many times in the past.[8] In his tent before launching his attack, Allenby opened his Bible to Isaiah 3:15,

As birds flying, so will the Lord of hosts defend Jerusalem; defending also he will deliver it; and passing he will preserve it.

This gave Allenby his battle plan. He ordered the British warplanes to fly low over the city repeatedly, while he and his army marched forward. The Turks, who had never seen an airplane, were amazed and frightened. Then they heard that "Allenby" was coming. This sounded to them like "Allah bey," or prophet of Allah.

These formidable warriors threw down their weapons and pros-
trated themselves before the approaching general, who captured
the city without firing a shot and with no destruction.[9]

The British took administrative control of the Holy Land after
World War I under the 1923 Palestine Mandate issued by the
League of Nations. By 1948 the number of Jewish settlers in
Palestine had grown to a little over 600,000, immigration having
been severely restricted by the British.

On May 14, 1948, the sovereign nation of Israel was established
once again by a mandate of the United Nations, with the fervent
support of U.S. President Harry Truman, who immediately granted
diplomatic recognition to the new provisional government, thus
fulfilling the promise of God in Isaiah 66:8 of a Jewish nation that
would be "born in a day."

On May 15 the tiny, fledgling Jewish state was attacked by the
combined armies of five surrounding Arab nations, including
Egypt, Jordan, and Syria, bent upon eradicating Israel from the face
of the Earth. But the outnumbered Israelis fought valiantly against
overwhelming odds. When a U.N.-brokered armistice was imposed
in 1949, Israel's boundaries encompassed almost 50 percent more
land than had been provided by the original partition mandate. In
1950, two years after the nation of Israel was formally established,
the Jewish population in Palestine was 1.2 million.[10]

In the Six-Day War of 1967 the Jews took over the West Bank
section of Palestine, and the Old City of Jerusalem. Then in 1973,
Israel miraculously survived the massive surprise attacks of her
enemies in the Yom Kippur War, emerging with even more territory, including the strategic Golan Heights region on her northern
border with Syria.[11]

The Aliyah, or Return of the Jews to Israel, got a big boost in
1989 when the Soviet Union collapsed, opening the doors for
Jewish emigration. More than 200,000 left the first year, and a total
of 500,000 former Soviet Jews had arrived in Israel by the midpoint
of 1994. At that time Russian Jews were arriving in Israel at the rate
of about 4,500 per month.

Many believe that this exodus of Soviet Jews to Israel is a partial
fulfillment of Jeremiah 16:14-16, which declares that God will
bring his people back to Israel "from the North." Between 2 and 4
million more Jews are estimated to remain in Russia and the former Soviet republics.

"This is probably one of the most powerfully prophetic events of modern times," said Michael Utterbach of the International Christian Embassy of Jerusalem, which assists Jews returning to Israel.[12]

As of 1993 an estimated 5.3 million Jews from all over the world had immigrated to Israel and were living in 8,000 square miles, an area about the size of the state of Massachusetts. An estimated 1.9 million Palestinians, over 90 percent of whom are Sunni Muslims, live there, too.[13]

Moslems on the Temple Mount

Since 1967, for the first time since the Babylonian captivity almost 2,600 years ago, Israel now exercises political control over the Old City of Jerusalem, which includes the site of the former Temple. This is important because key events of end-time prophecy—affirmed as valid by the words of Jesus Christ—are linked to the Jews' rebuilding of the Third Temple.

Today, reports from Israel indicate that a minority of Orthodox Jews still believe the Temple will be rebuilt and are actively preparing for that event. In the Old City of Jerusalem, the Ateret Kohanim Jewish seminary is teaching the Temple rituals, including animal sacrifice, as well as preparing the priestly robes and instruments needed to resume the rituals.[14]

And on the archaeological front, Hebrew University professor Dr. Asher Kaufman has discovered the actual northwest cornerstone of the Temple that existed when Jesus was alive. Dr. Kaufman has proven that the original Temple site is not covered by the Dome of the Rock but is actually 330 feet away. Therefore the Third Temple can be rebuilt without destroying the Moslem shrines now on the Temple Mount.[15]

Although modern Israel is a predominately secular state, even non-observant Jews seem to agree that the Temple should be rebuilt But for political reasons that event has not yet occurred, although a group of conservative Jews in Israel and their Christian supporters in the United States, known as the American Pro-Zionist Network, are trying to find a way to make it happen. So in a spiritual sense, Jerusalem is still "trodden under foot of the Gentiles."

Today the octagon-shaped Mosque of Omar, also called the Dome of the Rock, dominates the Temple Mount, although it is not actually on the spot where the Holy of Holies originally stood and where the Temple eventually must be rebuilt. This Muslim shrine is the third-holiest spot in Islam, after Mecca and Medina, and some Arab Moslems claim to believe that it was from this very spot that the Prophet Mohammed ascended alive into heaven mounted on his horse. The legend says that the rock also rose, and Mohammed had to push it back down.

The Israeli government has guaranteed the right of religious freedom, but not the right of proselytizing, to the adherents of various non-Jewish faiths, including the Moslems. It even spent $5 million dollars to restore the Christian churches damaged during the Six-Day War.

In August of 1986, the *New York Times* reported that a group of prominent Jewish rabbis in Jerusalem had issued a religious edict known as a halacha calling for both public Jewish prayers and the construction of a Jewish synagogue on the Temple Mount. That area has been off-limits to Jews since Israeli Defense Minister Moshe Dayan returned political control of the Temple Mount to the Arabs during the Six Day War of 1967.

According to the *New York Times* account,

> The call for prayers and the construction of a Synagogue came at a meeting led by Rabbi Shlomo Goren, a former Chief Rabbi of the Ashkenazim. He was rabbi of the Israeli Army when it seized the Wailing Wall in 1967....
>
> In their statement today, the rabbis called on "the Jewish nation and the Israeli authorities to guard and implement Jewish sovereignty of the Temple Mount and prevent its being turned over to and desecrated by foreigners"....
>
> The head of the Supreme Moslem Council in the city, Sheik Saad al-Din al-Alami, said that "the Moslems will never permit any Jew to pray in the area (meaning the Temple Mount)....
>
> "The Moslems are prepared to die for this."[16]

Rabbi Goren's demands were not met by the Israeli government, and the violent Palestinian *Intifada* came a year later.

I entered the nation of Israel on Christmas Day 1987, the day the *Intifada* began. I came out of Egypt by bus with a TWA tour, arriving in Tel Aviv about noon. For the next week I watched as Israel became an armed camp. Tourists visiting the Old City of

Jerusalem were allowed past Israeli check points beyond the Wailing Wall to tour the Dome of the Rock, but local Jews were not. In Bethlehem, the town square was surrounded by Israeli soldiers on the roofs armed with automatic weapons.[17]

On October 12, 1990—as Operation Desert Shield was in the process of becoming Operation Desert Storm—highly-publicized efforts by the Temple Mount Faithful to enter the Temple Mount and lay the cornerstone of the Third Temple were disallowed by the Israeli courts and rebuffed by Israeli police authorities. But the mere notion of such a thing caused the Moslem imams to issue proclamations that incited the Arabs to violent anger. A riot ensued on the Temple Mount and thousands of Arabs stormed and burned an Israeli police outpost. Embattled police, acting in self-defense, were forced to fire, killing 20 Arabs and wounding 200 more.

Biased media reports focused on Israeli violence toward Palestinians. Ultimately the United Nations, with U.S. approval, censured Israel for the incident and for failing to withdraw to her pre-1967 War boundaries.[18]

Because of the precarious status of negotiations in the ongoing peace accords between Israel and the Palestinians and their other Arab neighbors like Syria and Jordan, it is unlikely that the Israeli government will soon give any official sanction either to the removal of the Mosque of Omar or to the construction of a new Temple.

Nevertheless, the Bible says that must happen in the Last Days.[19]

Land For Peace

Land-for-peace negotiations in the wake of the Gulf War resulted in an agreement between Israel and the Palestinian Liberation Organization (PLO) signed at the White House on September 13, 1993. This Declaration of Principles called for Israel first to cede Gaza and Jericho to Palestinian autonomy and limited self-rule, and within five years to surrender control of the entire West Bank, which includes portions of Judea and Samaria.[20]

Jerusalem would remain, as it is today, the capital of Israel.

PLO leader Yassar Arafat, long branded an international pariah for the PLO's past terrorist actions, first agreed to acknowledge the right of the state of Israel to exist in 1988, in exchange for an autonomous Palestinian state. That concession earned Arafat a place at the table for the 1991 peace talks which followed the Gulf War, and ultimately led to the 1993 accord.

The PLO has been the implacable enemy of the Jews, with the destruction of the state of Israel as its avowed reason for existence, ever since its formation in 1964. Terror has been the tool used to achieve the goal, and PLO terrorists have been implicated in deaths of thousands in its campaign of random violence. Perhaps most widely known is the PLO attack which killed 11 Israeli Olympic athletes at the 1972 Summer Games in Munich.[21]

Prime Minister Yitzhak Rabin, the leader of the Labor Party coalition government that brokered the risky deal with the PLO, had campaigned in 1992 on the promise to produce a peace agreement within a year by trading "land for peace." The people of Israel, weary after 45 years of war, decided to take a chance on Rabin, ousting the long-time Likud government of Menachim Begin and Yitzhak Shamir, who had vowed never to give up any of the land Israel had won by conquest in her five wars with the Arabs.

After signing the long-awaited accord, Rabin still called the PLO a "terrorist organization," but he said the unsavory deal he had struck was necessary to the future security of Israel. "They are murderers, but you make peace with your enemies," Rabin said. "I can't tell you that some formulas in the agreement don't give me stomach pains. But I have to see the comprehensive picture. We have to take risks."

But the current Likud Party leader Benjamin Netanyahu, while not actively opposing the peace process, has warned that the agreement could result in serious breaches in Israeli security, leaving the borders vulnerable to attacks by both terrorists and enemy states.

Other critics of the plan have been more blunt. Former Army Chief of Staff Rafael Eitan said the government was "signing an agreement with the greatest murderer of Jews since Hitler."

"Peace agreement?" number two Likud leader Tzachi Hanegbi queried. "I don't see a peace agreement. I see a path leading to war."

Former Chief Rabbi Schlomo Goren expressed the feelings of many when he said, "Arafat is responsible for thousands of murders. Therefore, everyone in Israel who meets him in the streets has the right to kill him."

In early 1994, Israel began surrendering land to the PLO. This action produced violent reactions from Jewish settlers in the occupied territories, who will lose the protection of the Israeli army as the plan progresses. They believe their lives and property will be at risk under Arafat's rule.

"We are reacting with violence because the government has acted with violence by forcing this agreement on the nation," said Aaron Domb, spokesman for the Council of Settlements in Judea, Samaria, and Gaza.

More than 115,000 settlers have staked their claims to land in these regions at the urging of the previous Likud government. Now they feel they are being abandoned by the government to fend for themselves among the one million Palestinians who also live in the regions of Judea and Samaria.

Many Orthodox Jews are opposed to giving up any part of *Eretz Yisrael* (The Land of Israel) because they believe that the territories rightfully belong to the Jews, since God gave the land to Abraham.

But protests have also come from angry Palestinians, headquartered mostly in Gaza, who believe Arafat has abandoned their goal of eradicating Israel from the Earth. Leaders of *Hamas*, a militant Moslem fundamentalist group still committed to the destruction of Israel, have vowed to oppose the peace plan with a campaign of terror. Terrorist leader Ahmad Jibril warned Arafat from Damascus that he might be assassinated, and some of Arafat's top aides have died violent deaths in recent years.

"The Palestinian state is within our grasp," Arafat reassured his followers. "Soon the Palestinian flag will fly from the walls, the minarets, and the cathedrals of Jerusalem."

Israel sought and achieved a separate peace with Jordan and is still negotiating with Syria and Lebanon. Israel wants an exchange of embassies, free trade, and open borders. Syria wants the return of the strategic Golan Heights region of northern Israel, possession of which many military analysts believe to be essential for Israel's future self-defense.

"Despite recent peace overtures, Syria remains an extremely dangerous foe—one which cannot be trusted," observed military analyst Frank Gaffney at the Center for Security Policy. A former Assistant Secretary of Defense in the Reagan Administration, Gaffney confirms that Syria has at least 250 SCUD missiles, some of which could reach the Israeli population centers of Haifa, Jerusalem, and Tel Aviv. "We have reason to believe they are armed with chemical, perhaps biological weapons," Gaffney said.[22]

According to a 1989 report in the *Wall Street Journal*, Israel's Arab enemies have been busy building up their arsenals, buying more than $170 billion worth of modern weaponry since 1973. Total military expenditures of $450 billion during that time by the

Arab states at war with Israel have outstripped the Israelis by a margin of five to one. Today the combined armies of Syria, Iraq, Jordan, Saudi Arabia, and Egypt have 16,000 tanks, while Israel has only about 4,000.[23]

So Israel's hope of lasting peace may prove vain. Long-time Mideast observer Hal Lindsey has warned that "the risk of a nuclear exchange is heightened not diminished if Israel's borders become less defensible by conventional means," because Israel might be compelled to "go nuclear" to defend itself against an all-out Arab assault. There were two nuclear alerts reportedly called by Israel during the 1973 Yom Kippur War.[24]

As peace negotiations between Israel and Syria continued before the latest round of Arab terrorist attacks, indications from U.S. Secretary of State Warren Christopher were that a deal could come by the end of 1996. Secretary of Defense William Perry said during a recent trip to Israel that the United States would be willing to supply troops to monitor the peace on the Golan Heights if asked by Syria and Israel.

But as peace talks have continued and Palestinian self-rule has been partially implemented, tensions have continued to mount in the tiny nation of Israel, whose citizens seem to be about evenly divided as to the wisdom of the plan. The fuse burned short in late 1995, when an ardent Israeli nationalist shot and killed Rabin just before Christmas.

In the spring of 1996, Israel was reeling from the effects of four bomb blasts within nine days. Palestinian suicide bombers from the militant *Hamas* organization claimed more than 60 Israeli lives and wounded hundreds more, as bombs exploded on buses and in crowded shopping malls. Many of the casualties were children and even babies, and the people of Israel are both fearful and angry.

Israeli Prime Minister Shimon Peres, Rabin's successor, placed a temporary hold on the peace negotiations until a special anti-terrorism task force could bring the volatile situation under control. But public confidence in Peres was shaken and his Labor government fell to Likud in the May 1996 elections.

That development could drastically alter the peace process. "Our mistake was in believing that we can hire a subcontractor, Arafat, and he will take care of [security]," said Likud leader Benjamin Netanyahu. "We must take matters into our own hands."

Though Arafat has condemned the recent rash of bombings, he appears powerless to stop them. The *Hamas* militants are believed to be receiving support from Assad in Syria for their campaign of terror.[25]

The Temple Mount Faithful

Gershon Salomon, the founder of the Temple Mount Faithful, is a quiet-spoken, 58-year-old Oriental scholar at the Hebrew University in Jerusalem, where his specialty is Kurdish nationalist movements.

He is also a 10th-generation resident of that city, the descendant of Avraham Solomon Zalman Zoref, who came to Jerusalem in 1811. Zoref, a leader in Ashkenazi community, was killed by local Arabs because he rebuilt the Judah Hahassid synagogue in the Old City after Egypt took control of Palestine in 1831.

Salomon, with his unswerving commitment to rebuild the Third Temple in Jerusalem, is following in the spiritual footsteps of his ancestor. And like Zoref, he is high on the Arabs' hit list— Number One, in fact, according to "Leaflet 65," published by Palestinian *Intifada* leaders in 1991.

A war hero, Salomon was seriously wounded in 1958 while serving as a paratrooper officer, but later returned to his unit on crutches after spending a year in the hospital. In 1967 he took part in the liberation of East Jerusalem during the Six Day War and was assigned to guard the Temple Mount the night after the Jews captured the Old City.

Israel held the Temple Mount just 12 hours before Defense Minister Moshe Dayan decided to return the holy ground to the control of Arab Moslems, which Salomon has called a "national tragedy." That event was the catalyst which caused Salomon to form the Temple Mount Faithful.

I had the opportunity to interview Salomon during a fund-raising trip he made to the United States in 1992 under the auspices of numerous Christian leaders. He confirmed to me that his "basic goal is to liberate again the Temple Mount from Arab control," and he said that his 9,000-member organization enjoys popular support among the Israeli people.

"It is a duty, you know, it is a very basic duty of the Israeli people, when they are coming again to the chosen land, they must build a Temple," Salomon said. "I think that most Zionists have a very deep feeling that this is a condition for the coming of the Messiah."

I asked Salomon how he felt about the Camp David peace accords, which affirmed the demands of United Nations Resolution 242 requiring Israel to return to the boundaries that existed before the 1967 war.

"This resolution—I'm sorry to use this word, but I have not another word in my not good English—but it will be thrown into the garbage because this decision is against the law, against God, against history," Salomon responded.

"How can you say that Jerusalem and the Temple Mount, Judea and Samaria and Gaza and the Golan Heights and even Sinai—the heart, the soul, and the center of the focus of the Jewish people—are occupied territories?" he demanded.

Salomon believes that the Temple Mount is not really sacred to Arabs because they ran from it when the Israeli army approached, and did not defend the holy ground. By contrast, Salomon said that he and other Israeli soldiers "cried like little kids" when they first approached the rock where Abraham once laid Isaac as an offering to God.

As for the Arabs, "they are praying on the Temple Mount with their back to the Temple Mount and their face toward Mecca, and this symbolizes everything," he said.

"They don't need the Temple Mount, they don't need Jerusalem. Still, when they hold those places and control them, they think that they still have a chance to destroy the land of Israel," Salomon insisted. "The question is not the Temple Mount for them. For them the question is the existence of an Israeli Jewish state in the middle of the Middle East."

Salomon does not believe in the peace talks with Arab leaders—and this was before the 1993 agreement with the PLO—but he does believe in the sovereignty of God.

"God is the leader of the universe, He is the general of the universe, and only He controls the destiny of Israel," Salomon declared. "Not Yassar Arafat, not Saddam Hussein, not George Habbash, and not all of our enemies and not even George Bush and Baker. And this is why we shall succeed again and again.

"The history of Israel is the history of miracles," Salomon concluded. "In Israel, to be a realistic man, it means to believe in miracles."[26]

The Restoration of All Things

The miraculous return of Israel to the land of their inheritance has focused international attention on the Middle East and caused a renewed interest in Bible prophecy among Christians. Since Israel gained effective control of Jerusalem in 1967, that interest has been piqued even more.

Many Bible scholars believe that these events begin to fulfill a key prophecy, which was spoken by the Apostle Peter to Jews in Jerusalem:

> **Repent ye therefore, and be converted, that your sins may be blotted out, when the times of refreshing shall come from the presence of the Lord;**
> **And he shall send Jesus Christ, which before was preached unto you:**
> **Whom the heavens must receive until the times of restitution of all things, which God hath spoken by the mouth of all his holy prophets since the world began.**
>
> **Acts 3:19-21**

This passage speaks of a time when God will restore, or set back in right order, "all things" in the Earth, and it says that the Heavens must receive—and by implication, retain—the Lord Jesus Christ until this work of restoration is complete. In other words, until these things are done, Jesus cannot come back to Earth.

To serious students of Biblical prophecy, the restoration of Israel to the land in 1948 was a major work of God's restoration, and the deliverance of Jerusalem into her hands was a further fulfillment of this prophecy. All that remains is the restoration of the Temple and its sacrificial rituals.

According to a well-known prophecy newsletter, *The Gospel Truth:*

> Today in Israel there are two different schools of thought on the building of the Temple. Some believe the government should go ahead and build it next to the Dome of the Rock and risk another war with the Arabs. Others believe it is scriptural, and much safer, to wait for the Messiah to come and build it Himself. That the Messiah, whom we believe to be Jesus Christ, will build His own house is beyond question....

Also beyond doubt however, is that there must be a
Temple, or a building serving as a Temple in Jerusalem during the Tribulation period....

According to Revelation 11, the ministry of Elijah will
be associated with the Temple during the last half of the
Tribulation. It is prophetically important that Israel today
is praying for, and looking forward to, the restoration of
the Temple, another tremendous Messianic sign for the
present generation.[27]

The significance of the restoration of ritual Temple worship
will be discussed later, when we get to our study on the Antichrist.
For now, suffice it to say that the concept of restoration as a pre-
condition for the return of Christ is scripturally crucial both for
Israel and the Church.

But let us note that the Zionist movement (1898)—which has
now resulted in the re-establishment of Israel in the land of
Palestine in 1948 and restored Jerusalem to the Jews in 1967—
began historically at approximately the same time as the
Pentecostal movement in Topeka, Kansas (1900) and the Azusa
Street revival (1906)—which have now resulted in the ongoing
restoration of the gifts of the Holy Spirit to the Church, first
through the healing revivals of the late 1940s and later through the
Charismatic Renewal from about 1960 onward. The parallelism
is clear.[28]

The Parable of the Fig Tree

Toward the end of Matthew 24, Jesus spoke an important parable about the spiritual significance of a budding fig tree:

> *Now learn a parable of the fig tree; When his branch is
> yet tender, and putteth forth leaves, ye know that summer
> is nigh:*
> *So likewise ye, when ye shall see all these things, know
> that it is near, even at the doors.*
> *Verily I say unto you, This generation shall not pass,
> till all these things be fulfilled.*
> *Heaven and earth shall pass away, but my words shall
> not pass away.*
> **Matthew 24:32-35**

The fig tree in prophecy is a "type" or symbol for the nation of Israel. Jesus is saying that when we see Israel back in the land, with the Temple rebuilt, and all these other signs in evidence, the very end will be upon the world. Jesus placed that time within the context of a single generation, which could be our own.

Charismatic Bible teacher Derek Prince has gone so far as to say that

> This is *the* generation, above all other generations that have ever lived in the human race, this is *the* generation that cannot pass until all these things be fulfilled.[29]

So the generation that sees the budding of the fig tree Israel will be the generation that will see the fulfillment of all the other prophecies recorded in Matthew 24 as well.

A generation in the Bible is either 30 or 40 or 70 years, depending upon which commentator's interpretation you accept. The Bible, in Psalm 90:10, establishes a 70-year life span for mankind, so that is certainly a valid interpretation. Dr. Chriswell seems to favor 30 years.[30]

I personally believe that a Biblical generation is generally 40 years, because this is the period of time that Moses spent in the wilderness with the Children of Israel after they came out of Egypt. That is how long it took for the previous generation, which God would not allow into the Promised land because of their unbelief, to be replaced with a new one.[31] Jesus' prophecy of the destruction of the Temple was also fulfilled within 40 years.

Further scriptural support for this view comes from the ancient history of Israel. King David reigned 40 years as ruler over Israel. After King David took Jerusalem from the Jebusites, it was 37 years, or one generation, before his son Solomon began to build the Temple, and the project took him seven years to complete.[32]

Many prophetic Bible scholars date the beginning of the generation that will see these things come to pass from 1967, when Israel recaptured Jerusalem. If this view be correct, and if the 40-year generational pattern holds true, 2007 A.D. could be a very significant year for the world.

If the 70-year generation is the norm, then 2037 looms large.[33]

In any event, 1996 is the 3,000th anniversary of King David's initial designation of Jerusalem as the capital of Israel. The Middle East continues to smolder with unrelenting hostility, yet the time is pregnant with the promise of prophecies soon to be fulfilled, and of the Messiah's return.

—————⟫•⟪—————

[1]   Derek Prince, End-Time Prophecy, 4-tape series (Ft. Lauderdale, Fla.: Derek Prince, n.d.), Vol. 7004, "Israel and the Church: Parallel Restoration."

[2]   Genesis 12: 1-9 is known as the Abrahamic Covenant, an irrevocable, unconditional promise made by God that the land of Israel would belong to the descendants of Abraham forever. For a fuller discussion, see Pentecost, *Things to Come*, pp. 65-94.

[3]   Moses' predictions of God's judgment on Israel are found in Leviticus 27 and Deuteronomy 28. Restoration promises are Jeremiah 31:10, Isaiah 11, and Daniel 9 and 11.

[4]   Chronology is from Merrill F. Unger, *Unger's Bible Handbook* (Chicago: Moody, 1980), pp. 15-17, 387-389.

[5]   See Pentecost, *Things to Come*, pp. 314-318.

[6]   *Encyclopedia Americana*, 1957 ed., s.v. "Jewish History and Society — Social and Economic Developments in the 19th and 20th Centuries," by Jacob Lestschinsky.

[7]   For a discussion of the prophecies now being fulfilled concerning the Aliyah, or "In-Gathering" of the Jews to Israel from around the world, see Steve Lightle, *Exodus II: Let My People Go* (Kingwood, Texas: Hunter Books, 1983).

[8]   Jerusalem, which in Hebrew means the "city of peace," has been captured or destroyed 48 times in its long history. Its walls have been either rebuilt or repaired 18 times.

[9]   Winkler, Class Notes.

[10]   Early Jewish population figures are from *Encyclopedia Americana*, 1957 ed., s.v. "Jewish History and Society — Zionism," by Isidore Abramowitz.

[11]   A comprehensive history of the development of the modern Middle East can be found in Daniel C. Diller, ed. *The Middle East*, 7th ed. (Washington, D.C.: Congressional Quarterly, 1990). For a history of Mid-East conflict and arms race see pp. 7-68; for a profile of Israel see pp. 167-176.

[12]   "Exodus II: Jews Follow Prophetic Path To Israel," *The 700 Club Newswatch Fact Sheet*, June 23-24, 1994. See also Isaiah 43:5-6. See also Steve Lightle, *Exodus II: Let My People Go* (Kingwood, Texas: Hunter Books, 1983).

[13] Current (1993) population figures are from *Academic American Encyclopedia*, Electronic Version, s.v. "Israel Facts."

[14] Lindsey, *Planet Earth—2000 A.D.*, pp. 156-157.

[15] Asher S. Kaufman, "Where the Ancient Temple of Jerusalem Stood," *Biblical Archaeology Review*, March-April 1983, pp. 40-61. See also Lubrett Hargrove, "Temple, Temple — Where Was the Temple?" *The Gospel Truth*, July 1983.

[16] *The New York Times*, August 6, 1986, p. 7. See also "Tribulation Temple in View," *The Gospel Truth*, September 1986, p. 4.

[17] One thing about entering into Israel from Egypt was so striking that I must mention it here. After hours of driving through an absolutely barren desert of sand dunes inhabited only by scattered bands of nomadic goat herders living in tents among the rusted ruins of Egyptian tanks from previous wars, we passed through the border check point into Israel. Immediately the landscape came alive with endless fields of vegetables and citrus groves. The same soil that a few hundred yards away was desolate and barren had become lush and bountiful as a result of modern Israeli irrigation techniques. I saw with my own eyes the literal fulfillment of Isaiah 35:1, "and the desert shall rejoice, and blossom as the rose."

[18] Timothy J. Dailey, *The Gathering Storm* (Tarrytown, N.Y.: Fleming H. Revell, 1992), pp. 108-113.

[19] Matthew 24:15; 2 Thessalonians 2:3-4.

[20] John Wheeler Jr., "Peace in the Holy Land?: Israeli/Palestinian Accord Delayed By Doubts," *Christian American*, February 1994, pp. 1, 4. Most of the information in this section is from this article and/or in the September 15, 1993, issue of *Time* magazine.

[21] Hal Lindsey has reminded us that: "Arafat was the man who ordered innocent Arab brothers in Nablus hanged by their chins on butcher hooks until they were dead. He was the man who ordered the bellies of pregnant Arab women split open while their husbands looked on; he was the man who ordered the hands of Arab children cut off while their parents watched in horror. Remember, the PLO was created in 1964 with one objective in mind — destroying the Jewish state." Lindsey, *Planet Earth—2000 A.D.*, pp. 182-183.

[22] "America's Role in the Middle East: Ally or Peacekeeper?" *The 700 Club Newswatch Fact Sheet*, January 26, 1996.

[23] Ariel Sharon, *Wall Street Journal*, February 22, 1989, p. A-17.

[24] Lindsey, *Planet Earth—2000 A.D.*, pp. 174-175, 179.

[25] Information about terrorist bombings is from news reports. "Israel: Hamas Can't Hide," *USA Today,* March 5, 1996, pp. 1-2A. "Blast Rocks Israel Again: 14 Dead, 130 Hurt By Suicide Bomber," *Norfolk Virginian-Pilot,* March 5, 1996, pp. A1, A4.

[26] This section is based on an interview with Gershon Salomon, March 17, 1992.

[27] N.W. Hutchings, "Restoration of All Things," *The Gospel Truth,* March 1982, p. 5.

[28] "Some theologians, especially those who get more excited about the restoration of the Jews and the land of Israel than they do about the Restoration of the Church, apply these Scriptures only to the Nation of Israel. They get more excited about the rebuilding of the Temple in Jerusalem than they do about the Church being built as the Temple of God and the New Jerusalem. Christians today should get more excited about the Church and the prophecies being fulfilled in it than about any other prophetic fulfillment. The Church is the highest realm, the most privileged people, and the greatest race of beings in God's entire universe. Even Jews who become Christians are no longer Israelites in God's sight, but sons of God and members of the Body of Christ. 'In Christ there is neither Jew nor Gentile' (Gal. 3:28)." Hamon, *Eternal Church,* pp. 132-133. See also Chapter 5, "The Gospel of the Kingdom."

[29] Prince, Tape Series, Vol. 7001, "Climax in Four Phases: Repentance, Refreshing, Restoration, Return of Christ." Prince also teaches that the restoration of Israel to her spiritual inheritance in the land parallels a restoration of spiritual truth and power to the Church, both of which must be accomplished before Christ can return. See also Chapter 5, "The Gospel of the Kingdom."

[30] "The word in question in this verse is the term 'generation,' which usually means a period of only thirty to one hundred years. Several possible explanations for the observation are available: (1) Generation (*genea,* Gk.) refers to Israel as a nation and guarantees her perpetuity until the end of times. (2) Generation may mean 'age' or 'time period' and therefore be a reference to the dispensation of grace. (3) Finally, *genea* may carry its usual meaning of thirty years. If the latter is the case, then Jesus is saying that one generation would not have passed until all of these signs BEGIN to be fulfilled." W.A. Chriswell, ed., *The Chriswell Study Bible* (Nashville: Thomas Nelson, 1979), p. 1147.

[31] Deuteronomy 1:32-40, 29:5.

[32] 2 Samuel 5:4-7; I Kings 6:1, 37, 38.

[33] Steve Fitschen has pointed out that a few scholars believe that a Biblical generation is still 120 years, based on God's statement in Genesis 6:3 that man's "days shall be 120 years." The generation would not have passed away if a single member of it remained alive, which period of time could conceivably last 120 years. I personally consider this scenario unlikely.

Chapter 5
The Gospel
of the Kingdom

And this gospel of the kingdom shall be preached in all the world for a witness unto all nations; and then shall the end come.

Matthew 24:14

We have studied about lots of terrible things to come in the Last Days, from natural disasters and plagues to devastating wars and the rise of a wicked world ruler called Antichrist during the Great Tribulation. But not everything connected to the end times is bad, and in this section we will see that God has a glorious plan for His Church.

Jesus said that only one thing has to happen before the end comes. He said the Gospel of the Kingdom has to reach the whole Earth. I believe that with the modern communications technology now available to the Church and with the most remote areas of the world suddenly accessible to travel, we could see this happen in our lifetime.

If you don't believe the world is getting smaller, just look at the UPS commercials on television, with all those intrepid boxy brown vans darting from busy American metropolitan streets to thatched-roof huts in remote Asian villages. The major PR theme of our time is that we're all becoming part of an increasingly interconnected "global village."

The explosive combination of human knowledge and extensive travel—which has put men on the Moon in our lifetime and beamed the Gospel into the most remote recesses of the Earth—was also predicted in Daniel 12:4, where the prophet says that at the time of the end "many shall run to and fro, and knowledge shall be increased."

Taking the Gospel to the World

The first building constructed on the grounds of the Christian Broadcasting Network was the International Communications Center, dedicated on the eve of the Feast of Tabernacles in 1979 with a keynote address by Billy Graham.

Now known as the Studio Headquarters Building, it is a stately brick colonial-style structure which houses the executive offices as well as the sets and equipment for CBN's various television programs, including *The 700 Club.* Today that building is surrounded by an impressive array of similar colonial brick buildings, most of which contain the offices, classrooms and library of Regent University.

But still the Studio Headquarters Building is unique, for behind the massive marble columns that hold up the facade is a large brass plate, and inscribed on that plate are the words of Jesus from Matthew 24:14,

> **And this Gospel of the Kingdom shall be preached in all the world for a witness unto all nations, and then shall the end come.**

This was the foundational vision upon which was built one of the most successful and far-reaching Christian ministries in the world. It is a vision that, among other things, has produced a series of international "Gospel blitzes" that have won millions to Christ in the Philippines, Central and South America, and Eastern Europe since 1990. In Albania, almost one-third of that country's 3.2 million people reportedly came to Christ following a special CBN Christmas program.

"WorldReach" is CBN's aggressive evangelistic plan to take the Gospel to the whole world, and it is a vision that Pat Robertson, Michael Little, and other CBN ministry leaders are determined to fulfill while there is still time left and a window of opportunity open.[1]

CBN has made plans to join in a cooperative effort with Campus Crusade for Christ, which distributes the *Jesus Film* worldwide, as well as other international ministries, to take the Gospel to the world by the year 2000. Their optimistic goal, targeting the concentrated population band known as the "10-40 Window," particularly in Asia, is to reach three billion people with the Gospel and to see 500 million souls come to Christ within this five-year time frame.

Meanwhile, in June of 1995, evangelist Billy Graham's "Global Mission" broadcast the Gospel to one billion people simultaneously, the largest number of people ever to hear the message of salvation at one time. Graham's organization trained more than 500,000 counselors for a follow-up satellite broadcast from San Juan, Puerto Rico, in March of 1996, estimated to have reached 10 million people in 165 countries.

Other communications ministries are broadcasting Christian programming 24 hours a day, foreign missions groups are sending missionaries into the far corners of the globe, and Bible translators are working diligently to provide the Gospel in the native tongues of the estimated 11,874 separate "ethno-linguistic" people groups of the world.

There are approximately 6,528 distinct languages in the world, and by mid-1993 only about 2,000 had any portion of Scripture translated, while 1,199 other translations were in progress.[2]

But this is not bad news. One estimate by world missions sources says that while two-thirds of these languages have no Bible translations, those languages are spoken by only 6 percent of the world's population. And while only 4.2 percent of the Earth's languages have the whole Bible in translation, this 4.2 percent is spoken by 76 percent of the world's people. So the Word is going forth to the world.[3]

And people are seeing God answer their prayers. The largest prayer effort in history took place in October 1995, when 30 million Christians joined in prayer for the "gateway cities" of the 10/40 window, the world's largest unevangelized area. One month later, 800,000 souls came to Christ during a week-long rally in Hyderabad, India.

At home in America, over 500,000 men attended Promise Keepers rallies in 1995, and more than two million teenagers participated in last September's "See You at the Pole" prayer rally at their schools.[4]

So there are signs of spiritual life at home, the Gospel is going out around the world, and millions are coming to Christ. This is glorious and exciting. But there is even more to come.

Pat Robertson, one of the most prominent Christian leaders in America today, has accurately described the nature of the spiritual conflict that will characterize the decade of the 1990s. In his bestseller *The New Millennium*, Robertson explains the coming spiritual megatrend:

I believe we can expect to witness Satanic miracles, signs and wonders, and a host of demonic manifestations in the not-too-distant future. None of us should be surprised if during this decade we begin to see many more supernatural events taking place in our world.

Just as Jesus Christ foretold, demonic forces will be raging against the church of God, but the power of God will be alive in the church and we will also see incredible signs and wonders through the power of the Holy Spirit.

The clash we will experience, then, will not be between belief and unbelief but between one form of belief and another. It will be faith in God versus faith in the Devil, and it will be very clear where the people of God will have to make their stand.[5]

The Gospel of Power

I believe that we're going to see an even mightier manifestation of the power of God in these Last Days than we have seen in the past, precisely because of the specific words that Jesus said.

He said that a certain kind of Gospel, "this Gospel of the Kingdom," will be preached in all the world before the end shall come.

I believe that Jesus meant something very specific by this statement, something that much of the Church has been missing for about 1,900 years now, since the time of the Apostles and the Early Church.

We are going to see in these Last Days a restoration of the power of the Holy Spirit on the proclamation of the Word of God, unlike anything we have experienced heretofore. The last generation of Christians on this Earth will witness the power of God in a greater measure than even the first generation of Christians did.

This is going to be Present Truth for the Church of the end times.[6]

The Bible says plainly, "For this purpose the Son of God was manifested, that he might destroy the works of the devil" (1 John 3:8).

The blind are going to see, the deaf are going to hear, the lame are going to walk, and the dead are going to be raised, and it's all going to happen openly, for all to see. It is going to be a witness to the nations before the Lord returns.

That's the way it was with the Apostle Paul, who told the Corinthian Christians:

> **And my speech and my preaching was not with entic-
> ing words of man's wisdom, but in demonstration of the
> Spirit and of power:**
> **That your faith should not stand in the wisdom of
> men, but in the power of God.**
> 1 Corinthians 2:4-5

Paul said that the "signs of an apostle" followed him wher-
ever he preached the Word of God, and he told the church at
Thessalonica:

> **For our gospel came unto you not in word only, but also
> in power, and in the Holy Ghost, and in much assurance....**
> 1 Thessalonians 1:5

This is the way it's going to be again, in the Last Days, as the
Church of Jesus Christ takes the Gospel of the Kingdom to the
world. To understand this, we're going to have to understand what
the Kingdom of God is, because there is a lot of confusion among
the people of God.

The Spiritual Kingdom

First let me say that I believe whole-heartedly in the literal
Millennial reign of Jesus Christ on the Earth. He is coming back
visibly and personally as the King of Kings and Lord of Lords to
rule and reign from His throne in Jerusalem for a thousand years,
just like the Bible says. Not one jot nor tittle of the Scripture shall
fail, all shall be fulfilled. I'm a Premillennialist to the core.

But like the Amillennialists, I also believe that there is a spiritual
Kingdom of God, and it is present and active now. These two ideas
are complementary, not mutually exclusive. These concepts reinforce rather than contradict one another. If the opposing theological camps within Christendom could grasp this one simple truth,
they might be able to stop clashing verbal swords long enough to
accomplish something significant for God in these Last Days.

But this present Kingdom, while it impinges upon every aspect
of human life and culture, is not primarily institutional nor political, but truly spiritual. By that I mean that it is the manifestation of
the power of the Spirit of God living and working in and through

the individual members of the Body of Christ in the Earth, day by day, until Jesus finally returns in person and in power.

Christ In Us, Our Hope of Glory

It is that Spirit of Christ living in us that enables us both to live holy lives and to do the ministry of Jesus, and that is what God wants for His Church in these Last Days. This is not spiritual pride, merely scriptural obedience. That may sound radical to some, but that's what the Bible says.

The Apostle Paul said, "I can do all things through Christ which strengtheneth me." The power is not our own innate power, it is the supernatural power of God resident within us.[7]

Paul, warning the Corinthians against sexual sin, said that the Kingdom of God is within each disciple of Jesus Christ from the moment of regeneration, when we are joined spirit to Spirit with the Lord:

> **What? know ye not that he which is joined to an harlot is one body? for two, saith he, shall be one flesh.**
> **But he that is joined unto the Lord is one spirit.**
> **Flee fornication. Every sin that a man doeth is without the body; but he that committeth fornication sinneth against his own body.**
> **What? know ye not that your body is the temple of the Holy Ghost which is in you, which ye have of God, and ye are not your own?**
> **For you are bought with a price: therefore glorify God in your body, and in your spirit, which are God's.**
> **1 Corinthians 6:16-20**

The same Spirit that raised Jesus Christ from the dead now lives inside each regenerated disciple of Jesus. Understanding that truth is the key to moving in this realm of supernatural spiritual power.[8]

The Great Commission

The power to fulfill the Great Commission lies within each born-again Christian in the person of the indwelling Holy Spirit. But unfortunately, much of the Church has often failed to comprehend all that Jesus' commission to His disciples includes.

In Matthew 28, the resurrected Jesus delivered His instructions to the Church before He left for Heaven:

> **Then the eleven disciples went away into Galilee, into a mountain where Jesus had appointed them.**
>
> **And when they saw him, they worshipped him: but some doubted.**
>
> **And Jesus came and spake unto them, saying,** *All power is given unto me in heaven and in earth.*
>
> *Go ye therefore, and teach all nations, baptizing them in the name of the Father, and of the Son, and of the Holy Ghost:*
>
> <u>**Teaching them to observe all things whatsoever I have commanded you**</u>*: and lo, I am with you alway, even unto the end of the world. Amen.*
>
> **Matthew 28:16-20**

The Church historically has obeyed Jesus' commandment only partially. We have gone out into the world, and we have made disciples, and we have baptized them. Again, that much is good.

But we have never really taught those disciples "to observe all things whatsoever" Jesus commanded, and we certainly haven't presented ourselves to the world as the personal ambassadors of a sovereign King who has "all power...in heaven and in earth."

This may sound like a strange new doctrine to some, but I can prove what I am saying from the Bible.

The Example of Jesus Christ

First let's look at the ministry of Jesus Himself. The best place to start is in Luke 4, where Jesus' active ministry began. In verse 1 we read that

> **Jesus being full of the Holy Ghost returned from Jordan and was led by the Spirit into the wilderness, being forty days tempted of the devil.**

During that testing experience He successfully resisted every temptation and defeated the Devil with the Word of God.

> **And Jesus returned in the power of the Spirit into Galilee: and there went out a fame of him through all the region round about.**
>
> **And He taught in their synagogues, being glorified of all.**
>
>

Luke 4:14-15

Jesus then returned to His hometown, and in verse 21 declared Himself to be the Messiah, whose coming had been foretold by the prophet Isaiah.[9] The people of Nazareth rejected Jesus, and "he did not many mighty works there because of their unbelief."[10]

So Jesus went on to Capernaum, where He taught in their synagogues with a powerful anointing and cast out demons. This quickly got everyone's attention.

> **And they were all amazed, and spake among themselves, saying, What a word is this! For with authority and power he commandeth the unclean spirits, and they come out.**
>
> **And the fame of him went out into every place of the country round about.**
>
>

Luke 4:36-37

Afterwards Jesus rebuked a fever to heal Peter's mother, then ministered to multitudes of people, healing their diseases and casting out more demons, so that the people begged Him to stay in their city.

> **And he said unto them, _I must preach the kingdom of God_ to other cities also: for therefore am I sent.**
>
> **And he preached in the synagogues of Galilee.**
>
>

Luke 4:43-44

Jesus began His ministry by demonstrating His authority over sickness, disease, and Satan, and He called this "preaching the Kingdom of God." A similar incident also happened in another place early in Jesus' ministry, where Christ cast a demon out of a dumb man and restored the man's speech. This made the local religious leaders angry.

> **But the Pharisees said, He casteth out devils through the prince of the devils.**
> **And Jesus went about all the cities and villages, teaching in their synagogues, and <u>preaching the gospel of the kingdom</u>, and healing every sickness and every disease among the people.**
>
> **Matthew 9:34-35**

Again we see the direct scriptural connection between healing and deliverance in Jesus' ministry, and something called the "Gospel of the Kingdom." We can discern a pattern emerging here.

In the Power of the Spirit

But someone might object, "Yes, but that was Jesus. He was special, He was the Son of God. That's why He did those things."

Of course, that is true, Jesus was special. But the Bible also says that Jesus did all these things as a man "in the power of the Spirit," not merely because of His special status within the Godhead. The Apostle Peter declared in Acts 10:38 that Jesus' power came from the Holy Spirit:

> **<u>God anointed Jesus of Nazareth with the Holy Ghost and with power</u>: who went about doing good and healing all that were oppressed of the devil; for God was with him.**

In a similar incident in Matthew 12, Jesus cast out a demon and the unbelieving Pharisees again attributed His power to that of "Beelzebub the prince of devils." Jesus' response to their accusation is informative.

> *If I by Beelzebub cast out devils, by whom do your children cast them out? therefore they shall be your judges.*
> *But <u>if I cast out devils by the Spirit of God, then the kingdom of God is come unto you</u>.*
>
> **Matthew 12:27-28**

Here Jesus explicitly states that He casts out the demons "by the Spirit of God," and again He links this activity to the "Kingdom of God."

The Apostles' Example

In Matthew 10, Jesus sent His original 12 disciples out to do the same things that He was doing. These men are named, and they are the same (minus Judas) as the 11 mentioned previously as receiving the Great Commission from Jesus in Matthew 28.

> **And when he had called unto him his twelve disciples, he gave them power against unclean spirits, to cast them out, and to heal all manner of sickness and all manner of disease....**
> **These twelve Jesus sent forth, and commanded them, saying,** *Go not into the way of the Gentiles, and into any city of the Samaritans enter ye not:*
> *But go rather to the lost sheep of the house of Israel.*
> *And as you go,* <u>*preach, saying, the kingdom of heaven is at hand*</u>.
> *Heal the sick, cleanse the lepers, raise the dead, cast out devils: freely ye have received, freely give.*
> **Matthew 10:1, 5-8**

Here Jesus specifically instructs His original twelve disciples to go out and heal the sick, cleanse the lepers, cast out demons—and even raise the dead! And He tells them that while they are doing these things, they are to preach the "Kingdom of Heaven." The pattern is getting clearer.

Some people try hard to draw a distinction between the Kingdom of Heaven and the Kingdom of God, but that dichotomy is both artificial and unnecessary. Remember that Scripture will interpret Scripture. The parallel passage to Matthew 10 is found in Luke 9:

> **Then he called his twelve disciples together , and gave them power and authority over all devils, and to cure diseases.**
> **And** <u>**he sent them to preach the kingdom of God**</u>, **and to cure diseases....**
> **And they departed, and went through the towns,** <u>**preaching the gospel**</u>, **and healing every where.**
> **Luke 9:1-2, 6**

This latter incident is exactly the same event as the former, but here the Kingdom is said to be "of God," while there it is "of Heaven." Both Matthew and Luke wrote under the direct inspiration of the Holy Spirit, Who being God does not contradict Himself. By what authority do we attempt to split hairs and say the two Kingdoms are different?[11]

After all, God lives in Heaven. And He has given power and authority over Satan and sickness to those who declare His Kingdom to the world.

But wait a minute, someone may protest. Those men were the "Original Twelve Apostles." They were special, too, because they walked with Jesus. They wrote the Bible and got the Church started. That's why they could do those things, right? Read on.

The Disciples' Example

Lots of people don't consider the fact that the Bible names more than 12 apostles—it mentions 20, in fact. Matthias was an apostle, selected to replace Judas. Then came Paul, who never knew Jesus in the flesh and yet was equal to the "chiefest apostles." The Bible also says that Barnabas was an apostle. And so was Apollos. And Timothy and Silvanus. Two virtually unheard of apostles were named Andronicus and Junia. That's twenty, and those are just the ones mentioned by name.[12]

The fact is, an apostle is a special messenger of God. The word apostle in the Greek literally means "sent one." An apostle is a special messenger sent from God. Today we often call them "missionaries" and send them to foreign lands. There have been numerous apostles throughout the history of the Church, and there will be many more in the Last Days.

Besides, Jesus didn't limit His commission to the original apostles. In Luke 10, Jesus sent out some more.

> **After these things the Lord appointed other seventy also, and sent them two and two before his face into every city and place, whither he himself would come....**
>
> **And into whatsoever city ye enter, and they receive you, eat such things as are set before you; And heal the sick that are therein, and say unto them, <u>The kingdom of God is come nigh unto you</u>....**

> **And the seventy returned again with joy, saying, Lord,
> even the devils are subject unto us through thy name.**
> **Luke 10:1, 8-9, 17**

Jesus sent out 70 more average, garden-variety disciples to do exactly the same things He had first sent the original 12 to do. Those seventy simply went out and did what He said, preaching the "Kingdom of God." And when they got back, Jesus went even further. He told them:

> **Behold, <u>I give unto you power</u> to tread upon serpents
> and scorpions, and <u>over all the power of the enemy: and</u>
> nothing shall by any means hurt you.**
> **Notwithstanding in this rejoice not, that <u>the spirits are</u>
> <u>subject unto you</u>; but rather rejoice, because your names
> are written in heaven.**
> **Luke 10:19-20**

Jesus conferred specific authority upon these disciples "over all the power of the enemy" simply because of the fact that they were saved and their names were "written in heaven." Nothing could be clearer.

The Bible says that a matter may be established "in the mouth of two or three witnesses."[13] So far we have heard about half a dozen witnesses testify to the direct relationship between healing and deliverance and the preaching of the Gospel of the Kingdom by the disciples of Jesus.

These are the "all things whatsoever" that Jesus commanded His disciples to do and to teach their new converts to observe.

The Greater Works Ministry of Jesus

It remains only to be established that this same commission applies to Jesus' disciples today, and this is easily demonstrated from the Scriptures. In the Gospel of John, Jesus made a startling declaration:

> **Verily, verily, I say unto you, <u>He that believeth on me,
> the works that I do shall he do also; and greater works
> than these shall he do</u>, because I go unto my Father.**

> And whatsoever ye shall ask in my name, that will I
> do, that the Father may be glorified in the Son.
> If ye shall ask any thing in my name, I will do it.
>
> **John 14:12-14**

This is the solid Biblical basis for every disciple of Jesus Christ to do the works of Jesus in conjunction with the proclamation of the Gospel of the Kingdom. What Jesus did, we are to do also, and God will get the glory.

This was not spoken to the 12 apostles, nor to 70 specific disciples at a given point in time. This was spoken to any disciple who will receive it by faith. This is Jesus' promise to every man: "He that believeth."

It falls in the same category as another famous promise Jesus made: "<u>Whosoever will</u>, let him take of the water of life freely" (Revelation 22:17).

If "Whosoever will" applies to anyone who will receive it, so does "He that believeth." John 14:12 applies to all believers, just as John 3:16 does.

> *For God so loved the world, that he gave his only begot-*
> *ten Son, that <u>whosoever believeth in him</u> should not per-*
> *ish, but have everlasting life.*
>
> **John 3:16**

"He that believeth" is just like "whosoever believeth in him"—it is for anyone who will accept and receive it. It is for you and for me.

Days of Restoration

In the Book of Daniel, the prophet declares that in the Last Days,

> ...the people who do know their God shall be strong,
> and do exploits.
> And they that understand among the people shall
> instruct many...
>
> **Daniel 11:32-33**

As the demonic forces of Satan become more open and notorious in the Earth in the Last Days, the Bride of Christ will rise up "terrible as an army with banners."[14] As the darkness gets darker, the light will also get brighter, and the Church of God will shine as a beacon light in the midst of a crooked and perverse generation.[15]

These are the Days of Restoration spoken of by the prophet Joel, the "times of refreshing from the presence of the Lord" and the days of the "restoration of all things" proclaimed by the Apostle Peter.[16]

As the prophets have truly said concerning the outpouring of the Holy Spirit, the Latter Rain will be greater than the Former Rain, just as the glory of the latter house will be greater than that of the former house.[17]

The disciples who believe *will do* the Greater Works Ministry of Jesus Christ as they proclaim the Gospel of the Kingdom in the Last Days.

In the name of Jesus, the blind will see, the lame will walk, the deaf will hear, the dead will come back to life—all in the plain view of a wicked and unbelieving world that will reject God and His Christ anyway.

And when *this* Gospel of the Kingdom shall be preached in all the Earth, *then* shall the end come.

In the latter days ye shall consider it perfectly.
Jeremiah 23:20

═══❱●❰═══

[1] Pat Robertson has made a number of public statements, heard personally by this author, which indicate that he believes there is a special significance to the year 2007. That year is 400 years after the landing at Cape Henry, Virginia, by the British settlers who later established the colony of Jamestown in 1608. An Anglican priest, one of Robertson's ancestors, planted a cross in the sand at Cape Henry and prayed a prayer dedicating the new land to Jesus Christ. As has been previously mentioned, 2007 also will be 40 years after the restoration of the city of Jerusalem to the political control of the state of Israel in 1967, which Pat sees as significant. And he has also mentioned that he himself will be 77 years old in that year. See also Pat Robertson, *The New Millennium*, pp. 312-313.

[2] Patrick Johnstone, *Operation World: The Day-By-Day Guide to Praying for the World*, 5th ed. (Grand Rapids: Zondervan, 1993), p. 22.

[3] Ibid, p. 134.

[4] "1995 Year in Review: A World Searching for Answers," *The 700 Club Newswatch Fact Sheet*, December 31, 1995.

[5]   Pat Robertson, *The New Millennium: What You and Your Family Can Expect in the Year 2000* (Dallas: Word, 1990), p. 83. (Emphasis added.)

[6]   "Present Truth," 2 Peter 1:12. A prominent proponent of this view is Derek Prince, who sees this end-time manifestation of the power of the Holy Spirit as part of the parallel restoration of Israel and the Church in the Last Days. For a comprehensive history of God's restoration of "Present Truth" to the Church, see Bill Hamon, *The Eternal Church* (Phoenix: Christian International, [1981]).

[7]   Colossians 1:27, Philippians 4:13. See also John 15:5 and 1 Timothy 1:12.

[8]   Romans 8:9-11 and Galatians 3:2-5. Some people warn that we should not be seeking supernatural signs but merely seeking the Lord with pure devotion. (See David Hazard, "Classic Christianity: The Trap of Supernaturalism," *Charisma and Christian Life*, February 1996, p. 58.)
While it is true that our personal relationship with Christ is of paramount importance, my point is that power should flow from that relationship just like it did in the days of the Early Church. The problem with "classic Christianity" is that for hundreds of years it has enshrined the powerless traditions of men, rather than the dynamic power of the Spirit of the resurrected Christ, as the norm for Christian life and experience. It will be different in the Last Days, which will be unlike any time we have ever experienced before, and traditions will be of little use then.

[9]   Isaiah 61:1-2.

[10]   Parallel passage in Matthew 13:58.

[11]   While this is a departure from traditional Dispensationalism, I still believe that Dispensationalism is overall the most Biblically sound system of theological interpretation. However, no system can prosper by attempting to impose artificial restrictions on the Bible. I truly believe that the Holy Spirit is grieved by those on both sides of the theological debate who castigate one another for holding positions which have a clear Scriptural basis in fact.

[12]   For the apostleship of Matthias, see Acts 1:24-26; Paul, 1 Corinthians 9:1-2, 2 Corinthians 11:5 and 12:11; Barnabas, Acts 14:1-4, 14; Apollos, 1 Corinthians 3:22, 4: 6, 9; Timothy and Silvanus, 1 Thessalonians 1:1 and 2:6; Andronicus and Junia, Romans 16:7.

[13]   Matthew 18:16 and 2 Corinthians 13:1. See also Deuteronomy 19:15.

[14]   Song of Solomon 6:10.

[15]   Philippians 2:15. See also Hamon, *Eternal Church*, pp. 342-345, 375-77.

[16]   Joel 2:23-32; Acts 3:19-21.

[17]   Joel 2:23-26; Ecclesiastes 2:9; Haggai 2:9; Hamon, *Eternal Church*, pp. 138-139.

Chapter 6
Antichrist and Tribulation

Let no man deceive you by any means: for that day shall not come, except there come a falling away first, and that man of sin be revealed, the son of perdition;

Who opposeth and exalteth himself above all that is called God, or that is worshipped; so that he as God sitteth in the temple of God, shewing himself that he is God.

2 Thessalonians 2:3-4

For then shall be great tribulation, such as was not since the beginning of the world to this time, no, nor ever shall be.

And except those days should be shortened, there should no flesh be saved: but for the elect's sake those days shall be shortened.

Matthew 24:21-22

The Bible tells us that in the Last Days there will arise out of the Revived Roman Empire a powerful world ruler, a global dictator called the Antichrist, a man "whose coming is after the working of Satan, with all power and signs and lying wonders."[1] The open manifestation of this individual will mark the beginning of a seven-year period of misery and suffering which is called the Tribulation—the last half of this period is referred to as the Great Tribulation.[2]

The Tribulation will begin when the Antichrist—who will at that time be the head of the European Community and also a world ruler—signs a peace treaty guaranteeing the security of the nation of Israel.[3] Israel will then be invaded by Russia along with a confederation of Arab nations from Africa and the Middle East. The Antichrist will come to Israel's defense and Russia will be defeated with devastating losses. This battle probably will see the use of tactical nuclear weapons by both sides.[4]

But at the midpoint of the Tribulation period, the Antichrist will turn against Israel. He will enter into the Holiest of Holies in the Temple, declaring himself to be God and demanding to be worshipped. This blasphemy is what Jesus referred to in Matthew 24:15 as the "abomination of desolation, spoken of by the prophet Daniel."[5]

After this the "Kings of the East"—a phrase which refers to China—will cross the Euphrates River and invade the Holy Land with an army of 200 million men to challenge the Antichrist at the Plain of Megiddo.[6] The bloody fighting that will ensue is known as the Battle of Armageddon—though it is really an extended three and a half year military campaign—and it will most likely include the use of tactical nuclear weapons.[7] The Bible says that one-third of all living human beings will die in those gory battles, before the Lord Jesus comes in person to destroy the Antichrist.[9]

This capsule summary is derived from the many prophecies contained in the Books of Daniel and Revelation, as well as Ezekial 37 and 38 and various New Testament passages. To go into all these things in detail is, again, beyond the scope of this book.[9]

But I do want to explain some particular passages from Daniel and also to touch on some particular aspects of the Tribulation period that are being foreshadowed now by observable current events.

The Visions of Daniel

The visions of the prophet Daniel are the basis for much of our understanding about what is going to happen in the Last Days. We have already studied in Chapter 1 the dreams and visions relating to the succession of earthly kingdoms and the rise of the Revived Roman Empire in the Last Days.

But Daniel also had special, unique revelations from God about the timetable of human history, specifically relating to the coming of the Messiah and the seven-year Tribulation period at the end of time. A right understanding of the revelations God gave to Daniel about the Last Days is crucial to the correct interpretation of all Bible prophecy.

Daniel's Seventy Weeks

Daniel had been praying to God, confessing his sins and the sins of his people Israel, when the angel Gabriel appeared to him

and gave him the key to the timetable for all end-time events.[10]
The passage is in Daniel 9.

> **Seventy weeks are determined upon thy people and**
> **upon thy holy city**, to finish the transgression, and to
> make an end of sins, and to make reconciliation for ini-
> quity, and to bring in everlasting righteousness, and to seal
> up the vision and prophecy, and to anoint the most Holy.
>   Know therefore and understand, that <u>from the going</u>
> <u>forth of the commandment to restore and to build</u>
> <u>Jerusalem unto the Messiah the Prince shall be seven</u>
> <u>weeks, and threescore and two weeks</u>: the street shall be
> built again, and the wall, even in troublous times.
>   And after threescore and two weeks shall Messiah be
> cut off, but not for himself: and the people of the <u>prince</u>
> <u>that shall come</u> shall destroy the city and the sanctuary;
> and the end thereof shall be with a flood, and unto the
> end of the war desolations are determined.
>   And he shall confirm the covenant with many for one
> week: and <u>in the midst of the week he shall cause the sac-</u>
> <u>rifice and the oblation to cease, and for the overspreading</u>
> <u>of abominations he shall make it desolate</u>, even until the
> consummation, and that determined shall be poured
> upon the desolate.
>   **Daniel 9:24-27**

Gabriel told Daniel that "seventy weeks" had been "determined
upon thy people and upon thy holy city." This language clearly
indicates that God is talking about the Jewish people and the city
of Jerusalem. Once again this illustrates the crucial importance of
both the Jews and Jerusalem in God's historical timetable.

Bible scholars are agreed that the phrase "seventy weeks"
meant in Hebrew custom "seventy weeks *of years*"—or 490 years.
So all of the prophecies of God pertaining to the Jewish people and
their Messiah were to be wrapped up inside of a specified period of
490 years.[11]

This passage in verses 25 and 26 also told Daniel exactly when
the long-awaited Messiah would be manifested—after a total of 69
weeks of years, or 483 years, from "the going forth of the commandment to restore and to rebuild Jerusalem."

This historical event occurred long after Daniel's death, when the Medo-Persian King Artaxerxes Longimanus ordered the rebuilding of Jerusalem in 444 B.C.—an event recorded in the Bible in Nehemiah 2:1-8.[12] Exactly 483 years later, just as the prophet had predicted, the Messiah was "cut off" when Jesus Christ was crucified in 33 A.D.[13]

That leaves only the last week, Daniel's "seventieth week," still to be fulfilled for the Jewish people. Prophetically for the Jews, time has basically been standing still during the almost 2,000 years of their dispersion abroad upon the Earth since their rejection of their Messiah, Jesus Christ. During the intervening "times of the Gentiles," God has been actively dealing with the Church instead. According to Dr. Chriswell,

> Between the sixty-ninth and seventieth week there is an uncharted lapse of time not revealed to Daniel or to any other of the O.T. prophets. This intervening time span incorporates the age of the Church in which we now live and work. The events of the sixty-nine weeks, including the cutting off of Messiah are behind. The events of the seventieth week remain for the future and will be realized during the age of the Great Tribulation of seven years just prior to the bringing in of 'everlasting righteousness' (v. 24).[14]

The events of Daniel's seventieth week will begin with the open manifestation of "the prince that shall come," who is also the Beast from the sea of Revelation 13 and the "little horn" of Daniel 7:8—the man who commonly is called the Antichrist.[15]

Antichrist: Man of Sin

The Antichrist will serve Satan and blaspheme God.[16] The Bible speaks a great deal about this charismatic individual, also known as the Beast in Revelation 13, who will rise to world power through cunning and flattery with promises of peace. His ascent will be aided by a false religious system, known as the Great Whore of Revelation 17, but he will ultimately turn on that harlot system and destroy it. He will suffer a mortal head wound but will miraculously recover through the agency of the False Prophet,[17] and Satanic miracles will mark the last half of his reign.[18]

At the midpoint of the Tribulation period, he will even enter into the Jewish Temple in Jerusalem and declare himself to be God, demanding the worship of all the people of the Earth. Those who refuse to worship the Beast and to take his mark will be persecuted and killed.[19]

In the New Testament, the Apostle Paul described the way things will be on earth when the Antichrist comes to power. In 2 Thessalonians, Paul writes to Christians who were concerned that Jesus had already come and they had missed the Rapture. Paul encouraged those believers thus:

> **Let no man deceive you by any means: for that day shall not come, except there come a falling away first, and <u>that man of sin be revealed, the son of perdition</u>:**
>
> **<u>Who opposeth and exalteth himself above all that is called God, or that is worshipped; so that he as God sitteth in the temple of God, shewing himself that he is God</u>.**
>
> **Remember ye not, that, when I was yet with you, I told you these things?**
>
> **And now ye know what withholdeth that he might be revealed in his time.**
>
> **For the mystery of iniquity doth already work: only he that now letteth will let, until he be taken out of the way.**
>
> **And then shall that Wicked be revealed, whom the Lord shall consume with the spirit of his mouth, and shall destroy with the brightness of his coming:**
>
> **Even him, <u>whose coming is after the working of Satan with all power and signs and lying wonders</u>,**
>
> **And with all deceivableness of unrighteousness in them that perish; <u>because they received not the love of the truth</u>, that they might be saved.**
>
> **And for this cause <u>God shall send them strong delusion, that they should believe a lie</u>:**
>
> **That they all might be damned who believed not the truth, but had pleasure in unrighteousness.**
>
> **2 Thessalonians 2:3-12**

A number of crucial New Testament doctrines are contained in this critical passage of Scripture, and I'll touch on a few of them briefly.

Antichrist Revealed

First, in verse 3 we see the great "falling away" from the faith, the widespread apostasy of the Last Days. In Matthew 24:12, Jesus referred to this period of apostasy as the time when "iniquity shall abound." The falling away precedes the open manifestation of the Antichrist, who here is called the "man of sin" and the "son of perdition."

In Matthew 24:15, Jesus also mentioned the "abomination of desolation, spoken of by the prophet Daniel." This event, which is described here in verse 4, will occur when the Antichrist installs himself in the Jewish Temple and demands to be worshipped as God by the world.

Obviously, for this to happen, there has to be a Temple in Jerusalem, and this is why the plans of Jewish groups like the Temple Mount Faithful are so important today. Daniel 11:31 says that the Antichrist will also "take away the daily sacrifice," which means that the Jewish sacrificial worship system also must be resumed.[20]

According to 2 Thessalonians 2:7-8, the Antichrist spirit, or the "mystery of iniquity," is already at work in the world, but the Antichrist himself cannot be revealed in person until a powerful restraining force is removed. Most Bible scholars have traditionally interpreted the restrainer to be the Holy Spirit present in the Earth and indwelling the true believers of the Church.[21]

When the restrainer is removed, the Antichrist is revealed. Verse 9 reiterates the fact that this person will be Satanically empowered to do "signs and lying wonders." Daniel 8:25 says that "craft shall prosper in his hand," which refers to his skill at the "dark sentences" of witchcraft; and Daniel 11:38 says that "in his estate shall he honour the God of forces," which is a reference to Satanic worship.

As we see our world plunging into apostasy, occultism, witchcraft, and Satanism—while at the same time the Jewish Temple with its sacrificial system is on the verge of restoration—we can recognize that the Antichrist is about to make his entrance upon the world stage.

A Strong Delusion

Paul wrote that there would be great deception in these Last Days and that many would perish "because they received not the love of the truth, that they might be saved."

These are to me the most frightening words in the Bible. No, not because the Antichrist has come into the world, because we know that he will ultimately be defeated by Jesus. And not because of the supernatural Satanic power that will accompany his appearance, because we know that the power of God is greater than the power of the Devil.

No, it is not the Devil I fear, but God. The most frightening words in the Bible are quoted above, followed by these:

> **And for this cause <u>God shall send them strong delusion, that they should believe the lie:</u>**
> **That they might all be damned that believed not the truth, but had pleasure in unrighteousness.**
> **2 Thessalonians 2:11-12**

When God sends you the strong delusion, you have no choice but to believe the lie and follow the Antichrist to ultimate damnation. There is no hope and no escape. Your doom is sealed forever. This is the most horrible condition in which any person could ever find himself, because there is absolutely no way to get back to God.

And why does this happen to people? Because they "received not the love of the truth, that they might be saved." They rejected God's truth, preferring to choose evil and to have "pleasure in unrighteousness"—with the result that they will "all be damned."

This is what happened to Mohammed and to Joseph Smith: they rejected the true revelation from God about salvation through His only begotten Son, Jesus Christ. So Satan appeared to them as an angel of light and offered them a counterfeit revelation, an alternative religion to the one they had rejected. They believed his lie, and led millions to hell with them.

This is what will happen in the Last Days as well. The whole world will be faced with a choice between Jesus, God's true Christ, and the man of sin, Satan's Antichrist. The Greek prefix "anti-" carries a double meaning here: it connotes both "opposed to" and "in place of." The Antichrist will oppose himself to Jesus and at the same time try to take His place as God.

It will be the same kind of choice Pilate offered to the Jews two millennia ago: Will you choose Jesus, or Barabbas?[22] The choice will be between One Who is absolutely good, and another who is evil incarnate. And many, because they will choose not to believe the truth, will instead be deluded into believing the lie and choosing the Antichrist.

The prophet Joel had a vision of the Last Days. He wrote,

> **Multitudes, multitudes in the valley of decision: for the day of the Lord is near in the valley of decision.**
> **Joel 3:14**

The whole human race will soon find itself in the valley of decision, as the world will be presented with the same choice, just prior to Christ's Second Advent, that the Jews were given at His first.

As Derek Prince has aptly said, "No one will get out of that valley until he has made a decision.... Before this century closes, that matter will have been settled by every soul upon the face of the Earth. Which is it to be: the Christ or the Antichrist?"[23]

The Bible says that most people will choose the Antichrist:

> **And all that dwell upon the earth shall worship him, whose names are not written in the book of life of the Lamb slain from the foundation of the world.**
> **Revelation 13:8**

The Mark of the Beast

People will have to make a life and death choice about whether to worship the Antichrist and accept his rule. The Bible says that one requirement for participation in the worldwide Antichrist economic system will be receiving the "mark of the Beast." This mark will be imposed upon the world by the False Prophet, who will serve the Beast. Without the mark, no one will be allowed to buy or sell anything.

> **And I beheld another beast coming up out of the earth; and he had two horns like a lamb, and he spake as a dragon.**
> **And he exerciseth all the power of the first beast before him, and causeth the earth and them which dwell therein to worship the first beast, whose deadly wound was healed.**

And he doeth great wonders, so that he maketh fire to come down from heaven upon the earth in the sight of men,

And deceiveth them that dwell on the earth by the means of those miracles which he had power to do in the sight of the beast; saying to them that dwell upon the earth, that they should make an image to the beast, which had the wound by a sword, and did live.

And he had power to give life unto the image of the beast, that the image of the beast should both speak, and **cause that as many as would not worship the image of the beast should be killed.**

And he causeth all, both small and great, rich and poor, free and bond, to receive a mark in their right hand, or in their foreheads:

And that no man might buy or sell, save he that had the mark, or the name of the beast, or the number of his name.

Here is wisdom. Let him that hath understanding count the number of the beast: for it is the number of a man; and his number is Six hundred threescore and six.

Revelation 13:13-18

The False Prophet who serves the Antichrist will offer everyone only two choices: accept his mark, or perish. Without the mark, a person will be unable to participate in the normal commercial activities of the world. Those who refuse to worship the beast will be killed.

There is much speculation about what this mark will be, but it is obviously linked to the worldwide economic system.

Christian economist Larry Burkett has suggested that the ever-increasing burden of debt must eventually produce an international economic crash that will throw the world into an economic panic.

"If you can read the economic statistics of this country and see where we're headed and you aren't alarmed, you're brain dead," Burkett said.[24]

In such an emergency situation, it might be relatively easy for world leaders to justify abolishing cash and instituting electronic money to control counterfeiting and to bring order out of the chaos.

This idea is already being floated in some government circles as the only way to stem the financial bleeding from the estimated hundreds of billions of dollars worth of counterfeit U.S. $100 "supernotes" now widely circulating in the Middle East, Central Asia, and Africa.[25]

Smart Cards and 666

Many today believe that the mark could be a small computer chip the size of a grain of rice implanted in the body, a kind of a permanent reprogrammable "smart card" in the coming cashless society.

Already electronic banking has become commonplace worldwide, and smart cards are being widely used in Europe. They are expected to make a debut in America at the 1996 Summer Olympics in Atlanta and are being touted as the latest thing in convenience and safety.

"A chip implanted somewhere in our bodies might serve as a combination credit card, passport, driver's license, personal diary," speculated Edward Cornish, editor of *Futurist* magazine. "No longer would we worry about losing our credit cards while traveling."[26]

Others see a more sinister side to the coming electronic currency.

"The universal product code is a mark run by three sixes. It was designed as a boon to control and keep track of inventory for businesses," wrote Ken Klein in his book *The False Prophet*. "When the time is ripe, due to the many global problems, and the burgeoning world population, the mark will be applied to everyone for total world monetary control." [27]

A movie from 30 years ago, entitled *A Clockwork Orange*, depicted a futuristic scenario in which an electronic device was implanted into the brains of criminals to detect the chemicals that could trigger anger and to apply behavior-modifying pain stimuli, averting potential violence. Is it possible that some kind of hybrid device could serve the dual roles of electronic bankbook and mind-controller in a future Orwellian world?

I can't predict exactly how this scenario will develop, but I can see some stark possibilities looming on the horizon. The day will soon come when it is going to cost people a lot to take a stand for God.

Maybe even their lives.

Anti-Christian Persecution

One distinctive characteristic of the Tribulation period will be the persecution of all who do not accept the New Age world religion with the Antichrist as God. Those who refuse will be persecuted and even killed, just as early Christians were killed for refusing to worship the Roman emperors.

Christians have been persecuted throughout history, so this is nothing new. Oftentimes the persecution has caused the Church to grow stronger in faith, as was the case in the Early Church. It has also been the case in the 20th Century for many believers in Communist countries, where Marxist atheism was the official government doctrine. Thousands of Soviet Christians were sent to Siberian labor camps or to state-run psychiatric hospitals for thought rehabilitation.

Today new Christian converts in Moslem countries face social ostracism, rejection by their families and friends, and in some cases imprisonment and even death. Some militant Moslem countries have reportedly begun to make slaves of the Christians within their borders.

A recent feature article in *Charisma* magazine revealed that as many as 40 million Christians have been killed since the Church began. An estimated 156,000 Christians were martyred in 1995, including 52,000 women. The article carried this telling summary:

"Throughout the world today—in Pakistan, Rwanda, Colombia, Iran, and Peru—martyrs are paying the ultimate price for their faith."[28]

Sheltered American Christians

Compared to this kind of brutal treatment, Christians in America don't even know what persecution is. We have been sheltered from it for almost 400 years, for America has always had a strong Christian heritage. While there has never been a time when everyone in the United States was a Christian, nevertheless this country has been built on the solidly Judeo-Christian foundations of Western Civilization.

When the French aristocrat Alexis de Toqueville toured America in 1831, he sought to discover the source of her strength. He looked in vain in her public schools and commerce, her farms and forests, her Congress and Constitution. But he found it, he said, in her churches.

Not until I went into the churches of America and heard her pulpits flame with righteousness did I understand the secret of her genius and power.

America is great because America is good, and if America ever ceases to be good, America will cease to be great.[29]

The basic moral precepts of the Christian religion have always been accepted as the right standard for life in America, and Christianity has been regarded by the general populace as a good thing. So no real anti-Christian persecution has ever had the opportunity to rear its head in America.

That is, not until about 30 years ago, when the Supreme Court ruled that God had no place in the public education of American children. Since that time the moral tone of the society has radically changed. It used to be that Christians were generally acknowledged to be good people. Nowadays, increasingly, Christians are being regarded as somewhat suspect.

Blatant Media Bias

This development is, in large measure, the result of a conscious anti-Christian bias in the mainstream American media. That bias is real and growing, fueled in many cases by the rhetoric of special interest groups like radical feminists and gay rights activists whose ungodly political agendas are partially thwarted by the vocal opposition of concerned Christians.

One of the reasons that the Christian Coalition was founded in 1989 was to expose and protest anti-Christian bias in the schools and the media. As editor of all Christian Coalition publications for five years, I had the opportunity to observe just how pervasive that bias has become.

What I learned was truly shocking, as week after week the news clippings would come across my desk—another student suspended for reading a Bible or passing out a tract, another ACLU lawsuit to ban a creche or a hymn or a prayer, another strident assault from the liberal political left against the so-called "radical religious right." Another opinion piece on the *New York Times* editorial page castigating Christians for their homophobia and intolerance. Another pro-abortion feminist railing about the "religious fanatics" who were trying to "impose their morality on America" by restricting her Constitutional right to "choose" to murder her child.

The entertainment industry is saturated with anti-Christian themes in the degenerate lyrics and video images produced by ungodly musical groups. Madonna has made millions mocking Christian holiness and selling sleazy sex. Recent Hollywood movies like *The Handmaid's Tale* and *Leap of Faith* were negative caricatures of Christians, while Martin Scorsese's *Last Temptation of Christ* and *Cape Fear* crossed the line from insensitivity and bad taste into outright blasphemy and falsehood.

I began to realize that, for the mainstream liberal media, it is no longer politically correct to be a practicing Christian in America. That fact became crystal clear on February 1, 1993, when a front-page story in the *Washington Post* described the "gospel lobby" followers of Pat Robertson as "poor, uneducated, and easy to command."[30]

About the same time the Universal Press Syndicate distributed a cartoon by artist Pat Oliphant depicting Christians as rats dragging a reluctant GOP elephant into the "Fundamentalist Christian Mission." This is reminiscent of the Nazi propaganda films from 1939 which juxtaposed images of Jews praying with those of rats crawling out of sewers, thereby conditioning the German people in general, and the Hitler youth in particular, to regard Jews as social parasites.[31]

I began to wonder if a similar "ghettoizing" of Christians might be underway in America today.

Christian Bashing Politics

The Christian-bashing themes carried over into partisan politics. In Virginia, Christian constitutional attorney Mike Farris, who was running for Lieutenant Governor in 1993, became the target of an all-out character smear based on his past writings on Biblical topics. Similar assaults were launched in the Los Angeles mayoral contest, where alleged support from Christians was portrayed as evidence of corruption.

The anti-Christian political bigotry intensified in 1994 with the vicious mid-summer attacks leveled by top Democrats against conservative Christian candidates for political office and the grassroots activists who supported them. The plan was a calculated campaign strategy by political consultant James Carville, designed

to stigmatize Christian activists and to make them appear dangerous to the average American voters.[32]

Following the carefully crafted Carville plan, President Bill
Clinton solemnly warned the nation that obstructionist "right wing
fanatics" with a message of "hate and fear" were taking over the
Republican Party.

Congressman Vic Fazio (D-CA), chairman of the Democratic
National Congressional Committee, labeled the Christians in the
GOP as the "fire-breathing Christian radical right" and said that
"they are what the American people fear the most."

Democratic media consultant Mark Mellman called Christian
Republican nominees "card-carrying members of the flat-
earth society."

U.S. Surgeon General Joycelyn Elders and Texas Governor
Ann Richards joined in the national Christian-bashing chorus,
and the profane litany was repeated all over America at the state
and local levels.

In Washington, D.C., Democrats on Capitol Hill established a
"Radical Right Task Force" to investigate ways of removing the tax
exempt status from churches that get too involved in the political
process by allowing the distribution of nonpartisan voter guides to
their members.

The Anti-Defamation League got into the act as well, releasing a
shoddily-researched and highly partisan document entitled *The
Religious Right: The Assault on Tolerance and Pluralism in America.*
That blatantly biased report falsely accused conservative Christian
organizations and their leaders of anti-Semitism and theocratic
aims. It was quickly denounced as "liberalism, not Judaism" by a
host of conservative Jews.

Liberal journalists nationwide aided and abetted the summer
assault. Leading the attack in the *New York Times* were Michael
Kinsley ("Casting Stones," July 5); Anna Quindlen ("What They Stand
For," July 6); and Anthony Lewis ("Merchants of Hate," July 15).[33]

The Point and the Problem

By now you may be wondering why I am digressing, in the
middle of a Biblical analysis of the Tribulation, into a commentary
on political events from several years ago. After all, the Carville
strategy failed, the Christian candidates mostly won, and the
Republican Revolution is apparently moving full speed ahead with

the GOP in control of both houses of Congress. So what's the point, and what's the problem?

The point is simple. Some of the shrewdest political minds in America came up with that strategy because they thought it would work. They truly believed that American society had changed to such a degree that stigmatizing a candidate as a Christian would win them an election.

In the cases of high-profile candidates like Mike Farris and Oliver North, they were right. In the majority of 1994 elections, they were simply a little ahead of the curve, and their plan could not overcome their own unpopular President's negative drag on the Democratic ticket.

These same anti-Christian themes are likely to re-emerge in 1996, though probably in a more muted fashion. In fact, that is exactly what has already happened to Pat Buchanan's bid for the Republican presidential nomination. Only this time it is the Republican Establishment that is leading the charge against Buchanan's so-called conservative "extremism."

There is on the horizon an ideological convergence of the two major political parties in America. Those who place in the Republican Party their fond hopes for turning America around will be sadly disappointed. The pragmatic politicians who control both parties are going to continue to base their policies on polls rather than principles in order to stay in power.

The problem is obvious. Our culture no longer accepts Christian values as normative for American society. While the 1994 elections forced anti-Christian sentiments in the media to submerge for a while, they are still there under the surface.

Peter Jennings may have hired a religion reporter to cover the undeniable influence of self-described "mainstream" religious groups like the Christian Coalition within the newly ascendant Republican Party, but the basic anti-Christian bias in the media still remains.

Most working journalists in the liberal media still view Bible-believing Christians as the intellectual equivalents of apes swinging in trees.

Like leaven, the Antichrist spirit is still working through the mainstream media, gradually penetrating the society at large, subtly manipulating the masses and conditioning the culture.

Harbingers of Things to Come

If Clinton should be re-elected in 1996, and especially if Democrats should recapture control of one or more houses of Congress—which is possible, given the narrow margins of majority Republicans now hold—we can expect to see a resurgence of virulent anti-Christian rhetoric that makes everything in the recent past pale by comparison. Should a Republican capture the White House, this scenario will probably be delayed a little.

Whether it happens sooner or later, it will happen. Despite the good intentions and sincere efforts of many dedicated individuals, the vaunted Republican Revolution will not turn the historical tides of cultural disintegration at work in America today.

No great nation has ever fought its way back up the slippery slope of moral decadence to regain a position of pre-eminence in the world. It has never happened in history, and it isn't likely to happen in America. Both the cycles of history and the prophecies of the Bible militate against the vain Third Wave visions of Alvin Toffler, which have been embraced by Newt Gingrich.

Instead, as the culture continues to decline, Christians increasingly will be viewed as social pariahs who are holding back progress with their regressive superstitions and stubborn refusals to go with society's flow.

The New Age culture will gladly accommodate itself to the clamor of the pro-abortion feminists and the radical homosexual activists, and the Christians who oppose these ungodly agendas clearly will be "out of step."

A current example is the sympathetic media attention being devoted to an ongoing smear campaign against Pat Robertson by a group of radical homosexual activists. They claim that Robertson's public statements labeling homosexual practices as sin have resulted in "hate crimes" against gays. Free speech is to be allowed only if it is politically correct.[34]

Demonizing Christians

In April 1993 at Waco, Texas, 81 members of the Branch Davidian sect, including 24 children, perished in a fiery inferno after a 51-day standoff with federal agents. The leader of the group, David Koresh, was the target.

Koresh was not your model Christian. He exerted total mind control over the members of his group, slept with any woman he chose (including young girls), and reportedly considered himself the Messiah. Obsessed with end-time prophecy and the Book of Revelation, he also stockpiled a large cache of weapons, some of which authorities believed to be illegal. Koresh anticipated a violent conflict with the government, and he got one.

A chilling incident occurred in the wake of the tragedy at Waco. Upon first hearing of the disastrous conclusion of the stand-off, President Bill Clinton denied any personal involvement and shifted the blame onto the willing shoulders of newly-appointed Attorney General Janet Reno.

But then Clinton made some amazing and ominous statements:

> I hope very much that others tempted to join cults and to become involved with people like David Koresh will be deterred by the horrible scenes they have seen over the last seven weeks....
>
> There is unfortunately a rise in this sort of fanaticism all over the world. And we may have to confront it again.[35]

Clinton's comments communicated an unmistakable message that dissident religious beliefs will not be tolerated by the all-powerful state.

Without trying to defend Koresh—whose ideas were wrong and whose conduct was reckless and foolhardy—one can still discern a dangerous mindset developing in the nation in the wake of Waco.

"Fundamentalist Christians," like fundamentalist Moslem terrorist bombers, are now being viewed as a threat by the government, the media, and the public. Especially suspect are those who express a belief in the literal truth of Bible prophecy and the imminent return of Jesus Christ.

Just as the Jews in Germany were ghettoized by the Nazis, Bible-believing Christians in America are being demonized today by the statist socialists of the liberal left and their apologists in the mainstream media.

Cult Watcher's Handbook

A recent book on the beliefs of American Christians about end-time Bible prophecy has been published by the Harvard University

Press and is quietly making its presence felt in the academic institutions of America. *When Time Shall Be No More,* by historian Paul Boyer, gives a detailed, essentially accurate account of the general themes of literal Biblical prophetic interpretation. But Boyer is skeptical of their conclusions and warns that they could be dangerous to the stability of the society.

For example, Christians who believe in the literal fulfillment of prophecy reject globalist trends because they associate world government with the Antichrist. In a similar way they are wary of a computerized cashless society which could be a vehicle for mass social control. Because they can see the likelihood of nuclear war in the prophetic Scriptures, they tend to be less supportive of unilateral disarmament initiatives.[36]

Boyer's book will likely become the authoritative reference source for future social engineers trying to understand the alien prophetic mindset of those stubborn, troublesome Christians who will refuse to cooperate with the marvelous new programs of the Antichrist's global regime.

It is possible that the blame for many of the world's future problems may be laid at the feet of the strange Christian sect, just as it was in Rome.

That is when the real anti-Christian persecution will begin with a vengeance. We should be able to discern these signs of the coming times.

Plagues and Natural Disasters

The Tribulation period described in the Book of Revelation will be a time of terrible plagues and intense natural disasters. The beginning of the Tribulation plagues is described in Revelation 6 with the opening of the six seals. The first four seals describe four riders, commonly called the Four Horsemen of the Apocalypse.

The white horse in verse 2 represents the emerging Antichrist, who goes forth "conquering and to conquer." The red horse represents war, and the black horse represents the famines that follow after war. The pale horse represents death, and verse 8 says that one-fourth of the people on the Earth will perish "with the sword, and with hunger, and with death, and with the beasts of the earth."

War, famine, disease, and wild beasts will kill between them at least 1.5 billion people during the seven years of the Tribulation period.

In Revelation 6:12, the sixth seal is opened:

> **...and, lo, there was a great earthquake; and the sun became black as sackcloth of hair, and the moon became as blood;**
> **And the stars of heaven fell unto the earth, even as a fig tree casteth her untimely figs, when she is shaken as of a mighty wind.**
> **And <u>the heaven departed as a scroll when it is rolled together</u>, and every mountain and island were moved out of their places.**

The language referring to the heaven rolling up like a scroll is similar to that in 2 Peter 3:10, which says that

> **the heavens shall pass away with a great noise, and the <u>elements shall melt with a fervent heat</u>, the earth also and the works that are therein shall be burned up.**

Many Bible scholars believe that these words could be describing what a nuclear explosion would look like to someone from the first century, seeing an actual vision of the things that would happen at the end of time.

Ezekial 38:22 describes the similar manner in which the armies of Gog, the ruler of Russia, will be destroyed on the mountains of Israel:

> **And I will plead against him with pestilence and with blood; and I will rain upon him, and upon his bands, and upon the many people that are with him, an overflowing rain, and great hailstones, fire, and brimstone.**

These passages could be describing natural calamities like massive earthquakes and volcanic eruptions, since the lava and volcanic ash from one or more major eruptions could fall like fire and brimstone and the ash filling the air could also obscure the sun and moon.

But they could also be describing chemical or biological weapons, or a widespread nuclear holocaust directed against not only the armies of Gog but also "his bands" and the "many people with him." This could refer to the home-based populations of all the nations involved in the conflict.[37]

Ezekial 39:6 says that during the fierce destruction of the Russian armies, God will "send a fire on Magog, and upon them that dwell carelessly in the isles." Many believe that this could be a reference to the escalation of the nuclear conflict into far-off countries which think themselves secure—particularly the United States of America.[38]

The seventh seal is opened in Revelation 8:1, and this introduces a series of seven trumpet judgments. These result in "hail and fire, mixed with blood" falling upon the Earth and burning up one-third of the vegetation, as well as a "great mountain burning with fire" falling into the sea, turning one-third of the water to blood, and killing fish and destroying ships. Many believe that this could be describing the effect of a giant meteor hitting the Earth's oceans, producing devastating tidal waves and setting off a series of volcanic eruptions and earthquakes.[39]

A similar occurrence is described in verses 10 and 11, where "there fell from heaven a great star, burning as it were a lamp," which poisoned the waters of the rivers and made them bitter, killing the people who drank the water. The name of this star is called "Wormwood."

Many believe that this refers to what an incoming ICBM might look like, with its subsequent explosion and radiation poisoning. Recall the massive nuclear disaster at Chernobyl in the Soviet Union in 1986, which spread radioactive fallout all across northern Europe for a distance of 1,300 miles—noting that "Chernobyl" in Russian means "Wormwood."

Nuclear War, Nuclear Winter

Revelation 16 describes the seven last plagues, the outpouring of the "vials of the wrath of God" upon the Earth. Men who have the mark of the beast are smitten with sores, and all the waters of the oceans are turned to blood, as well as all fresh water.

Then in verses 8 and 9, the sun is affected and "men were scorched with great heat, and blasphemed the name of God, which hath power over these plagues, and they repented not to give him glory." It has been suggested by some that this could be describing intense heat from solar flares, or that it this could be a kind of skin cancer from increased solar radiation due to erosion of the Earth's ozone layer.

Next the Earth is smitten with darkness, which again could be produced by volcanic ash, by smoke from numerous fires burning out of control, or even by the implosion of our sun into a dark star after having briefly flared into a nova.

Or it could be the description of a desolate nuclear winter that would follow a massive nuclear war, as all the debris filling the atmosphere after the nuclear explosions would blot out the light from the sun and moon.

Revelation 16:17-21 describes the final plague that accompanies the outpouring of the last vial of God's wrath upon the Earth. It is a time of massive and unprecedented devastation, apparently separate and unique from the previously described plagues of the Tribulation.

> **And the seventh angel poured out his vial into the air; and there came a great voice out of the temple of heaven, from the throne, saying, It is done.**
>
> **And there were voices, and thunders, and lightnings; and there was <u>a great earthquake, such as was not since men were upon the earth, so mighty was the earthquake, and so great</u>.**
>
> **And the great city was divided into three parts, and <u>the cities of the nations fell</u>: and great Babylon came into remembrance before God, to give unto her the cup of the wine of the fierceness of his wrath.**
>
> **And every island fled away, and the mountains were not found.**
>
> **And <u>there fell upon men a great hail out of heaven</u>, every stone about the weight of a talent: and men blasphemed God because of the plague of the hail; for the plague thereof was exceeding great.**
>
> **Revelation 16:17-21**

This passage has been interpreted by Hal Lindsey as "a nuclear war that wipes out every major city in the world."[40]

The scenario described occurs at the very end of the Tribulation period, at the time when Jesus Himself shall return to Jerusalem and touch His foot upon the Mount of Olives. It is also found in Zechariah 14:12,

And this shall be the plague wherewith the Lord shall smite all the people that have fought against Jerusalem; <u>Their flesh shall consume away while they stand upon their feet</u>, and their eyes shall consume away in their holes, and their tongue shall consume away in their mouth.

This is an exact description of what a neutron bomb does to men.

This is the most frightening scenario imaginable, and one which I do not like to contemplate for anyone. To my mind, however, it is the only explanation that makes sense. One-third of the remaining population of the Earth, or about 1.5 billion people, will perish at this time.[41]

I would love to be wrong about this.

But I don't think so.

New World Order

The Bible plainly says that the Antichrist, also called the Beast, will rule over all the Earth. Yet it also reveals that there will be other kings who will still have huge armies, with which they will attempt to resist his power and make war against him. This seeming contradiction can be explained by understanding the globalist agenda now at work in the world.[42]

U.S. President George Bush announced that agenda to the world on September 11, 1990, in an address to a Joint Session of Congress. He was explaining why America had to send troops to rescue Kuwait from Saddam Hussein, and he spoke of establishing a New World Order.

Later, on March 6, 1991, after the conclusion of Operation Desert Storm, Bush again addressed Congress to announce his success:

Now, we can see a new world coming into view. A world in which there is <u>a very real prospect of a new world order</u>. In the words of Winston Churchill, a world order in which "the principles of justice and fair play protect the weak against the strong." A world <u>where the United Nations—</u> freed from Cold War stalemate—<u>is poised to fulfill the historic vision of its founders</u>....[43] (Emphasis added.)

According to Bush, the New World Order was to establish justice for all according to the historic vision of the United Nations. But many prominent Christians responded to Bush's remarks with alarm. Taking the lead was Pat Robertson, who warned,

> Implicit in all of the debate and discussion of the war was the fact that "United Nations sanctions" gave the war legitimacy....
>
> Without a clear vote of any of our elected representatives on the matter, and without any clear understanding among the people of the future ramifications, <u>the United States has taken a giant step toward submitting its decisions and policies to the control of a one-world government under the United Nations</u>.
>
> A one-world government, a common central bank-managed currency, and three common market trading blocs—Europe, Asia, and North America—has been the goal of the Council on Foreign Relations and its offshoot, the Trilateral Commission, for decades.[44] (Emphasis added.)

The United Nations is an international organization formed in 1945 for the purpose of promoting world peace through collective security, but for half a century it has proven ineffectual in accomplishing that goal.

The years since the 1991 Persian Gulf War—which was conducted against Iraq by an international coalition of nations under the umbrella of a UN resolution—have seen a global proliferation of UN "peacekeeping" operations. These have resulted in notable failures in Somalia and Bosnia and no notable successes.

Each year that passes, however, is taking the United Nations a few steps further along the path to its actual goal of world domination through world government—a goal fervently desired and actively promoted by groups like the World Federalist Association, who see such an official governmental structure as essential for ending war in the world.

The stated goal of the UN is "general and complete disarmament under effective international control." What this really means is a world in which no nation has the military might effectively to resist the will of the UN's world peace-keeping forces. Individual nations will retain only the military capabilities necessary to effectively police their own people and to supply a quota of troops and equipment to the UN. The year 2000 is the tentative target date for achieving this lofty goal of global disarmament.[45]

Despite the UN's past failures, the globalist agenda of a New World Order remains intact, with the United States taking the lead. Since taking office in 1993, Bill Clinton has weakened the United States through massive cutbacks in the U.S. military. Yet he strengthened the United Nations when he committed U.S. troops to serve under UN command in Somalia, and later signed Presidential Decision Directive 25 (PDD-25), which says that this will be the future U.S. military policy.[46]

When Army Specialist Michael New, a 22-year-old U.S. service-man stationed in Germany, recently refused to obey an order to submit himself to UN authority—saying that his sworn allegiance was to the U.S. Constitution—he was court-martialed and dishon-orably discharged.[47]

While wealthy international businessmen and financiers may believe that the UN can keep the peace and make the world safe for Trilateral trade, others believe that the hard-line Communists in Russia and China still desire world domination and will never voluntarily surrender their massive nuclear arsenals to the UN.

For example, intelligence analyst Don McAlvaney believes that the so-called demise of Soviet Communism is merely an elaborate ruse by Russian strategists. He envisions a Red Dawn scenario in which Russia will wait for a complacent America to lower her defenses, and then attack suddenly:

> But at a point in time (this writer believes in the mid- to late-1990s) the Russians, the greatest masters of deception in history, will launch their final drive for world dom-ination, will double-cross their liberal Western capitalist benefactors, and will attack the United States of America.[48]

Struggle for the World

Given the foregoing set of circumstances and the international geopolitical developments discussed previously in Chapter One, let me suggest a possible political scenario for the Tribulation period, assuming that such a time were to begin in the foresee-able future.

I do not say that these events must or will happen exactly this way—this fictitious scenario is merely a reasonable possibility.

The Beast and the Harlot

Let us assume that the Beast, whoever he may happen to be, has come to power as the head of the European Community during a time of worldwide economic crisis. He will propose a brilliant plan to stabilize the global economic system, promising to end the chaos and produce world peace. He will be accepted by the leaders of the world and elected head of the United Nations. In this capacity he will be the titular "ruler of the world," although each nation will still retain its own limited sovereignty.

This Antichrist's ascendancy will be promoted by a blessing from a corrupt Pope—an apostate, Satanically empowered successor to John Paul II. This false Pope, still claiming unique authority as the vicar of Christ, will speak ecumenically on behalf of all the world's religions, which will then be united by common New Age themes of universal brotherhood and world peace in the Age of Aquarius.

The Beast will appeal to those desires for global security and will implement sweeping international treaties to guarantee peace, especially in the tumultuous Middle East. The Jews, eager for a respite from war and the threat of annihilation by the Arabs, will gladly accept his protection.

The Nuclear Club

There will be five major nuclear powers in the world: the United States of America, the Russian Federation (including Kazakhstan), the European Community, Communist China, and Israel. Other nations will have limited nuclear capabilities but not enough to pose a global threat.

Each of these five nuclear powers will be faced with a ticking clock: the nuclear disarmament timetable of the United Nations. Each one will be aware that fully submitting itself to the terms of the UN disarmament plan will effectively end any lingering hope it might have for world empire.

Only the United States, a decadent nation in moral and economic decline under the inept leadership of an ardent internationalist, will unilaterally begin to dismantle its military machine. The rest will posture and pontificate about peace and disarmament but will really be doing all they can to strengthen their geopolitical hands at every opportunity.

The Battle of Gog and Magog

Russia will come under the leadership of an ardent nationalist like Vladimir Zhirinovsky. Faced with ever-increasing economic woes at home and smarting under the impending humiliation of seeing Russia reduced to Third World status when his nuclear weapons have been surrendered, this demented demagogue will seek a way to save the Fatherland. In desperation, he will make covenant with an Islamic Fundamentalist alliance headed by Iran. They will agree to strike swiftly at Israel and the wealthy moderate Arab oil states in the Gulf, dividing the spoils of war and establishing Russian hegemony in Central Asia and the Middle East.

The assault on Israel will include a pre-emptive nuclear strike against the weakened, complacent United States, Israel's nominal ally and a long-time Russian nemesis. The Russian "Gog" will see the U.S.A. as his only real obstacle to world empire, believing the fledgling European Union to be a paper tiger still intimidated by half a century of Russian continental dominance and incapable of decisive action against him.

In his lust for power, Gog will underestimate both the U.S.A. and the Beast. America will be severely crippled by the surprise attack, suffering tremendous casualties, but will still manage to launch a one-time retaliatory strike before the Russian missiles hit. The American counter-attack will destroy much of the Russian heartland, killing millions.

Nevertheless, Gog will stubbornly press on into Israel. There Gog's armies will be destroyed on the mountains of northern Israel by a combination of Israeli tactical nuclear weapons and surprise air assaults from the Beast, who will then move his armies into Israel.

All totaled, 80 percent of the population of Russia—and possibly that of his allies—will perish in this exchange. So great will be the carnage that it will take seven months to bury the dead and seven years to collect and burn the weapons.

Of the 6 billion souls alive on the Earth, one-quarter will die.

The Abomination of Desolation

The Beast will then fight against Egypt and the remnants of the Islamic coalition that had joined the Russian assault on Israel. Because of his continued fighting in violation of the peace treaties he had previously signed, the Beast will be censured by the false Pope, who will assert his spiritual authority. The Beast will respond by destroying the false Pope.

In the course of the fighting in Israel, the Beast will receive a mortal head wound. The wound will miraculously be healed by a Jewish False Prophet, who may even profess to be acting on special instructions from "ascended masters" or extremely wise creatures from advanced civilizations in other galaxies. The False Prophet will proclaim the Beast to be the divine messiah, or New Age avatar embodying the "Christ office."

From the moment he recovers from his mortal head wound, the Beast will be totally possessed by Satan. His reign for the next three and a half years will be marked by Satanically empowered signs and wonders. At this midpoint in the Tribulation period, the Beast will break his covenant with Israel. He will enter into the Temple and cause the Jewish sacrificial rituals to cease, and declaring himself to be God will demand the worship of the whole world—which will require that everyone accept his mark.

Those who accept the mark will be allowed to buy and sell but will forfeit their eternal souls. Those who refuse will be persecuted and in some cases killed. Many will turn to Christ during the seven-year Tribulation period, despite the intense persecution they will suffer.

God will send two witnesses to oppose the Beast during the last half of the seven years, which will be known as the Great Tribulation. These men will have the power to do supernatural miracles and to bring plagues upon the Earth as a testimony to the power of God.

During this time no rain will fall upon the Earth, the water will turn to blood, and men will be visited with great plagues from God, but still they will not repent and turn to Christ.

The Battle of Armageddon

With Russia and the U.S.A. destroyed and Israel occupied by the Beast—who will appear weakened from his campaign against Russia and Egypt and then his mortal wound—China will see her great chance to emerge as the only remaining superpower in the world. China will send an army of 200 million men across the dried-up Euphrates River to launch human wave attacks against the armies of the Beast assembled at Armageddon. As head of the

UN, the Beast will conscript soldiers from every nation on Earth to resist the Asian hordes bearing down upon him.

The fighting will last continuously for the greater part of the Great Tribulation period. The carnage will be so great that blood will run up to the horses' bridles. An exchange of neutron bombs by both sides will kill millions. The intense radiation from these explosions will cause the flesh literally to melt off the soldiers' bones as they stand on their feet. Of the 4.5 billion people on the planet, one-third will die in this conflagration.

Counting those who died during the Russian invasion, that adds up to 3 billion people—half the population of the planet—who will die within 7 years' time.

Unless something drastic happens, no one will remain alive.

The Day of the Lord

The Day of the Lord exactly coincides with the seven-year Tribulation period of Daniel's Seventieth Week. I use this phrase here because in the Old Testament, the Day of the Lord was always understood to be a time of wrath and judgment. Jesus Himself described the way it is going to be:

> **Immediately after the tribulation of those days shall the sun be darkened, and the moon shall not give her light, and the stars shall fall from heaven, and the powers of the heavens shall be shaken:**
> **And then shall appear the sign of the Son of man in heaven: and then shall all the tribes of the earth mourn, and they shall see the Son of man coming in the clouds of heaven with power and great glory.**
>
> **Matthew 24:29-30**

Suddenly there will be great signs in the heavens. A rider on a white horse will appear at the head of vast armies of angels and glorified saints clothed in fine linen, clean and white. The Apostle John saw the vision:

> **And I saw heaven opened, and behold a white horse; and he that sat upon him was called Faithful and True, and in righteousness he doth judge and make war.**

His eyes were as a flame of fire, and on his head were many crowns; and he had a name written, that no man knew, but he himself.

And he was clothed with a vesture dipped in blood: and his name was called the Word of God.

And the armies which were in heaven followed him upon white horses, clothed in fine linen, white and clean.

And out of his mouth goeth a sharp sword, that with it he should smite the nations: and he shall rule them with a rod of iron: and he treadeth the winepress of the fierceness and wrath of Almighty God.

And he hath on his vesture a name written, KING OF KINGS, AND LORD OF LORDS.

And I saw an angel standing in the sun: and he cried with a loud voice, saying to all the fowls that fly in the midst of heaven, Come and gather yourselves together unto the supper of the great God;

That ye may eat the flesh of kings, and the flesh of captains, and the flesh of mighty men, and the flesh of horses, and of them that sit on them, and the flesh of all men, both free and bond, both small and great.

And I saw the beast, and the kings of the earth, and their armies, gathered to make war against him that sat on the horse, and against his army.

And the beast was taken, and with him the false prophet that wrought miracles before him, with which he deceived them that had received the mark of the beast, and them that worshipped his image. These both were cast alive into a lake of fire burning with brimstone.

And the remnant were slain with the sword of him that sat upon the horse, which sword proceedeth out of his mouth: and all the fowls were filled with their flesh.

Revelation 19:11-21

This is the end of both the Antichrist and the Tribulation. Even so, come quickly, Lord Jesus.

[1]   2 Thessalonians 2:9. See also Daniel 8:23-26 and 11:36-39.

[2]   While many use these terms interchangeably to refer to the whole seven-year period, the chronology of Matthew 24 places the Great Tribulation (verse 21) after the Abomination of Desolation (verse 15). The latter event occurs at the mid-point of the seven-year Tribulation.

[3]   Daniel 9:27 and 11:21-23.

[4]   Ezekial 38 and 39; Daniel 11.

[5]   Daniel 9:27 and 11:30-31.

[6]   Revelation 9:13-19; Daniel 12:44-45.

[7]   Zechariah 14:12.

[8]   Revelation 9:18 and 19:11-20.

[9]   The broad outline I have described is basically agreed upon by virtually all conservative Premillennial Bible scholars, with only minor points of disagreement. These scenarios match pretty closely the perspectives of both Prof. Winkler and prophecy expert Hal Lindsey, although at some points I may have a slightly different slant. I encourage the readers of this book to purchase Hal Lindsey's newer books, *Planet Earth — 200 A.D.* and *The Final Battle*, to gain a deeper understanding of these events.

[10]   There is a deep spiritual truth here. Daniel is described in the Bible as a man "greatly beloved" of God, a man given supernatural abilities by God, a man who prayed to God in defiance of a royal decree and was willing to die rather than deny God. There is no recorded instance in the Bible where Daniel ever committed any sin. He could easily have adopted a self-righteous attitude. Yet he was praying, confessing his sins, when God sent an angel to give him perhaps the single most crucial prophetic revelation in the Bible — the exact date of the coming of the Messiah. We can learn from this that honesty and humility gain God's special favor.

[11]   See Chriswell, *Chriswell Study Bible,* p. 995, and Unger, *Unger's Bible Handbook,* pp. 391-392.

[12]   See also Ezra 7:13-26.

[13]   Unger gives a slightly different time frame but the same basic interpretation. Here I am following Chriswell's detailed chronology: "Calculating from 444 B.C. to 33 A.D., one arrives at 478 years rather than the 483 years required. However, this is due to our reckonings, which are based upon the solar year of 365 days; whereas the Jewish calendar was based upon lunar years of 360 days. When the two calendars are adjusted, and one must do so for accuracy, a difference of

about eight years will be discovered. Allowing an additional year for the transition from B.C. to A.D., the date of 33 A.D. is the date at the end of the sixty-ninth week when Christ is cut off (v. 26)." *Chriswell Study Bible*, p. 995.

[14] Ibid. See also Unger, who agrees: "The final week of seven years constitutes the climax of Jewish history prior to the establishment of the messianic kingdom, 27. It is divided into two half periods (three and a half years each). During the *first half* the 'prince' (world ruler, 'little horn' of 7:8, 24-25) will make a covenant with the Jews, who are restored in Palestine with a resumption of temple worship. In the *middle of the week* the covenant is broken, worship for the Jews ceases (2 Thess. 2:3-4), and the time of the Great Tribulation ensues. The *advent of Christ* the Messiah consummates this period of desolation, bringing everlasting righteousness to Israel, 24, and judgment upon the 'desolator,' the prince, and his hosts (Rev. 19:20).

[15] Ibid. See also Pentecost, *Things to Come*, pp. 332-336, for detailed information about the Antichrist. Much of the information in this chapter is derived from Pentecost.

[16] Daniel 11:36-39.

[17] Revelation 13:3-7.

[18] Revelation 13 and 17.

[19] Daniel 11:31; Matthew 24:15; 2 Thessalonians 2:3-4; Revelation 13:16.

[20] See also Daniel 9:27.

[21] Pentecost explains, "The fact that the Holy Spirit is the restrainer, to be removed from the earth before the Tribulation period begins, must not be interpreted to mean that the Holy Spirit is no longer omnipresent, nor operative in the age. The Spirit will work in and through men. It is only insisted that the particular ministries of the Holy Spirit to the believer in this present age ... do terminate." *Things to Come*, pp. 261-263.

[22] Matthew 27:15-26.

[23] Prince, "Israel and the Church: Parallel Restoration."

[24] Paul English, "Burkett Predicts Hard Times: Christian Economist Urges Church to Take Initiative," *Christian American*, January 1994, pp. 8-9.

[25] These bills are believed to have been printed and distributed by the government of Iran as a means of destabilizing the U.S. economy. Many also believe that eliminating cash could help to control tax fraud, stop the lucrative drug trade, and eliminate money laundering.

[26] "1996: Changes, Choices, and Challenges," *The 700 Club Newswatch Fact Sheet,* January 1, 1996.

[27] My friend Ken Klein has suggested that the False Prophet may really be a global electronic money system, pointing out that the three guard bars in the UPC codes have the numerical values of 6-6-6. Ken Klein, *The False Prophet: Evil Architect of the New World Order* (Eugene, Ore.: Winterhaven, 1992), p. 183

[28] Kim A. Lawton, "Killed in the Line of Duty," *Charisma,* October 1995, pp. 54-59.

[29] William J. Federer, *America's God and Country Encyclopedia of Quotations* (Coppell, Tex.: FAME, 1994), p. 205.

[30] Heidi Scanlon, "Fashionable Bigotry Against Evangelicals," *Christian American,* March 1993, p. 7; Don Feder, "Christian Bashing Reaches New Heights," April 1993, p. 6.

[31] "Cartoon Portrays Christians as Rats," *Christian American,* April 1993, p. 6.

[32] Information about the 1994 political campaigns is from John Wheeler Jr., "Assault on Faith: Liberals Launch Campaign of Bigotry," *Christian American,* September 1994, pp. 1,4.

[33] For an excellent rebuttal of these attacks, see Charles Krauthammer, "Demonizing the Religious Right," *Washington Post,* July 8, 1994, p. A23. See also William J. Bennett, "Credit the Christian Right," *Washington Post,* June 26, 1994, p. C7.

[34] Steve Stone, "Fighting Words: CBN vs. Gay Groups," *Norfolk Virginian-Pilot,* March 1, 1996, p. B1. See also full page anti-Robertson advertisement June 6, 1995, p. E8.

[35] White House Press Conference, April 20, 1993. Quoted in Don McAlvaney, "The Waco Massacre: A Case Study on the Emerging American Police State," *The McAlvaney Intelligence Advisor,* July 1993, pp. 17-18.

[36] Paul Boyer, *When Time Shall Be No More: Prophecy Belief in Modern American Culture* (Cambridge, Mass.: Harvard University Press [Belknap ed.], 1992), pp. 145-146, 254-290. Boyer' thesis is that prophetic and theological beliefs have social consequences: "one cannot fully understand the American public's response to a wide range of international and domestic issues without bearing in mind that millions of men and women view world events and trends, at least in part, through the refracting lens of prophetic belief" (xii). Boyer also claims that "My aim throughout is not to ridicule or trivialize beliefs espoused by millions of Americans, but to understand them and to reflect upon their meaning and implications" (18). However, the tone of condescending skepticism and unbelief permeates the pages of his book.

[37] There is a difference of opinion among Bible scholars as to the exact time of the battle of Gog and Magog. Some think it comes in the middle of the Tribulation period, while others believe it comes at the very beginning. I tend to agree with the latter.

[38] See Hal Lindsey, *The Final Battle*, pp. 246-247.

[39] This is the scenario described in Pat Robertson's fictionalized account of the Tribulation period. If we can derive his doctrine from this book, Pat apparently does not expect massive nuclear warfare to occur. He instead attributes the destruction of those days primarily to the unleashing of powerful natural forces. Robertson, *The End of the Age* (Dallas: Word, 1995), pp. 365-371.

[40] Lindsey, *The Final Battle*, pp. 254-258. Lindsey also notes that Zephaniah 1:15-18 describes a similar scenario, but that no armies are mentioned, just a day of thick darkness and clouds. "Again, it sounds just like the portrait you would expect if you transported an ancient prophet into the 20th or 21st century to witness a nuclear attack," p. 255.

[41] Revelation 9:18.

[42] Information is from John L. Wheeler, Jr., "Collective Security in the New World Order: Biblical and Constitutional Perspectives," Master's Thesis, Regent University, 1991.

[43] President George Bush, "Address to Joint Session of Congress," March 6, 1991 (White House Information Office).

[44] Pat Robertson, *Perspective*, March/April 1991, p. 4. See also his later book , *New World Order* (Dallas: Word, 1991). Robertson opined that Bush was sincere but misguided:
"I know George Bush. I have met with him in the White House, and I personally believe that President Bush is an honorable man and a man of integrity. Nevertheless, I believe that he has become convinced, as Woodrow Wilson was before him, of the idealistic possibilities of a world at peace under the benign leadership of a forum for all nations.
"But I am equally convinced that for the past two hundred years the term *new world order* has been the code phrase of those who desire to destroy the Christian faith and what Pope Pius XI termed the 'Christian social order.' They wish to replace it with an occult-inspired world socialist dictatorship" (p. 92).

[45] United Nations, *Report of the Conference on Disarmament, General Assembly, Official Records: Forty-first Session*, Supplement No. 27 (A/41/27) (New York: United Nations, 1986), pp. 145-150.

[46] White House Press Office, *Executive Summary: The Clinton Administration's Policy on Reforming Multilateral Peace Operations*, May 3, 1994. See also

New York Times News Service, "Clinton Sets Rules for U.S. Involvement in U.N. Peacekeeping," *Norfolk Virginian-Pilot,* May 6, 1994, p. A9.

[47] Rowan Scarborough, "Medic Tainted by Guilty Finding," *Washington Times,* January 26, 1996, p. A6. See also William Norman Grigg, "I Am Not a UN Soldier," *New American,* October 2, 1995, pp. 5-8.

[48] Donald S. McAlvaney, *Toward a New World Order: The Countdown to Armageddon* (Phoenix: Western Pacific, 1992), pp. 342-348.

Chapter 7
Our Blessed Hope

For the grace of God that bringeth salvation hath
appeared to all men,
Teaching us that, denying ungodliness and worldly
lusts, we should live soberly, righteously, and godly, in
this present world;
Looking for that blessed hope, and the glorious
appearing of our great God and Saviour Jesus Christ;
Who gave himself for us, that he might redeem us from
all iniquity, and purify unto himself a peculiar people,
zealous of good works.

Titus 2:11-14

Every true Christian has as his ultimate destination a life of
eternal peace and blissful, glorious existence with God. No matter
what hardships we may have to endure here on Earth, Jesus has
given His disciples the promise of eternal life with Him.

What Is the Rapture?

The blessed hope of every Christian is the return of the Lord Jesus
Christ to redeem His people. This is commonly known as the Rapture.
Jesus told His disciples shortly before He was crucified:

Let not your heart be troubled: ye believe in God,
believe also in me.
In my Father's house are many mansions: if it were not
so, I would have told you. I go to prepare a place for you.
And if I go and prepare a place for you, I will come
again, and receive you unto myself; that where I am, there
ye may be also.

John 14:1-3

This is Jesus' promise to all those who put their trust in Him—He will come again and receive them unto Himself, and for all of eternity they will be with Him. It has been said truly that this Scripture is the first New Testament revelation of the Rapture of the Church.

For the Christian, death does not hold terror because death is not the end of existence but a new beginning of a much better life than he has ever known before. This agrees with the words of the Apostle Paul, who wrote to the Corinthians of his confident assurance that "to be absent from the body" is "to be present with the Lord" (2 Corinthians 5:8).

While some, unfortunately, have chosen to characterize a heavenly focus as "escapist mentality," the fact is that in the Bible, such a focus is presented as a source of hope, comfort and encouragement to those believers who, as Jesus also said, were suffering persecution in the world for the sake of their faith in Him.

The Apostle Paul is the human author of the doctrine of the Rapture, which is derived from two prominent and irrefutable passages of Scripture. The first describes what will happen when Jesus comes for His people.

> **But I would not have you to be ignorant, brethren, concerning them which are asleep, that ye sorrow not, even as others which have no hope.**
>
> **For if we believe that Jesus died and rose again, even so them also which sleep in Jesus will God bring with him.**
>
> **For this we say to you <u>by the word of the Lord</u>, that we which are alive and remain unto the coming of the Lord shall not prevent them which are asleep.**
>
> **For <u>the Lord himself shall descend from heaven</u> with a shout, with the voice of the archangel, and with the trump of God: and <u>the dead in Christ shall rise first</u>:**
>
> **Then <u>we which are alive and remain shall be caught up together with them in the clouds, to meet the Lord in the air</u>: and so shall we ever be with the Lord.**
>
> **Wherefore <u>comfort one another with these words</u>.**
>
> 1 Thessalonians 4:13-18

Paul says that Christians should not be ignorant of this doctrine, but should take comfort from the knowledge that Jesus is going to come for them, and that they should "comfort one another with these words." He points out that Christians are not like the rest of the people in the world, who "have no hope" at death.

Paul gives the sequence of events for the Rapture: first those believers in Christ who have died in previous times will be raised, then all those who are still alive when Jesus comes, will be "caught up" to meet the Lord in the air and to remain with Him forever.[1]

This is actually a two-fold event happening at one time. First there is the resurrection of the dead in Christ, then the Rapture of the living saints. This Rapture is actually a "translation" of a certain group of living people into the Eternal State without the necessity of their experiencing physical death, as also happened to Enoch and Elijah.[2]

Why God has chosen to change these particular saints in this way, we do not know. But that He has so determined, we cannot doubt.

Paul—perhaps anticipating some future opposition to the doctrine—also takes great pains to point out that this message is not something he made up, but it comes directly "by the word of the Lord."

Who Goes In the Rapture?

And in another famous passage dealing with the resurrection of the dead, Paul describes exactly what will happen when this same event occurs.

> **Now this I say, brethren, that flesh and blood cannot inherit the kingdom of God; neither doth corruption inherit incorruption.**
>
> **Behold, I shew you a mystery; We shall not all sleep, but we shall all be changed,**
>
> **In a moment, in the twinkling of an eye, at the last trump: for the trumpet shall sound, and the dead shall be raised incorruptible, and we shall all be changed.**
>
> **For this corruptible must put on incorruption, and this mortal must put on immortality.**
>
> **So when this corruptible shall have put on incorruption, and this mortal shall have put on immortality, then shall be brought to pass the saying that is written, Death is swallowed up in victory.**
>
> **O death, where is thy sting? O grave, where is thy victory?**
>
> **1 Corinthians 15:50-55**

What Paul is clearly saying here is that, at a certain point in time, all the believers in Jesus Christ—whether previously dead or still alive—are going to be changed from the mortal state to the glorified immortal state. The earthly bodies in which we have lived our mortal lives are going to be changed into glorified resurrection bodies in which we shall live for all of eternity. This also corresponds to the First Resurrection of Revelation 20:5.

The most glorious part of this is that we will then have the same kind of body as the Lord Jesus since His resurrection. According to 1 John 3:2,

> **Beloved, now are we the sons of God, and it doth not yet appear what we shall be: but we know that, <u>when he shall appear, we shall be like him; for we shall see him as he is</u>.**

Every born-again believer who has trusted Christ and has been placed by the Holy Spirit into the Body of Christ, which is the Church, is one day going to have a glorified resurrection body just like Jesus now has. This is the plain teaching of the Scripture. We have looked at four different passages dealing with this event, and they all agree.

Still, the libraries are filled with books by men teaching various theories of partial or multiple Raptures. Some say that only those who are watching and waiting will go with Jesus—the wise virgins with oil in their lamps. Others say only the spiritually mature will go, and the immature will be left behind to have their faith purified by the Tribulation.

Others say that there will be multiple raptures at different points in time, and they count Enoch and Elijah, and sometimes even Moses and Jesus, as separate raptures.

For example, Albert Batts, a truly saintly man of God who faithfully preached the Word of God for more than 60 years, taught that Moses must have been raptured in a chariot of fire because Elijah was translated from Moses' grave site "in a whirlwind," so what else could the chariot have been for?[3] I can't accept this flawed premise.

Hilton Sutton, a prominent Word of Faith Bible teacher, counts seven raptures: Enoch, Elijah, Jesus, the Church, the Mid-Tribulation saints, the 144,000 Jewish evangelists, and the Two Witnesses of Revelation 11.[4]

I certainly can acknowledge that Enoch and Elijah were translated because the Bible clearly says so, and this is a "type" of the Rapture of the Church. But I have no scriptural evidence that they have received glorified resurrection bodies as yet. As for Jesus and the Two Witnesses, these are strictly speaking resurrections, not translations. As for the evangelists and the Mid-Tribulation saints, this appears to be pure speculation, because the Bible never describes how these people get to heaven. One might just as easily assume that they had been martyred as translated.

My personal belief is that the Rapture will be a unique event in history, just as was the resurrection and ascension of Jesus Christ, whom the Bible calls the "firstfruits of them that slept." I believe that Jesus Christ is the only Person who presently has a glorified resurrection body, and no one else will get one until the Rapture, and then we'll all go together.

I do not believe that there will be separate raptures for spiritual versus immature Christians. There have been plenty of Christians who have died spiritually immature, like the thief on the cross, and while they may have limited rewards in heaven, they'll be there just the same.[5] And they also will be part of the First Resurrection that accompanies the Rapture.

Paul said that when the Rapture occurs, first the dead in Christ will be resurrected, and then immediately, along with those who are alive, they will all be changed in a moment of time, in the twinkling of an eye, and all will be caught up to be with the Lord in the air.

That is indeed a blessed hope and a reason to be both comforted and encouraged, and that's good enough for me.

When Does the Rapture Occur?

There are a lot of different opinions in the Church, even among committed Premillennial Bible scholars, as to the exact time of the Rapture. Sincere men of God disagree, sometimes strongly. While everyone may have good intentions, everyone cannot be right. Let's examine the evidence.

The Post-Tribulation Rapture

One prominent view, which appears to be growing more prevalent all the time, is the Post-Tribulation position, which holds that the Church will go through the entire seven-year Tribulation period and will be Raptured to meet Jesus in the air when He returns at the end of that time to destroy the Antichrist and to establish His Kingdom.

This view, which is sometimes called "classical Premillennialism," is held by many outstanding men of God in the mainstream Evangelical and Independent Charismatic camps.

Pat Robertson's newest book, a novel called *The End of the Age,* offers a fictionalized but very detailed version of what it might be like for some Christians to go through the Tribulation period.[6]

The Post-Trib doctrine is based upon the fact that the Bible does not clearly say in unmistakable terms that the Rapture will occur before the Tribulation, while several Scriptures seem to suggest that it will come at the end. Nowhere does the Bible say the Second Coming is in two parts.

One of the passages often cited is in Matthew 24, where Jesus says:

> **<u>Immediately after the tribulation of those days</u> shall the sun be darkened, and the moon shall not give her light, and the stars shall fall from the heaven, and the powers of the heavens shall be shaken:**
>
> **And then shall appear the sign of the Son of man in heaven: and then shall all the tribes of the Earth mourn, and <u>they shall see the Son of man coming in the clouds of heaven with power and great glory.</u>**
>
> **And <u>he shall send his angels with the sound of a great trumpet, and they shall gather together his elect</u> from the four winds, from one end of heaven to the other.**
>
> **Matthew 24:29-31**

For Post-Tribs, this passage clearly shows that Jesus comes at the end of the Tribulation and sends His angels out to gather up all of his disciples. Revelation 7:14 describes a "great multitude" in white robes who came out of "great tribulation." Coupled with other verses like "He that shall endure to the end, the same shall be saved" (Matthew 24:13), it is obvious to Post-Tribs that the Church will go through this Tribulation period.

And why should it not? Jesus said that in the world His disciples will have tribulation (John 16:33). Christians have been horribly persecuted throughout history, with many martyrs choosing to die agonizing deaths rather than to renounce their faith in Christ. Why should the pampered Church of the Last Days seek to escape the honor of suffering for the Lord?

Objections to the Post-Trib Rapture

Those who disagree with this position point out that Matthew 24:31 does not define who the "elect" are, but many believe this verse applies to natural Jews who will be regathered to the land of Israel, especially since verse 32 begins the parable of the fig tree. Up until verse 26, Jesus was talking to His disciples, using the word "you." But in verse 30, He says that "they" shall see the Son of man coming in the clouds.

Anyway, the Church is not scattered all over Heaven at this point in time, but is part of the army returning with Jesus.[7]

While it is true that Christians are called upon to endure much persecution in the world, Jesus also said that His disciples should "Watch ye therefore, and pray always, that ye may be accounted worthy to escape all these things that shall come to pass, and to stand before the Son of man" (Luke 21:36). If Jesus said it, that must mean there's something to escape.

One distinctive aspect of Post-Trib apologetics seems to be an outright and growing hostility toward the Pre-Trib Rapture doctrine. Usually it takes the form of a disparaging comment to the effect that, after all, this Pre-Trib Rapture idea is a fairly recent development in church history, and it came as a spurious prophecy around 1830 from a so-called "female teenage mystic" named Margaret MacDonald. In its most virulent form, the attack charges that there is an active conspiracy to hide the possibly demonic origins of the doctrine and to deceive the average Christian as to its pernicious and false nature.[8]

Both of these charges are untrue. First of all, the girl in question never taught a Pre-Trib Rapture. That doctrine has been derived over time as men of God have diligently studied the Word of God. There has been no conspiracy and no cover-up. The fact that the doctrine has arisen in the past 200 years is easily explained by the progressive revelation of Present Truth to the Church by the Holy Spirit.[9]

I highly recommend Dr. Tim LaHaye's excellent book *No Fear of the Storm* for those interested in learning more about the accurate historical and theological details of the Pre-Tribulation Rapture doctrine.

The Mid-Tribulation Rapture

Those who hold to a Mid-Tribulation Rapture believe that the Church will go through the first part of the Tribulation period, but will then be raptured at the midpoint, thus escaping the terrible plagues of the last three and a half years of Great Tribulation. This position, which has been called the "new Protestant Purgatory" by Hal Lindsey, is also flawed.

The distinctive characteristic of the Mid-Trib view is that it spiritualizes the interpretation of the Two Witnesses of Revelation 11 and identifies them as either Israel and the Church or as the dead and living Christians. Either way, Mid-Tribs view the Church as enduring the first half of the Tribulation, which they view as the "wrath of man," and escaping the "wrath of God" during the last three and a half years of Great Tribulation.

The problem with this view is that it unnecessarily complicates the interpretation of the passage, which is obviously referring to two literal individuals. Moreover, the first part of the Tribulation has its share of terrible plagues, so the distinction is somewhat artificial.

The Mid-Trib Rapture theory therefore is really just a modified version of the Pre-Tribulation view, so the other arguments for and against it are essentially the same.

This position is the least popular of the three major views.

The Pre-Tribulation Rapture

The most prevalent view among traditional Dispensationalists—which now includes most Fundamentalists and Pentecostals, and some Evangelicals and independent Charismatics—is that Jesus comes back for the Church before the beginning of the seven-year Tribulation Period.

This view is called Pre-Tribulation Rapture, and it is based in part on the words of Jesus in Revelation 3:10 to the Church at Philadelphia:

> *Because thou hast kept the word of my patience, I also will keep thee from the hour of temptation, which shall come upon all the world, to try them that dwell on the earth.*

Here Jesus is promising to "keep from the hour of temptation" the faithful Church that had kept His Word.[10]

Remember that the Tribulation period coming upon the Earth is a time of absolutely unprecedented misery and grief, such as has never been before and will never be again. It is called the time when the "vials of the wrath of God" will be poured out upon the Earth (Revelation 16:1).

This matches another teaching of the Apostle Paul concerning the Day of the Lord, which he likened to the coming of a "thief in the night." The phrase "Day of the Lord" has a specific meaning derived from the Old Testament, and it corresponds to the entire seven-year Tribulation period.[11] But Paul said that this did not apply to the true Church.

> **But of the times and seasons, brethren, you have no need that I should write unto you.**
>
> **For yourselves know perfectly that the day of the Lord so cometh as a thief in the night.**
>
> **For <u>when they shall say, Peace and safety; then sudden destruction cometh upon them</u>, as travail upon a woman with child; and they shall not escape.**
>
> **<u>But ye, brethren, are not in darkness, that that day should overtake you as a thief.</u>**
>
> **Ye are all children of light, and the children of the day: we are not of the night, nor of darkness.**
>
> **Therefore let us not sleep, as do others; but let us watch and be sober.**
>
> **For they that sleep sleep in the night; and they that be drunken are drunken in the night.**
>
> **But let us, who are of the day, be sober, putting on the breastplate of faith and love; and for an helmet the hope of salvation.**
>
> **<u>For God hath not appointed us unto wrath</u>, but to obtain salvation by our Lord Jesus Christ,**
>
> **Who died for us, that, whether we wake or sleep, we should live together with him**
>
> **<u>Wherefore comfort yourselves together</u>, and edify one another, even as also ye do.**
>
> **1 Thessalonians 5:1-11**

Paul is here drawing a clear distinction between the one group "they" and "them," who will say "Peace and safety" but instead reap sudden destruction, and the other group "you" and "us," who are "not appointed unto wrath, but to obtain salvation." Paul says that the believers can take comfort from these facts and edify one another. They would hardly be comforted by the thought of having to endure the Tribulation period soon.

The Types of Noah and Lot

A "type" in the Bible is a kind of pattern which foreshadows something else which is to come. We have already considered the fact that the Great Tribulation period is a time of God's severe judgment on the Earth for its exceeding wickedness, as it was in the Days of Noah. But the Biblical story of Noah and the Flood is also a "type" of the Church and the Rapture. Jesus said in Matthew 24:38-39 that

> *For as in the days that were before the flood they were eating and drinking, marrying and giving in marriage, <u>until the day that Noe entered into the ark,</u>*
> *And <u>knew not until the flood came,</u> and took them all away; so shall also the coming of the Son of man be.*

Noah and the Ark are a "type" of the Church and the Rapture. Noah entered into the Ark, a place of safety and absolute security prepared by God. No one else even knew what was going on, until the Flood suddenly came and carried the wicked away to judgment.

In the same way the Church will be caught up in the safety of the Rapture, and the people in the world won't have a clue that judgment is about to begin until suddenly it breaks out all around them.

Some people say they don't believe in a "secret Rapture." I don't either. Jesus is going to come for His Bride with the voice of an archangel and the Trump of God, and I believe that it will attract some attention. So it may not be secret, but it will most certainly be sudden and unexpected. While the Church will be caught up into Heaven, the world will be caught completely unawares and swept into judgment.

Another Old Testament "type" is Lot in Sodom. According to Jesus, this is how conditions in the world will be when He returns:

> *Likewise also as it was in the days of Lot; they did eat, they drank, they bought, they sold, they planted, they builded;*

> But *the same day that Lot went out of Sodom, it rained fire and brimstone from heaven, and destroyed them all.*
> *Even thus shall it be in the day when the Son of man is revealed.*
>
> Luke 17:28-30

Lot was a righteous man living in the midst of great wickedness. God told Abraham that He was going to destroy Sodom and Gomorrah because of their grievous sins, and there were not enough righteous people found in those cities to avert the predetermined destruction of God.

And yet God could not release that divine judgment until Lot had left the city and was safely removed. In the same way, the only thing now restraining the awful judgment of God on this sin-cursed Earth is the presence of the Church. And when that restraint is removed in the Rapture, the judgment will be released.[12]

Some will object to this typology, arguing that God can protect His people through the Tribulation, just as He protected the Israelites who lived in the land of Goshen during the plagues God sent upon Egypt. God judged Pharaoh's people but the people of God were spared.[13]

Of course this is true. God can and does protect His people in the midst of circumstances that devastate others. But I personally see this kind of providential preservation as more typical of God's dealing with men in the normal course of the events of life, rather than in the context of the unique period of Tribulation which is to come upon the Earth.

The clear Biblical typology of the Last Days is deliverance out of the time of wrath, as described above, not merely protection through it.

The Rapture is a Mystery

The Bible says this doctrine of the Rapture is a mystery.[14] It was not revealed in Old Testament times, and it is not understood today except by revelation of the Spirit of God.[15]

The religious leaders of the Old Testament could not discern the fact that the coming of the Messiah was a two-part event, in which He would come first in mercy as a suffering servant to die on the Cross, and later in judgment as a King to rule in glory, although the prophecies revealing these truths were right there in the Scriptures.

Likewise today many religious leaders do not seem to be able to discern that the Second Coming of Jesus is a two-part event, in which He comes once in mercy *for* His saints and later returns in judgment *with* His saints. The Rapture of the Church will occur before the Tribulation period and the glorious Return of Christ will occur at the very end.

These facts are also plainly in the Scriptures.

But let me reiterate at this point the central truth of our Blessed Hope: Jesus Himself is coming back in person for His people, and when that time comes, we're all going to meet Him together.

It won't matter then what our theology was, or how we thought it was going to happen, because it will be a sovereign act of Almighty God.

———◦———

[1] Some people object to the term "Rapture" because they can't find it in their concordance. But this in no way affects the scriptural truth of the doctrine, which is clearly taught in the Bible. Dr. Ryrie points out that the term is derived from the Latin word *rapturo,* which is the literal translation of the Greek *harpazo,* which means "to snatch or take away." So the word "Rapture" is perfectly in harmony with the literal Biblical text. Charles C. Ryrie, *What You Should Know About the Rapture* (Chicago: Moody, 1981), pp. 27-28.

[2] Genesis 5:21-24; 2 Kings 2:11.

[3] Albert Batts, *Doctrine and Qualifications for the Rapture,* 2nd ed. (Chattanooga, Tenn.: Albert Batts, n.d.), pp. 11-12.

[4] Hilton Sutton, *He's Coming! The Glorious Appearing of Jesus and the Seven Raptures of God* (Tulsa: Harrison House, 1983), pp. 9-72.

[5] Luke 23:39-43.

[6] Pat Robertson, *The End of the Age* (Dallas: Word, 1995).

[7] See Zechariah 14:5; Revelation 19:8, 14; 2 Thessalonians 1:10.

[8] The latter position is advanced by Dave MacPherson, *The Incredible Cover-Up* (Plainfield, N.J.: Logos, 1975. Rpt. ed, Medford, Ore.: Omega, 1980).

[9] LaHaye, *No Fear of the Storm,* pp. 115-134.

[10] Greek scholar Kenneth Taylor, who has done several paraphrased versions of the Bible from original texts, has pointed out that "keep from" is not the only acceptable translation of this verse. According to Taylor, "The inference is not clear in the Greek as to whether this means 'kept from' or 'kept through' the coming horror." Kenneth Taylor, *Living Prophecies: The Minor Prophets Paraphrased, with Daniel and Revelation* (Wheaton, Ill.: Tyndale House, 1965), p. 189.

By contrast, both Dr. Ryrie and Dr. LaHaye argue persuasively that not only does the Greek preposition ek normally mean "out of," the promise of Revelation 3:10 involves much more than merely being kept from the *events* of the Tribulation, but from the *time* of the Tribulation as well. Ryrie, *What You Should Know About the Rapture*, pp. 112-118. See also LaHaye, *No Fear of the Storm*, pp. 229-231.

[11] Ryrie, *What You Should Know About the Rapture*, pp. 93-106.

[12] Genesis 19:1-29.

[13] Exodus 7-12.

[14] 1 Corinthians 15:51.

[15] Ephesians 1:17-19.

Afterward
Are You Ready?

Therefore be ye also ready: for in such an hour as ye think not the Son of man cometh.

Matthew 24:44

People loved Ronald Reagan because he made them feel good, smiling kindly and speaking from his heart about "morning in America." He believed that things were going to get better and he made others believe it, too. The Great Communicator was an inveterate optimist, and he knew how to win friends and influence people.

Reagan was also keenly aware of Bible prophecy and the great destruction that was predicted for the Last Days, and he equated that destruction with nuclear warfare. As the leader of the Free World, he felt a moral obligation to do all within his power to prevent that calamity from coming upon the people of America and the rest of the world. That is why he signed the nuclear arms reduction treaties with the Soviets.[1]

I believe that Ronald Reagan's intentions were good but that he was the victim of his own optimism. I think that because he wanted so desperately to believe that men are basically good, he allowed himself to be manipulated by his enemies, who were basically evil.

History will judge whether Reagan's good-hearted efforts will ultimately prove successful. Personally, I would place my bets on the prophets of the Bible who were inspired by the Spirit of God.

Most people don't like to hear bad news, they want someone to promise them peace. That's why God's prophets were rejected in their own day, and that is the same way it will be at the very end. The Antichrist will promise to bring peace to the world, and the people will believe him.

But the Bible says that when men least expect it, calamity will srike.

For yourselves know perfectly that the day of the Lord so cometh as a thief in the night.

> For **when they shall say, Peace and safety; then sudden destruction cometh upon them,** as travail upon a woman with child; **and they shall not escape.**
>
> 1 Thessalonians 5:2-3

Don't tell us these things, some will object. This is just "doom and gloom" fear-mongering. Tell us something pleasant. Let's party.

Counting Down to 2000

Lots of people have their attention focused on the coming year 2000. For the New Agers, that date signifies the dawning of the "Age of Aquarius."

Some of them have even planned a big New Years Eve party for December 31, 1999, at the Great Pyramid of Cheops in Giza, Egypt, to ring in not just the new year but the New Millennium as well. Some of the top celebrity entertainers and many of the most famous people in the world are expected to attend the 3,000-person World Millennium Charity Ball.[2]

Those who can't make it to Giza on the specially chartered Queen Elizabeth II ocean liner will have to party someplace else. Ballrooms at the world's most famous hotels—the Rainbow Room in Manhattan, the Savoy Hotel in London, the Space Needle in Seattle, the Kaiser Ball in Vienna, the Waldorf-Astoria in New York, even the 17 Walt Disney World hotels in Orlando—are already sold out with waiting lists.[3]

Meanwhile, the United Nations is waiting for all the nuclear powers to turn in their guns, while the Russians and Chinese are eyeing each other warily and inching toward the Middle East, and Iran is racing Iraq to build a bomb. The Pope is looking for another Fatima, and the Jews are waiting for a Temple and a Messiah. Somewhere in Europe, the future Antichrist is waiting in the wings, already at work behind the scenes.

All over the world, for most folks, life goes blithely on. People are buying and selling, marrying and giving in marriage, living their lives for themselves, with scarcely a thought for God. Except for the millions who are starving, dying of AIDS, or being sliced to pieces inside the womb.

Still the questions we have raised confront us.

Will Christians ultimately be persecuted in America like defenseless Jews were in Nazi Germany?

Will the Big One finally hit San Francisco? Will California crumble off into the Pacific Ocean?

Will the world's economy crash? Will they call in all the cash?

Will an evil Antichrist soon seize power over Europe?

Will Russia's nuclear arsenal fall into the hands of Zhirinovsky or another demented demagogue who wants to be "Master of the World"?

Will Russia really invade Israel between now and the year 2000, as some analysts expect? Will a slumbering America be on the target list?

Will the world survive a global nuclear holocaust?

Will Jesus come back today?

Nobody knows for sure when any of these things will happen, but their outline is visible ahead, looming on the horizon of history.[4]

After reading this book, you should be able to discern these "signs of the times" and understand that we truly are living in the Last Days.

But the Bible says that many people will choose denial.

> **Knowing this first, that <u>there shall come in the last days scoffers, walking after their own lusts</u>,**
> **<u>And saying, Where is the promise of his coming?</u> for since the fathers fell asleep, all things continue as they were from the beginning of the creation.**
> **For <u>this they are willingly ignorant of</u>, that by the word of God the heavens were of old, and the earth standing out of the water and in the water:**
> **Whereby the world that then was, being overflowed with water, perished:**
> **But the heavens and the earth, which are now, by the same word are kept in store, reserved unto fire against the day of judgment and perdition of ungodly men.**
> **2 Peter 3:3-7**

We need not be "willingly ignorant" of God's revealed truth. The signs of our times show plainly that Jesus is coming back soon. Denying these facts will neither change them nor make them go away.

Trust in God

These "things to come" that we have studied are awful and frightening, especially to someone who does not know the love of

God. But to those who are His, the return of Jesus Christ to Earth is not a cause for alarm or a reason for fear, but a source of strength, hope, and joy.

Yes, I feel sorry for all those who will perish during this terrible time of Tribulation. But I am not responsible for their sins nor for their choices to reject God. It is my hope and prayer that this book will serve as a warning and that God will use it to save as many as possible.

I didn't write the prophecies, I am just a messenger attempting to explain the meaning of the Word of God. God doesn't need me to try to defend Him or His plans for history and eternity. It's beyond me.

However, I encourage you to be like the Bereans in Acts 17:11, who "searched the scriptures daily, whether those things were so." If I have said something wrong, don't listen to me. But if you see it in the Word, let God speak to your heart and reveal His truth to you.

I can only say two things. First, in my own experience, the Lord Jesus Christ has proven Himself a loving and faithful "friend that sticketh closer than a brother." He will do the same for anyone who will let Him.

Second, there is no unrighteousness with God, and His ways are perfect. The Bible says in Genesis 17:25, "Shall not the Judge of all the earth do right?" All of God's dealings with men are perfectly fair and just.

Those who know Jesus personally, know that He is good and that they can trust Him totally. And that brings us to the crucial question that every person who reads this book must answer individually.

The Bible says in Romans 14:12,

So then every one of us shall give account of himself to God.

Are You Ready?

What about you? Do you know Jesus Christ as your Savior? Are you ready to meet Him when He comes?

He is coming soon. Will He return as your Savior or as your Judge? That choice is yours alone.

The game is almost over for this weary old world. The "two minute" warning has sounded. The clock is ticking off the seconds until the end.

The Bible says in 2 Corinthians 6:2,

> **Behold, <u>now is the accepted time</u>; behold, <u>now is the day of salvation</u>.**

Right now, today, God offers His mercy and forgiveness freely to all who will accept it. To receive Jesus Christ as your Savior and His free gift of eternal life, you must do two simple things.

First, you must repent of your sins. The Bible says in Romans 3:23,

> **For <u>all have sinned</u> and come short of the glory of God.**

Men don't like to admit that they are sinners, but that is what God's Word says. To repent means literally to "change your mind," confess your sins, and turn to God for forgiveness.

The second thing you have to do is simply to ask Jesus to be your Savior. Romans 10:13 says plainly that

> **Whosoever shall call upon the name of the Lord shall be saved.**

"Whosoever" applies to everyone. It applies to you. The name of the Lord is Jesus Christ. He died on the Cross for your sins because He loves you. He rose from the dead and is alive today on the right hand of power.

Call on the name of Jesus now. Simply ask Him, by faith, to forgive your sins, to come into your heart, and to be your Savior.

Then, when He comes again, He'll be coming for you.

> **The word is nigh thee, even in thy mouth, and in thy heart: that is, <u>the word of faith, which we preach</u>;**
> **That if thou shalt <u>confess with thy mouth the Lord Jesus</u>, and shalt <u>believe in thine heart that God hath raised him from the dead</u>, thou shalt be saved.**
> **For with the heart man believeth unto righteousness; and <u>with the mouth confession is made unto salvation</u>.**
> **Romans 10:8-10**

Will you take a public stand for Jesus Christ as the rightful King of all Creation? Jesus said that if you will confess Him before men, He will confess you before His Father in Heaven.[5]

To choose Jesus Christ in the Last Days will not be an easy thing to do. The pressure to reject Him will be intense, and following Him will be costly. But the reward of faith is eternal life with God, and the alternative is eternal damnation in the lake of fire with Satan and his demons.

The choice is yours. Will you choose Jesus, God's true Christ, or the coming Antichrist, Satan's servant?

⟶➤●◄⟵

[1]   Boyer, *When Time Shall Be No More,* p. 142. See also Martin Anderson, *Revolution* (New York: Harcourt, Brace, Jovanovich, 1988), pp. 70-79.

[2]   Lindsey, *Planet Earth — 2000 A.D.,* p. 305.

[3]   Prodigy News Service, January 10, 1996. Quoted in N.W. Hutchings, "Countdown 2000," *Prophetic Observer,* February 1996, p. 4.

[4]   Setting dates invariably fails. One writer sold two million copies of a book, predicting that the Rapture would occur at the Jewish holiday of Rosh Hashana in September 1988 and that Russia's invasion of Israel would come three weeks later. False predictions such as this unfortunately have caused some to reject the legitimacy of all prophetic writing. Edgar C. Whisenant, *88 Reasons Why the Rapture Will Be in 1988: New Expanded Edition* (Nashville: World Bible Society, 1988). See also Boyer, *When Time Shall Be No More,* p. 130.

[5]   Matthew 10:32-33.

Selected Bibliography with Notes

The following reference materials represent a variety of perspectives on end-time Bible prophecy. Some have been quoted in this book, while most have served as general background material. For those who wish to explore these matters in greater detail, notes have been supplied to indicate what type of information each source contains. Other peripheral sources are referenced in footnotes but are not listed here.

Academic American Encyclopedia, Electronic Version. Danbury, Conn.: Grolier, 1995.

Encyclopedia Americana, 1957 ed. S.v. "Israel"; "Jewish History and Society—Zionism," by Isidore Abramowitz; "Jewish History and Society—Social and Economic Developments in the 19th and 20th Centuries," by Jacob Lestschinsky.

The 700 Club **Newswatch Fact Sheets.** Virginia Beach, Va.: Christian Broadcasting Network, 1995-1996. Various topics. Cutting-edge news items from a Christian perspective.

Bahnsen, Greg L. *By This Standard: The Authority of God's Law Today.* Tyler, Texas: Institute for Christian Economics, 1985. An articulate introduction to Reconstructionist theology.

Bass, Clarence B. *Backgrounds to Dispensationalism: Its Historical Genesis and Ecclesiastical Implications.* Grand Rapids: Eerdmans, 1960. Rpt. ed., Grand Rapids: Baker Books, 1977. A scholarly treatise attacking Dispensational theology as a break with traditional church history and positions. For reference only.

Batts, Albert H. *Doctrine and Qualifications for the Rapture.*
2nd ed. Chattanooga, Tenn.: Albert Batts, n.d.
A series of Rapture sermons by a Church of God radio preacher.

Bennett, William J. *The Index of Leading Cultural Indicators.*
Washington, D.C.: Heritage Foundation/Empower America, 1993.
Statistics reflecting American cultural trends over the past
30 years.

Benware, Paul N. *Understanding End Times Prophecy: A Compre-hensive Approach.* Foreword by Charles Ryrie. Chicago:
Moody Press, 1995.
A balanced, scholarly, yet understandable overview of the
different theological perspectives on Biblical prophecy.

Boyer, Paul. *When Time Shall Be No More: Prophecy Belief in
Modern American Culture.* Cambridge, Mass.: Harvard
University Press [Belknap], 1992.
An essentially skeptical academic analysis of American
prophecy believers, whose obsession with end-time eschatology could be unhealthy and socially dangerous, written by a
professing Christian.

Byers, Marvin. *The Final Victory: The Year 2000.* Foreword by
Gen. Jose Efrain Rios Montt. Shippensburg, Pa.: Companion
Press, 1991.
Lots of diligent Bible study represented here, but it sets the
date of the Rapture at 1996 "in the Church" and 2000 "for the
Church."

Chriswell, W.A. *The Chriswell Study Bible.* Nashville: Thomas
Nelson, 1979.
Enlightening textual notes by an eminent Bible teacher.

Dake, Finnis Jennings. *God's Plan For Man: The Key to the
World's Storehouse of Wisdom.* Lawrenceville, Ga.: Dake Bible
Sales, 1977.
Like trying to drink from a fire hose. Lots of Scriptures to study
for yourself. Some conclusions drawn are questionable.
Pentecostal.

Dailey, Timothy J. *The Gathering Storm.* Foreword by D. Stuart Briscoe. Tarrytown, N.Y.: Fleming H. Revell, 1992.
An eyewitness account of dramatic events in the Middle East.

Erickson, Millard J. *Contemporary Options in Eschatology.* Grand Rapids:Baker, 1977. Paperback ed., 1987.
An exhaustive overview of major eschatological systems.

Fitschen, Steven W. "An Evaluation of Covenant Theology and Dispensationalism." M.Div. research paper, Regent University, 1989. Includes "On Paul and Reconstruction: Two Views of the Law," 1988.
Scholarly theological research which finds flaws in both Covenant theology and Dispensationalism and proposes a synthesis.

Gaebelin, Frank E., gen. ed. *The Expositor's Bible Commentary.* 12 vols. Grand Rapids: Zondervan, 1981. Vol. 12: Hebrews— Revelation. Alan F. Johnson, "Revelation," pp. 399—603.
Scholarly exposition line by line through the Book of Revelation.

Hamon, Bill. *The Eternal Church.* Phoenix: Christian International Publishers, [1981].
An excellent resource on progressive revelation in church history from the Charismatic perspective. Easily understood by laymen.

Hunt, Dave. *The Cult Explosion.* Irvine, Cal.: Harvest House, 1980.
Analysis of the New Age doctrines behind the proliferation of cults.

Hutchings, N.W. *Petra in History and Prophecy.* Foreword by Dave Breese. Oklahoma City: Hearthstone Publishing, 1991.
Tells where Israel will hide during the Great Tribulation period.

_____, ed. *The Gospel Truth.* Oklahoma City: Southwest Radio Church, 1981-89. "Restoration of All Things," March 1982.
Prophecy newsletter from Dispensational perspective. Deals with the restoration of Israel to the land and the necessity of rebuilding the Jewish Temple before the return of Christ. Also other issues on a variety of topics related to end-time Bible prophecy.

Irvine, Doreen. *Freed From Witchcraft.* Nashville:
  Thomas Nelson, 1973.
  The true story of a practicing witch who came to Christ.

Johnstone, Patrick. *Operation World: The Day-By-Day Guide to
  Praying for the World.* 5th ed. Grand Rapids: Zondervan, 1993.
  Definitive reference resource on world missions.

Kah, Gary H. *The Demonic Roots of Globalism.* Lafayette, La.:
  Huntington House, 1995.
  Reveals New Age doctrines that undergird the globalist movement.

Klein, Ken. *The False Prophet.* Eugene, Ore.: Winterhaven, 1992.
  Analyzes the occult roots of the coming world banking system.

Koch, Kurt. *Occult Bondage and Deliverance.* Grand Rapids:
  Kregel, 1970.
  A respected scholar examines the occult phenomena of today.

LaHaye, Tim. *No Fear of the Storm: Why Christians Will Escape
  All the Tribulation.* Sisters, Ore.: Multnomah, 1992.
  An outstanding defense of the Pre-Trib Rapture by a con-
  temporary Christian leader. Highly recommended.

Larkin, Clarence. *The Book of Revelation: A Study of the Last
  Prophetic Book of the Holy Scriptures.* Philadelphia:
  Larkin Estate, 1919.
  A classic of early Dispensational prophetic interpretation.

Lightle, Steve. *Exodus II: Let My People Go.* Kingwood, Tex.:
  Hunter Books, 1983.
  Gives insight into God's sovereign move to return the Jews
  to Israel.

Lindsey, Hal. *The Late Great Planet Earth.* Grand Rapids:
  Zondervan, 1970. Rpt. ed., New York: Bantam, 1980.

_____. *The Liberation of Planet Earth.* Grand Rapids: Zondervan,
  1974. Rpt. ed., New York: Bantam, 1980.

_____. *The Terminal Generation.* Old Tappan, N.J.: Revell, 1976. Rpt. ed., New York: Bantam, 1980.

_____. *The 1980's: Countdown to Armageddon.* New York: Bantam, 1981.
Four popular earlier books on Pre-Trib prophecy, written for laymen.

_____. *Planet Earth—2000 A.D.* Palos Verdes, Cal.: Western Front, 1994.
This is *The Late Great Planet Earth* revisited 25 years later. Very good.

_____. *The Final Battle.* Palos Verdes, Cal.: Western Front, 1995.
Lindsey's latest, with keen insights into geopolitical developments setting the stage for Battle of Armageddon. Highly recommended.

McAlvany, Donald S. *Toward a New World Order: The Countdown to Armageddon.* Phoenix: Western Pacific, 1992.
Hard-hitting factual analysis of imminent dangers of globalism. Highly recommended.

MacPherson, Dave. *The Incredible Cover-Up.* Foreword by Jim McKeever. Plainfield, N.J.: Logos, 1975. Rpt. ed., Omega, 1980.
A reporter attacks Dispensationalism generally and the Pre-Trib Rapture particularly as a conspiracy and a fraud. Not convincing.

Martin, Malachi. *The Keys of This Blood: The Struggle for World Dominion Between Pope John Paul II, Mikhail Gorbachev, and the Capitalist West.* New York: Simon and Schuster, 1990.
An insightful analysis of geopolitics and the Pope. Roman Catholic.

Martin, Walter. *The Kingdom of the Cults.* Minneapolis: Bethany, 1977.
The classic work on modern day pseudo-Christian cults.

Mather, George A. and Larry A. Nichols. *Dictionary of Cults, Sects, Religions, and the Occult.* Grand Rapids: Zondervan, 1993.
A good quick reference work packed with pertinent facts.

Overbey, Scot. *Vladimir Zhirinovsky: The Man Who Would Be Gog.* Oklahoma City: Hearthstone, 1994.
Biographical sketch of the ultranationalist Russian hardliner.

Pentecost, J. Dwight. *Things to Come: A Study in Biblical Eschatology.* Introduction by John F. Walvoord. Findlay, Ohio: Dunham, 1958. Rpt. ed., Grand Rapids: Zondervan, 1981.
The ultimate systematic study from Dallas Seminary. Pre-Trib.

Pfeiffer, Charles F. and Everett F. Harrison, eds. *The Wycliffe Bible Commentary.* Chicago: Moody, 1962.
An excellent one-volume commentary on the whole Bible.

Prince, Derek. End-Time Prophecy Series. 4 cassette tapes. Vol 7001. "Climax in Four Phases: Repentance, Refreshing, Restoration, Return of Christ." Vol. 7002. "Divine Destiny for This Nation (USA) and This Generation." Vol. 7003. "Prophecy: God's Time Map." Vol. 7004. "Israel and the Church: Parallel Restoration." Ft. Lauderdale, Fla.: Derek Prince Ministries, [1982].
A clear, comprehensive presentation of end-time events and God's plan for restoration of both Israel and the Church, leading to a Pre-Trib Rapture, by an excellent Bible teacher. Charismatic.

Ryrie, Charles C. *What You Should Know About the Rapture.* Chicago: Moody, 1981.
Evangelical answers attacks on the Pre-Trib Rapture from the Greek.

Robertson, Pat. *The New Millennium.* Dallas: Word, 1990.
Perspectives on global megatrends reshaping the world.

_____. *The New World Order.* Dallas: Word, 1991.
Insights on the rise of globalism and world government.

_____. *The End of the Age.* Dallas: Word, 1995.
A novel giving a fictionalized account of the end times.
Post-Trib.

Scofield, C. I. *The Scofield Study [Reference] Bible.* New York:
Oxford University Press, 1945.
Original notes by one of the all-time great Bible scholars.

Strong, James. *The Exhaustive Concordance of the Bible.* Iowa Falls,
Iowa: Riverside, n.d.
The one indispensable resource for personal Bible study.
Contains all the words in the Bible plus Greek and Hebrew
dictionaries.

Sutton, Hilton. *He's Coming! The Glorious Appearing of Jesus
and the Seven Raptures of God.* Tulsa: Harrison House, 1983.
A prominent Word of Faith teacher with unique ideas
on Rapture.

Taylor, Kenneth G. *Living Prophecies: The Minor Prophets, with
Daniel and Revelation, Paraphrased.* Wheaton, Ill.: Tyndale
House, 1965.
Shows how clear Bible prophecy can be when taken literally.

Unger, Merrill F. *Unger's Bible Handbook.* Chicago: Moody, 1980.

_____. *Unger's Bible Dictionary.* Chicago: Moody, 1966.
Two excellent resources for Bible study by a renowned
Bible scholar.

_____. *Demons In the World Today: A Study of Occultism in the
Light of God's Word.* Wheaton, Ill.: Tyndale House, 1971.
An in-depth look at the way Satan and his demons operate.

Wheeler, John L. Jr. "Collective Security in the New World Order:
Biblical and Constitutional Perspectives." Master's Thesis,
Regent University, 1991.
Author's study of implications of modern globalist development.

_____., Ed. *Christian American.* Chesapeake, Va.: Christian
Coalition, 1990-1995. Articles on various topics.
A Christian perspective on social, cultural and political events.

Winkler, Alan. Author's Notes from Class Lectures. "Prophecy and
End Times." Dayton, Tenn.: William Jennings Bryan College,
1982-83.
Detailed, knowledgeable explanations of every aspect of
end-time events in a comprehensive theological framework.
Current to 1983.

About the Author

John Wheeler Jr. is a journalist, author, and evangelist who has studied end-time Bible prophecy extensively. He has a B.A. degree from William Jennings Bryan College, where he studied history, theology and Bible, and an M.A. in Public Policy from Regent University.

This solid Christian educational background, plus his five years of experience as the founding editor of *Christian American*, the flagship publication of the Christian Coalition, have given John unique insights into the tumultuous times in which we live.

Miraculously converted to Christ at the age of 32, John was delivered from a background of drugs and occultism. He was licensed as a Southern Baptist evangelist in 1982 and ordained by a Spirit-filled independent fellowship in 1996. He travels extensively, speaking in churches and public gatherings, giving anointed testimony to the power of the Blood of Jesus Christ and the prophetic signs of His imminent personal return.

John currently resides in Chesapeake, Virginia, with his wife Cheryl and their seven children.

To schedule John Wheeler Jr. for a speaking engagement, please call

(804) 465-4068

To receive a free trial copy of John's ministry newsletter, write your name, address, and telephone number on a piece of paper and mail it to:

John Wheeler Jr.
Ministry Newsletter
4809 Phoenix Drive
Chesapeake, Virginia 23321

To support this ministry, send tax-deductible contributions to the above address. Make checks payable to Believers' Fellowship Church.